The Routledge Course in Modern Mandarin Chinese is a two-ye
students with no prior background in Chinese study. Designed ˘˘ ˘˘˘˘ ˘ ˘˘˘˘˘g
in both the spoken and written language it develops all the basic skills such as pronunciation, character writing, word use, and structures, while placing strong emphasis on the development of communication skills.

The complete course consists of Textbook Level 1, Workbook Level 1—including free CDs, and Textbook Level 2 and Workbook Level 2—including free CDs. All books are available separately in simplified as well as traditional characters and take the students from complete beginner to post-intermediate level.

Workbook Level 2 is designed to accompany *Textbook Level 2* lesson by lesson, and offers exercises for homework, independent study, and classroom use. Each lesson focuses on the skills of listening and speaking, as well as reading and writing.

The course is also fully supported by an interactive companion website which contains a wealth of additional resources for both teachers and students.

- Teachers will find lesson plans in both English and Mandarin, providing a weekly schedule and overall syllabus for fall and spring, as well as activities for each lesson, and answer keys for all workbook exercises.
- Students will be able to access downloadable character practice worksheets, along with interactive vocabulary and character practice exercises. All the audio material necessary for the course is also available online and conveniently linked on screen to the relevant exercises for ease of use.

For more information about the course and to access these additional resources, please visit the companion website at http://www.routledge.com/textbooks/9780415472500.

Claudia Ross is Professor of Chinese at the College of the Holy Cross, Massachusetts. She has served as President of the Chinese Language Teachers Association and as Director of the CET Chinese Program in Beijing. Her publications include *Chinese Demystified* (2010); *The Lady in the Painting, Expanded Edition* (2008); *Modern Mandarin Chinese Grammar: A Practical Guide*, co-authored with Jing-heng Sheng Ma; *Modern Mandarin Chinese Grammar Workbook*, co-authored with Jing-heng Sheng Ma and Baozhang He (both Routledge, 2006); *Outline of Chinese Grammar* (2004); and *Traditional Chinese Tales: A Course in Intermediate Chinese* (2001).

Baozhang He is Associate Professor of Chinese at the College of the Holy Cross, Massachusetts. He has served as Director of the Chinese Language Program at Harvard University and as Head Instructor in the "Princeton in Beijing" language program. His publications include *Modern Mandarin Chinese Grammar Workbook* (Routledge, 2006), co-authored with Claudia Ross and Jing-heng Sheng Ma, and *Elementary Chinese* (2006), co-authored with Pei-Chia Chen.

Pei-Chia Chen is Lecturer in Chinese at UC San Diego and has previously taught at Harvard University. Her publications include *Elementary Chinese* (2006), co-authored with Baozhang He.

Meng Yeh is Senior Lecturer in Chinese at Rice University, Texas. She has served as a Board Member of the Chinese Language Teachers Association and is a founding member of CLTA-TX. She is an AP Chinese consultant for the College Board and a certified Oral Proficiency Interviewer in Chinese for Language Testing International, ACTFL. Her publications include *Advancing in Chinese* (2010) and *Task-based Listening Workbook: Communicating in Chinese Series* (1999).

"*The Routledge Course in Modern Mandarin*, Level 2, offers a step-by-step introduction to the Chinese language for real-life scenarios. It is a fantastic resource which effectively assists both autonomous learning while offering practical guidance for teachers."

Wei Jin, *The School of Oriental and African Studies, University of London, UK*

"*The Routledge Course in Modern Mandarin Chinese* is a valuable addition to the field of Chinese language textbooks. Thorough and careful pedagogical considerations continue to be evident throughout the second volume of this two-year series. Students using this series will be provided with strong and clear guidance for their learning, both in terms of form and function connection and in developing their four skills in a spiraling fashion that has been meticulously designed to reflect the most up-to-date knowledge in second language acquisition. I highly recommend this series."

Cecilia Chang, *Williams College, USA*

THE ROUTLEDGE COURSE IN
Modern Mandarin Chinese
现代汉语课程

Workbook Level 2: Simplified Characters
练习本　　第二册
简体版

Claudia Ross
Baozhang He
Pei-Chia Chen
Meng Yeh

Routledge
Taylor & Francis Group
LONDON AND NEW YORK

First published 2012
by Routledge
711 Third Avenue, New York, NY 10017

Simultaneously published in the UK
by Routledge
2 Park Square, Milton Park, Abingdon, Oxon OX14 4RN

Routledge is an imprint of the Taylor & Francis Group, an informa business

© 2012 Claudia Ross, Baozhang He, Pei-Chia Chen, and Meng Yeh

Library of Congress Cataloging in Publication Data
Ross, Claudia.
  The Routledge course in modern Mandarin Chinese. Textbook level 2 : Simplified
characters / Claudia Ross . . . [et al.]. — 1st ed.
    p. cm.
  1. Chinese language—Textbook for foreign speakers—English. 2. Mandarin dialects.
I. Title. II. Title: Modern Mandarin Chinese.
  PL1129.E5R678 2011
  495.1'82421—dc22

                                                            2010052079

British Library Cataloguing in Publication Data
A catalogue record for this book is available from the British Library

ISBN: 978-0-415-47246-3 (Textbook Level 2, Traditional characters)
ISBN: 978-0-415-47250-0 (Textbook Level 2, Simplified characters)
ISBN: 978-0-415-47253-1 (Workbook Level 2, Traditional characters)
ISBN: 978-0-415-47247-0 (Workbook Level 2, Simplified characters)

Typeset in 12/15pt Scala
by Graphicraft Limited, Hong Kong

Printed and bound in the United States of America on acid-free paper.
Printed by Sheridan Books, Inc.

Contents

Acknowledgments

We thank all of the people who have been involved in the development of this course. We give a special thanks to Jessica Lee, who provided the illustrations for the textbooks and workbooks for Levels 1 and 2. The photographs in the textbook are originals supplied by the photographers Wenze Hu, Jin Lu, and Claudia Ross, and are used with their permission. We thank Wenze Hu and Jin Lu for their contributions. Thanks also to the students in the intermediate Chinese classes at the College of the Holy Cross 2008–2010 for their patience and feedback as we field-tested and revised each lesson, and to Sun Shao-Hui, Yao Shu-Ting, Ho Chia-Jung, and Chang Yu-Lun, foreign language assistants in Chinese at Holy Cross during those years, for their help on many aspects of the project. We are grateful to the College of the Holy Cross for its generous support in the way of released time and resources, and to the members of the Audio-Visual Department at the College for their help in producing audio recordings that enabled field-testing. We thank our editors for their guidance and for their help in keeping us on track. Last but not least, we thank our families for their ongoing support and their confidence in our work.

The stroke order flow charts in this book were produced with eStroke software and are included with the permission of EON Media Limited:

http://www.eon.com.hk/estroke

Introduction

The Routledge Course in Modern Mandarin Chinese is an innovative two-year course for English-speaking learners of Chinese as a foreign language that guides students to build a strong foundation in Mandarin and prepares them for continued success in the language. The course is designed to address the five goals (the 5 C's) of foreign language learning highlighted by the American Council on the Teaching of Foreign Languages (ACTFL). Each *communication*-focused lesson is grounded in the *cultural* context of China, guiding students to make *comparisons* between language and social customs in the United States and the Chinese-speaking world, and providing activities that *connect* their language study to other disciplines and lead them to use Chinese in the wider *community*.

Set in China, the course introduces themes that students encounter in their first experience abroad and prepares them to converse, read, and write in Chinese on everyday topics. The themes in Level 2 include *courses and majors, getting sick and seeing a doctor, weather, sports and exercise, shopping and bargaining, celebrating the Chinese New Year, cooking and eating out, travel, job hunting, and talking about the Chinese language.*

The Routledge Course in Modern Mandarin Chinese is available in Simplified or Traditional characters and includes:

- A textbook with narratives, dialogues, vocabulary and character lists, stroke order tables, jargon-free explanations of use and structure, *Sentence Pyramids* to illustrate phrase and sentence structure, and notes on Chinese culture and language use.
- A comprehensive workbook with extensive information-focused and skill-focused exercises that target all aspects of each lesson.
- Alphabetically arranged indices for vocabulary, characters, and structures.
- A student website with character and vocabulary flashcards, downloadable character practice sheets, and easily accessible audio files for the *Structure Drills* and *Listening for Information* exercises provided in the Workbook.
- A *Teacher Resources* section of the website containing a wealth of communication-based classroom activities, project suggestions, lesson plans, and teaching tips.

Innovative features of *The Routledge Course in Modern Mandarin*

- Separate introduction of *words* and *characters*. Vocabulary items are presented in Pinyin in the lesson in which they are introduced so that students learn the pronunciation and meaning of new words before they learn to read and write them in characters. Character introduction is staggered and selective. Characters are introduced at the second or later occurrence of a vocabulary item in the text, with a focus on the introduction of high-frequency characters. Level 1 introduces approximately 575 words and 180 characters. Level 2 introduces an additional 800 vocabulary items and 330 characters. Since a single character often serves as a component in many different words, by the end of Level 2, the gap between written and spoken vocabulary is small.

- Complete replacement of Pinyin by characters. When a character is introduced, it replaces the Pinyin form in all subsequent occurrences without additional Pinyin support. Students must focus on the character as the primary written form of the Chinese word or syllable.
- Character literacy instruction. Once characters are introduced, workbook exercises guide students to understand the structure of characters and to develop reading and writing strategies.
- Integration of form and function. Structures are introduced to support communication.
- "Basic to complex" introduction of grammatical structures. Students build a solid foundation in basic structures before learning more complex variations.
- Recycling. Vocabulary and structures are recycled in successive lessons to facilitate mastery.

Features of Level 2

Level 2 begins the transition from the study of colloquial Chinese to that of the formal written and spoken language. Features include:

- Presentation of themes in *colloquial* and *formal* contexts. Each lesson includes a dialogue that develops a theme in conversational format, and a narrative that develops the same theme in a more formal written style. This presentation facilitates the *introduction of features of formal literary language*, including vocabulary, sentence structures, and narrative conventions, and serves as a *transition* to the reading and discussion of formal written texts in subsequent levels of Chinese language study.
- Development of written narrative skills in a variety of rhetorical modes: description, narrative, explanation, and persuasion. Lessons introduce features of written narrative, including the development of a topic, text cohesion, and parallel structure, and use a variety of exercises to guide students to write progressively longer and more complex narratives in a variety of rhetorical modes.
- Continued focus on an understanding of the structure of characters including the recognition of radicals, and the development of dictionary skills.
- Continued focus on strengthening listening comprehension skills through longer and more complex narratives in the form of speeches, reports, and instructions.
- Continued focus on the strengthening of oral presentation skills through tasks involving responses to oral messages, and summarizing explanations, arguments and descriptions.
- Continued focus on the strengthening of interpersonal speaking skills through tasks involving interviews, negotiations, and shared responsibilities.

引言

《Routledge 现代汉语课程》是针对母语为英语的学习者编写的一套创新汉语教材。本教材为两年的课程，帮助学生打下坚实的汉语基础并为他们继续在语言学习的成功上做好准备。教材的设计上力求全面反映全美外语教学学会(ACTFL)倡导的外语学习的五项目标(5 C's)。每一课以语言交际为中心，以中国文化为背景，引导学生做中美语言及社会习俗方面的对比，并提供大量的教学活动使学生把语言学习与其他专业知识的学习贯穿起来，以使他们能在更广的范围内使用汉语。

教材的背景是在中国，给学生介绍第一次到中国通常会遇到的情景。第二册教材的情景包括课程与专业、看病、天气、运动与健身、购物与讨价还价、欢度春节、做饭、去饭馆、旅游、找工作及中国语言。

《Routledge 现代汉语课程》有简繁体两种版本，内容包括：

- 课本中每一课有叙述、对话、生词、所学的汉字及汉字笔顺表、通俗易懂的用法和结构的介绍、句型扩展、语言常识及中国文化点滴。
- 综合练习本内有大量的针对每课所学内容的信息交际及语言技能的练习。
- 以字母顺序安排的生词、汉字及语法点的索引。
- 学生学习网页：汉字和生词学习卡、可以下载的汉字练习表格、及练习本中的句型操练和听力练习等语音档案。
- 教师资源网页：大量的语言交际的课堂活动、教学建议、课程安排及教学技巧。

《现代汉语课程》的创意性特点：

- "词"、"字"分开介绍。生词在第一次出现的时候，只以拼音的形式介绍。这样，学生可以先把精力集中在发音、意思及用法上，然后再学汉字。介绍哪些汉字是有步骤有选择的。所介绍的汉字一定在课文的词汇中出现过两次以上，重点介绍使用频率高的汉字。第一册介绍了575个生词，180个汉字。第二册介绍800个生词330个汉字。因为一个汉字往往在不同的生词中出现，到第二册结束的时候，学生所能说的词汇和能写的词汇（汉字）差距是很小的。

- 汉字全部代替拼音。某一汉字一经介绍，该字的拼音形式就不再出现。学生必须学着把注意力集中在汉字上，因为只有汉字才是汉语的词或音节的真正书写形式。
- 识字教学：针对每课所介绍的汉字，课本和练习本都有相应的练习帮助学生了解汉字的结构，并培养学生阅读和书写的策略。
- 形式和功能结合：句型结构的介绍是为了便于交际。
- "由简到难"引进语法结构。学生在充分掌握了简单的语法结构后，再逐步学习较为复杂的结构。
- 重复。为帮助学生掌握运用，句型和生词在后续几课的课文和练习中尽量重复。

第二册的特点

第二册开始从学习白话的口语过渡到正式的口语和书面语。其特点包括：

- 在正式和非正式的语境中介绍主题。每课都有对话，以对话的形式发展情景，及一段叙述，同样的情境但以正式的书写的形式呈现。这样的安排易于引进正式的书面语的特征，其中包括词汇、句型、叙述的格式，为学生以后阅读讨论正式书面语起一个过渡的作用。
- 培养学生叙述不同的情景的语言能力：描写、叙述、解释及说服。课中介绍书写体的特征，包括发挥主题、起承转合、对称结构等，并通过不同的练习引导学生逐步以更长更复杂的段落书写不同情境。
- 继续强调了解汉字的结构，包括识别偏旁部首、学习使用字典等。
- 通过更长的，更复杂的讲话、报告及指令等不同的听力材料继续加强听力理解的能力。
- 通过对口头信息的回答、对解释性文字的总结、辩论及描述继续增强学生的口头表达能力。
- 通过完成提问、面谈、协商及职责等教学任务继续加强学生人际交流的能力。

引言

《Routledge 現代漢語課程》是針對母語為英語的學習者編寫的一套創新漢語教材。本教材為兩年的課程，幫助學生打下堅實的漢語基礎並為他們繼續在語言學習的成功上做好準備。教材的設計上力求全面反映全美外語教學學會(ACTFL)倡導的外語學習的五項目標(5 C's)。每一課以語言交際為中心，以中國文化為背景，引導學生做中美語言及社會習俗方面的對比，並提供大量的教學活動使學生把語言學習與其他專業知識的學習貫穿起來，以使他們能在更廣的範圍內使用漢語。

教材的背景是在中國，給學生介紹第一次到中國通常會遇到的情景。第二冊教材的情景包括課程與專業、看病、天氣、運動與健身、購物與討價還價、歡度春節、做飯、去飯館、旅遊、找工作及中國語言。

《Routledge 現代漢語課程》有簡繁體兩種版本，內容包括：

- 課本中每一課有敘述、對話、生詞、所學的漢字及漢字筆順表、通俗易懂的用法和結構的介紹、句型擴展、語言常識及中國文化點滴。
- 綜合練習本內有大量的針對每課所學內容的信息交際及語言技能的練習。
- 以字母順序安排的生詞、漢字及語法點的索引。
- 學生學習網頁：漢字和生詞學習卡、可以下載的漢字練習表格、及練習本中的句型操練和聽力練習等語音檔案。
- 教師資源網頁：大量的語言交際的課堂活動、教學建議、課程安排及教學技巧。

《現代漢語課程》的創意性特點：

- "詞"、"字"分開介紹。生詞在第一次出現的時候，只以拼音的形式介紹。這樣，學生可以先把精力集中在發音、意思及用法上，然後再學漢字。介紹哪些漢字是有步驟有選擇的。所介紹的漢字一定在課文的詞彙中出現過兩次以上，重點介紹使用頻率高的漢字。第一冊介紹了575個生詞，180個漢字。第二冊介紹800個生詞330個漢字。因為一個漢字往往在不同的生詞中出現，到第二冊結束的時候，學生所能說的詞彙和能寫的詞彙（漢字）差距是很小的。

- 漢字全部代替拼音。某一漢字一經介紹，該字的拼音形式就不再出現。學生必須學著把注意力集中在漢字上，因為只有漢字才是漢語的詞或音節的真正書寫形式。
- 識字教學：針對每課所介紹的漢字，課本和練習本都有相應的練習幫助學生瞭解漢字的結構，並培養學生閱讀和書寫的策略。
- 形式和功能結合：句型結構的介紹是為了便於交際。
- "由簡到難"引進語法結構。學生在充分掌握了簡單的語法結構後，再逐步學習較為複雜的結構。
- 重復。為幫助學生掌握運用，句型和生詞在後續幾課的課文和練習中盡量重復。

第二冊的特點

第二冊開始從學習白話的口語過渡到正式的口語和書面語。其特點包括：

- 在正式和非正式的語境中介紹主題。每課都有對話，以對話的形式發展情景，及一段敘述，同樣的情境但以正式的書寫的形式呈現。這樣的安排易於引進正式的書面語的特徵，其中包括詞彙、句型、敘述的格式，為學生以後閱讀討論正式書面語起一個過渡的作用。
- 培養學生敘述不同的情景的語言能力：描寫、敘述、解釋及說服。課中介紹書寫體的特徵，包括發揮主題、起承轉合、對稱結構等，並通過不同的練習引導學生逐步以更長更複雜的段落書寫不同情境。
- 繼續強調瞭解漢字的結構，包括識別偏旁部首、學習使用字典等。
- 通過更長的，更複雜的講話、報告及指令等不同的聽力材料繼續加強聽力理解的能力。
- 通過對口頭信息的回答、對解釋性文字的總結、辯論及描述繼續增強學生的口頭表達能力。
- 通過完成提問、面談、協商及職責等教學任務繼續加強學生人際交流的能力。

How to use the resources in this course to learn Chinese

This course consists of a textbook, workbook, and website with a wealth of material designed to help you to learn to speak Mandarin and read and write in Chinese. Here is an overview of the resources, with suggestions to help you to do your best work.

Textbook

The textbook presents new material and explanations.

- *Narratives* and *Dialogues* illustrate the use of words and structures, and also the cultural conventions of communication associated with each topic.
- *Stroke Order Flow Charts* show you how to write each new character, stroke by stroke.
- *Use and Structure* notes explain how new structures function, and how structures and phrases are used.
- *Sentence Pyramids* show you how words and phrases are grouped into sentences, and help you to understand Chinese word order.
- *Narrative Structure* explanations show you how to organize information into cohesive essays for different communicative functions.
- *Language FAQs* and *Notes on Chinese Culture* provide additional information about language use and Chinese culture related to the topic of the lesson.

Workbook

The workbook provides exercises that you can do as homework or in class to practice the words, structures, and themes introduced in each lesson. These include:

- *Structure Drills*
- *Listening for Information*
- *Focus on Chinese Characters*
- *Focus on Structure*
- *Focus on Communication*

Website

The website includes listening files that you need in order to complete workbook exercises and additional resources that help you practice and review. Resources include:

- Character and vocabulary flash cards
- Character practice sheets
- Listening files for *Structure Drills*
- Listening files for *Listening for Information*

Study tips

- Learn vocabulary and characters. If you don't know the words in a lesson, you can't participate in class and you cannot do the homework. You need to begin each lesson by learning the new vocabulary and characters. *Regularly review* vocabulary and characters from earlier lessons. Use the resources provided with this course to help you study. Download the character practice sheets from the course website to practice writing characters. Pay attention to the stroke order presented on the practice sheets so that you learn to write characters correctly. Using the same stroke order each time you write a character helps you to remember the character. Conversely, if you write a character differently each time you write it, your brain will have a hard time remembering it. Use the vocabulary and character flash cards on the website to help you review vocabulary and characters, but be sure to write down your responses in Chinese to make sure that you really know the tones in each vocabulary item, or the correct way to write each character.
- Learn the structures. Notice that most of the *Focus on Structure* exercises refer to a specific *Use and Structure* note. Read the *Use and Structure* note before you do the exercise, and follow the model sentences in the note as you complete your work. Work through the *Sentence Pyramids* in the textbook to see how phrases are built up into sentences in Chinese. Use the *Sentence Pyramids* to test yourself, translating the Chinese column into English and checking your answers, and then translating the English column into Chinese. Work through the *Structure Drills* on the website to practice new structures on your own.
- Use the listening resources. If you could understand a sentence or narrative in Chinese the first time you heard it, you wouldn't need to study Chinese. Do not expect to understand listening files on your first try. Instead, listen to the same texts over and over again in order to train your brain to understand what it hears. When you work on the *Listening for Information* exercises, expect to listen to each 'clip' multiple times until you are sure that you understand it. Help your brain to focus on information by reading the instructions and the answer choices before you listen. The *Structure Drills* provided on the website will exercise your listening skills as they increase your control of new structures and vocabulary.
- Focus on communication. Many of the exercises in this section require you to read or write longer passages in Chinese. Before you read, identify the sentence structures so that you know how words and phrases in the text are related. Identify word boundaries

so that you group characters correctly, and look for connecting words that tell you if the text is presenting a sequence, or a description, or an explanation, etc. Before you write, think of what you want to say, and jot down the Chinese structures that you can use to express your meaning. Think of how you want to organize your ideas, and make a list of the connecting words or structures you need for the organization you are planning. After you write, proofread your work. Be sure to write characters where you have learned them, and be sure that the characters you write are correct. When reading or writing, if you cannot remember a character or a vocabulary item, use this as an opportunity to review.

If you spend the time you need to prepare and review, you will have a successful and satisfying Chinese-learning experience. Good luck in your studies!

How to use the resources in this course to teach Chinese

The textbook, workbook, and website material in this course are designed to be used together to help students learn to communicate in Mandarin Chinese in speech and writing. We suggest the following approach to maximize your students' success in learning Chinese. (More detailed suggestions are provided in the lesson plans that are included on the course website.)

Coordinating the textbook with workbook assignments

- *Focus on Chinese Characters.* Require students to learn the new characters in each lesson at the start of the lesson. The exercises in the *Focus on Chinese Characters* section of the workbook rely on grammar introduced in previous lessons, so students can do these exercises before new grammar is presented in class.
- *Focus on Structure.* The text in each lesson is presented in modules: a *Narrative*, and a *Dialogue* divided into several parts. Each module has its own list of new vocabulary, and modules are sequentially linked to *Use and Structure* notes. Present each lesson module by module, and assign relevant *Focus on Structure* homework as you complete a module. You can assign a few structure exercises at a time, after the introduction of the targeted structures in each module.
- *Listening for Information.* Assign *Listening for Information* exercises for homework after the relevant structures have been introduced. You can assign a few exercises at a time, after you have introduced and practiced the targeted structures in class.
- *Focus on Communication.* Use *Focus on Communication* exercises as classroom activities or homework after all modules have been covered to help students apply what they have learned in the lesson to new situations.

Classwork or homework?

Distinguish between activities that students can do on their own and activities that are appropriate for the classroom setting. *Do not use valuable class time for activities that students can do on their own.*

Activities that students should do on their own include:

- Memorization of vocabulary and characters. Do not explain vocabulary in class. English definitions and structure notes in the textbook provide the information that students need to understand the meaning and use of vocabulary.
- Reading of narratives and dialogues. Have students read the text at home and discuss the content in class. Discussion can take a question-answer format.
- Exercises involving identification, completion, and stroke count in the *Focus on Chinese Characters* section of the workbook.
- *Listening for Information* exercises. Listening exercises are designed to help students develop listening skills at their own pace, and students should be encouraged to listen to audio files as many times as necessary in order to complete each listening task. In-class listening practice deprives students of the opportunity to listen at their own pace and should not be used as a classroom activity.
- *Focus on Structure* exercises involving the use of targeted structures in individual sentences. These should always be assigned as homework after the structures are introduced in class. Problematic structures can be reviewed in class after homework assignments are complete. In short, follow these steps: presentation (in class), practice (at home), review (in class).
- Essay writing.

Activities that can be done in class include:

- Communication-based activities such as those suggested in the *Dialogue Practice* section of the textbook.
- *Structure Drills.*
- Communication-focused activities that lead students to practice new structures in context. Detailed suggestions are presented on the lesson plans in the *Teacher Resources* section of the course website.
- Discussion of the lesson's *Narrative* and *Dialogue* in Chinese.
- Brainstorming in preparation for essay writing.
- Small-group editing sessions in which students correct essays written by their peers.
- Problem-solving. The *Focus on Chinese Characters* and *Focus on Communication* sections of the workbook include a number of activities that lend themselves to group work. See the lesson plans in the *Teacher Resources* section of the course website.
- Group presentations of projects or skits.

How much homework?

The workbook includes extensive listening, reading, and writing practice, and you may choose to assign all or part of the exercises for homework. Meaningful homework, including preparation and review, expands the time that students work on Chinese outside of the classroom and accelerates the learning process.

Typing or handwriting?

Require students to complete some assignments by hand and some by computer. Writing Chinese by hand makes students focus on the structure of Chinese characters. Typing helps strengthen character recognition and proofreading skills.

练习本教师使用指南

练习本为培养和巩固学生的汉语语言技能及每课所介绍的交际功能提供练习。这些练习是作为课外功课设计的，使学生能在课外有更多的用汉语互动的机会。有的练习也可以在课堂上作为小组活动。

如何使用练习本我们提出如下建议。更加具体的建议在课程网页教案和"教学活动"的栏目中提供。

- 把学生可以自己独立完成的练习和最好在课堂上做的练习分开。不要把课堂上宝贵的时间用来做学生自己可以做的练习。
- 练习均匀分配，让学生在上每一节课之前做不同的活动，同时也使学生一周内每节课课前的预习时间均等。

学生自己可以独立完成的练习包括：

- 生词和汉字的记忆。课堂上用少量的时间"测验"生词和汉字，但不要花很多时间"解释"。
- 聚焦汉字的练习，包括识别、完成、笔画数目。
- 掌握信息的听力练习。听力练习是为帮助学生按照自己的进度提高听的能力而设计的。应鼓励学生在完成某一听力任务时尽量多听。我们建议不要利用课堂时间练习听力。
- 聚焦结构的练习在单句中使用某一特定的结构。这一练习应在课上介绍了该结构后作为课外作业。容易出错的结构可以在学生完成作业后课堂上集体讲评。简言之，遵循如下步骤：介绍（课上），练习（课下），复习（课上）。
- 作文。作文应该是家庭作业。但是，作文也可以在课堂上分小组学生相互修改。

利用课堂时间作学生不能自己作的练习。这些有：

- 以交际为基础的活动，如课本中介绍的对话练习。
- 新结构介绍。句型操练可以在课堂上练习新句型。教师资源网页也介绍很多帮助学生掌握新句型的交际活动练习。
- 课堂上讨论课文。让学生讲课文的内容、回答问题、或让学生针对课文内容准备问题在课堂上问别的同学。

- 集思广益准备作文。在布置家庭作业作文时，课堂上的讨论帮助学生明确思路、观点。
- 解决问题。练习本中<u>聚焦汉字</u>和<u>交际</u>部分都有可以作为课堂活动的练习。在<u>聚焦汉字</u>中有识别和改错字，识别形旁和声旁。在<u>信息交际</u>中有访问同学后做作文、选择词汇或短语完成句子、句子组合成段落等。
- 小组汇报和短剧。

课文的每一组成部分：叙述、对话的每一段可以视为相对独立的部分。每部分的生词和语法点都单独列出。我们建议每一课时完成一小部分。要求学生课前掌握所要学习部分的生词。上课开始时用几分钟生词测验以确保学生课前预习。另外，要求学生课前预习语法点的解释，课后复习。不建议学生在课上做语法解释的笔记，因为做笔记分散学生精力，降低学习效果。学生所需要掌握的每一语法点在<u>用法与结构</u>中均有讲解。

每课的新汉字都有一个汉字表。让学生从认字到发音，再到书写分为不同的步骤在几个课时中学完。

在课堂上介绍语法点时，让学生做学习网页（练习本）上的<u>结构操练</u>，以使学生更好地掌握本课介绍的语法结构。

练习本中有大量的听力、阅读和书写的练习。可以让学生做部分或所有的练习。下面建议布置作业的顺序。

- <u>聚焦汉字</u>练习中所涉及的语法点都是本课前出现的，所以可以在学完全部课文前做。
- 课堂上介绍了语法结构后再布置练习本中的<u>结构练习</u>。
- 在所有的新语法点都介绍以后再布置<u>听力练习</u>。
- 用<u>信息交际</u>练习帮助学生在新情景中使用本课所学的内容。

練習本教師使用指南

練習本為培養和鞏固學生的漢語語言技能及每課所介紹的交際功能提供練習。這些練習是作為課外功課設計的，使學生能在課外有更多的用漢語互動的機會。有的練習也可以在課堂上作為小組活動。

如何使用練習本我們提出如下建議。更加具體的建議在課程網頁教案和"教學活動"的欄目中提供。

- 把學生可以自己獨立完成的練習和最好在課堂上做的練習分開。不要把課堂上寶貴的時間用來做學生自己可以做的練習。
- 練習均勻分配，讓學生在上每一節課之前做不同的活動，同時也使學生一周內每節課課前的預習時間均等。

學生自己可以獨立完成的練習包括:

- 生詞和漢字的記憶。課堂上用少量的時間"測驗"生詞和漢字，但不要花很多時間"解釋"。
- 聚焦漢字的練習，包括識別、完成、筆畫數目。
- 掌握信息的聽力練習。聽力練習是為幫助學生按照自己的進度提高聽的能力而設計的。應鼓勵學生在完成某一聽力任務時盡量多聽。我們建議不要利用課堂時間練習聽力。
- 聚焦結構的練習在單句中使用某一特定的結構。這一練習應在課上介紹了該結構後作為課外作業。容易出錯的結構可以在學生完成作業後課堂上集體講評。簡言之，遵循如下步驟: 介紹（課上），練習（課下），復習（課上）。
- 作文。作文應該是家庭作業。但是，作文也可以在課堂上分小組學生相互修改。

利用課堂時間作學生不能自己作的練習。這些有:

- 以交際為基礎的活動，如課本中介紹的對話練習。
- 新結構介紹。句型操練可以在課堂上練習新句型。教師資源網頁也介紹很多幫助學生掌握新句型的交際活動練習。
- 課堂上討論課文。讓學生講課文的內容、回答問題、或讓學生針對課文內容準備問題在課堂上問別的同學。

- 集思廣益準備作文。在佈置家庭作業作文時，課堂上的討論幫助學生明確思路、觀點。
- 解決問題。練習本中<u>聚焦漢字</u>和<u>交際</u>部分都有可以作為課堂活動的練習。在<u>聚焦漢字</u>中有識別和改錯字，識別形旁和聲旁。在<u>信息交際</u>中有訪問同學後做作文、選擇詞彙或短語完成句子、句子組合成段落等。
- 小組彙報和短劇。

課文的每一組成部分：敘述、對話的每一段可以視為相對獨立的部分。每部分的生詞和語法點都單獨列出。我們建議每一課時完成一小部分。要求學生課前掌握所要學習部分的生詞。上課開始時用幾分鐘生詞測驗以確保學生課前預習。另外，要求學生課前預習語法點的解釋，課後復習。不建議學生在課上做語法解釋的筆記，因為做筆記分散學生精力，降低學習效果。學生所需要掌握的每一語法點在<u>用法與結構</u>中均有講解。

每課的新漢字都有一個漢字表。讓學生從認字到發音，再到書寫分為不同的步驟在幾個課時中學完。

在課堂上介紹語法點時，讓學生做學習網頁（練習本）上的<u>結構操練</u>，以使學生更好地掌握本課介紹的語法結構。

練習本中有大量的聽力、閱讀和書寫的練習。可以讓學生做部分或所有的練習。下面建議佈置作業的順序。

- <u>聚焦漢字</u>練習中所涉及的語法點都是本課前出現的，所以可以在學完全部課文前做。
- 課堂上介紹了語法結構後再佈置練習本中的<u>結構練習</u>。
- 在所有的新語法點都介紹以後再佈置<u>聽力練習</u>。
- 用<u>信息交際</u>練習幫助學生在新情景中使用本課所學的內容。

List of abbreviations

V	verb
AdjV	adjectival verb
ActV	action verb
Adj	adjective
Adv	adverb
VP	verb phrase
N	noun
NP	noun phrase
S	sentence
NEG	negation
PP	prepositional phrase
CL	classifier
QW	question word

Lesson 17 Workbook

 Listening and speaking

Structure drills

(audio online)

1. 有的 NP…有的 NP (Use and Structure note 10.9)

You will hear a question asking about some person or thing. Use 有的…有的 to say that the description is true for *some* and not others, as in the example.

> **Example:**
> *You will hear:* 课本都很 **guì** 吗？
> *You will say:* 有的 **guì**，有的不 **guì**。
> *Click "R" to hear the correct response:* 有的 **guì**，有的不 **guì**。

(a)   (b)   (c)   (d)   (e)   (f)   (g)   (h)

2. It hasn't happened in a while (Use and Structure note 17.4)

> **Example:**
> *You will hear:* 这三个月我没说中文。
> *You will say:* 我有三个月没有说中文了。
> *Click "R" to hear the correct response:* 我有三个月没有说中文了。

(a)   (b)   (c)   (d)   (e)   (f)   (g)   (h)

3. Yīn 为…suǒ 以 *because…therefore* (Use and Structure note 17.5)

You will hear a statement. Rephrase the statement, adding **yīn** 为 and **suǒ** 以 to emphasize cause and effect, as in the example.

> **Example:**
> *You will hear:* 我很忙，没有给你打电话。
> *You will say:* **Yīn** 为我很忙，**suǒ** 以没有给你打电话。
> *Click "R" to hear the correct response:* **Yīn** 为我很忙，**suǒ** 以没有给你打电话。

(a)   (b)   (c)   (d)   (e)   (f)   (g)   (h)   (i)   (j)

4. What did they say? 说 and **gàosu** (Use and Structure note 17.7)

You will hear a statement indicating what someone said to someone. If the verb used is 说, rephrase the statement with **gàosu**; if the verb used is **gàosu**, rephrase the sentence with 说, as in the examples.

Example:

You will hear: 他跟我说明天没有 **kǎoshì**。
You will say: 他 **gàosu** 我明天没有 **kǎoshì**。
Click "R" to hear the correct response: 他 **gàosu** 我明天没有 **kǎoshì**。
Or
You will hear: 他 **gàosu** 我明天没有 **kǎoshì**。
You will say: 他跟我说明天没有 **kǎoshì**。
Click "R" to hear the correct response: 他跟我说明天没有 **kǎoshì**。

(a)   (b)   (c)   (d)   (e)   (f)   (g)   (h)   (i)   (j)

5. What did he say? Asking indirect questions (Use and Structure note 17.9)

Xiao Zhang is asking you some questions. Tell me what he asked you, using an indirect question in each of your reports, as in the example.

Example:

You will hear: 那个老师 **yán** 吗？
You will say: 他问我那个老师 **yán** 不 **yán**。
Click "R" to hear the correct response: 他问我那个老师 **yán** 不 **yán**。

(a)   (b)   (c)   (d)   (e)   (f)   (g)   (h)

6. Practice with intensifiers: 有一点 AdjV, **bǐjiào** AdjV (Use and Structure note 17.13)

You will hear a question followed by an intensifier. Reply to the question, adding the intensifier right before the adjectival verb, as in the example.

Example:

You will hear: **Jiāo** 文 **huà** 课的老师 **yán** 吗？　（有一点）
You will say: **Jiāo** 文 **huà** 课的老师有一点 **yán**。
Click "R" to hear the correct response: **Jiāo** 文 **huà** 课的老师有一点 **yán**。

(a)   (b)   (c)   (d)   (e)   (f)   (g)   (h)   (i)

7.   What are you interested in? (Use and Structure note 17.14)

You will hear a question asking what someone is interested in followed by a noun phrase. You will use that noun phrase to answer the question.

>   **Example:**
>   *You will hear:* 小高对什么有 **xìngqu**?　（中国文 **huà**）
>   *You will say:* 小高对中国文 **huà** 有 **xìngqu**。
>   *Click "R" to hear the correct response:* 小高对中国文 **huà** 有 **xìngqu**。

(a)　　(b)　　(c)　　(d)　　(e)　　(f)　　(g)　　(h)

8.   Not interested (Use and Structure note 17.14)

You will hear a person's name followed by a place, thing, or action. Say that the person is not interested in the place, thing, or action, as in the example.

>   **Example:**
>   *You will hear:* 小高，**lǔyóu**
>   *You will say:* 小高对 **lǔyóu** 没有 **xìngqu**。
>   *Click "R" to hear the correct response:* 小高对 **lǔyóu** 没有 **xìngqu**。

(a)　　(b)　　(c)　　(d)　　(e)　　(f)　　(g)　　(h)

Listening for information

1.   Class schedule

He Fang is telling her friends the classes that she is taking this semester. Listen carefully (CD1: 3) and present He Fang's class schedule on the following form, indicating the name of each course and its meeting time.

星期一	星期二	星期三	星期四	星期五

2.   What are they busy doing?

(CD1: 4) You will hear five statements stating what five people are busy doing. Write the name of each person underneath the picture of his or her activity. Listen carefully so that you can transcribe the names accurately in pinyin.

3.   Yuan Kai's week

(CD1: 5) The following is Yuan Kai's weekly schedule. You will hear six questions. Based on his schedule, answer the questions in English.

time	星期一	星期二	星期三	星期四	星期五
9:00–10:00 a.m.		Chinese Culture class		Chinese Culture class	
10:00–11:00 a.m.	Math class		Math class		
1:00–2:00 p.m.		Computer class		Computer class	
7:00–9:00 p.m.	Work in the library	German class	German class	Work in the library	

a.

b.

c.

d.

e.

f.

4. Interviewing YOU

You are having a conversation with your classmate, Yu Shi, who is asking about your **(CD1: 6)** semester. Answer each question in Mandarin, based on your real-life situation, using characters where we have learned them.

a.

b.

c.

d.

e.

f.

g.

5. Comparisons

You will hear five questions, one for each picture. Answer each question in Mandarin, **(CD1: 7)** based on the pictures.

a. Xiao Chen's   Lao Wang's

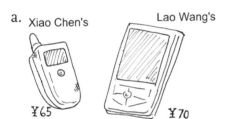

¥65   ¥70

c.

Bob   Eric

e.

Carl   Max

b.

Bao Kang   Shu Wen

Sam

d.

a.

b.

c.

d.

e.

6.   Listen and reply

(CD1: 8) This is the first day of the Chinese course and Teacher Wu is describing the basic structure of the class. Listen to her description, and then answer the six questions that follow in English, based on the information that she gives.

a.

b.

c.

d.

e.

f.

7.   Dialogue I

(CD1: 9) You will hear a telephone conversation between two students who attend different schools. Answer the questions based on the dialogue.

a. When did/does the woman's school start?
  1) in another three days
  2) three days ago
  3) next week

b. Why is the woman taking Chinese this semester?
  1) She is required to take two years of Chinese.
  2) She has been taking Chinese for two years and wants to continue.
  3) She needs to take five courses this semester.

c. What is the main topic of this conversation?
  1) studying Chinese
  2) starting a new semester
  3) planning a trip to China

8.   Dialogue II

You will hear a dialogue between a man and a woman. Answer the questions based on the (CD1: 10) dialogue.

a. What is the main topic of their conversation?
   1) where to eat tonight
   2) what the new restaurant is like
   3) which dish to order in the new restaurant
   4) how to get to the new restaurant

b. Based on the information in the dialogue, what do we know about the restaurant?
   1) It is far away. They need to take the subway.
   2) It is a bit pricey, but the food is excellent.
   3) We do not know much, since neither of them has been there.
   4) The dumplings in that restaurant are pretty good.

 # Reading and writing

Focus on Chinese characters

1.   Number of strokes

Indicate the number of strokes used in writing each of the following characters.

a. 课 _____   f. 些 _____

b. 思 _____   g. 意 _____

c. 听 _____   h. 直 _____

d. 为 _____   i. 校 _____

e. 忙 _____   j. 每 _____

2.   Which character?

Circle the character in each line that corresponds to the meaning on the left.

a. **zhí** (**yīzhí** *continuously*)   直   真

b. **guān** (**guānxi** *connection*)   关   半

c. **gōng** (**gōngkè** *course work*)   工   功

d. **měi** *every*   每   母

e. **tīng** *listen*   听   吓

f. **xiào (xuéxiào** *school*)   饺   校

g. **xiē** *several*   此   些

h. **zhōng** *clock*   钟   种

i. **kè** *class*   颗   课

j. **sī (yìsi** *meaning*)   思   想

k. **cái** (*less than expected*)   才   寸

l. **yòng** *use*   用   月

3.   First strokes

Write the first two strokes of each of the following characters.

a. 思 _____   f. 关 _____

b. 校 _____   g. 意 _____

c. 才 _____   h. 系 _____

d. 些 _____   i. 忙 _____

e. 为 _____   j. 钟 _____

4.   Missing strokes

Complete each character by writing in the missing strokes.

a.   丁   **gōng (gōngkè** *course work*)

b.   叮   **tīng** *listen*

c.   诅   **kè** *class*

d.   乞   **měi** *every*

e.   乙   **xì (guānxi** *connection*)

f.   亠   **yì (yìsi** *meaning*)

g.   斗   **xiē** *several*

h.   古   **zhí (yīzhí** *continuously, straight*)

i.   乍   **zhōng** *clock* (**yīdiǎn zhōng** *1 o'clock*)

j.   月   **yòng** *use*

5. Total strokes

Rewrite this list of characters, arranging the characters in terms of their total number of strokes. Begin your list with the character with the fewest strokes.

为	校	每	意	些	才	课	思	直	用	忙	钟	听	功	系	关
4	10	8	12	8	3	10	9	8	5	6	9	7	5	7	6

6. Radicals

Here is a list of characters that we have learned through this lesson. Rewrite each character in the row next to its radical.

叫　课　钟　听　快　请　思　您
意　校　忙　怎　想　本　钱　慢

心	
木	
钅	
口	
忄	
讠	

7. Character sleuth

Group the following characters in terms of a part that they share in common. The shared part need not be the radical in each character. Write the shared part first, and then list the characters that share the part afterward, as in the example. You can use a character more than once.

给　钟　系　用　朋　意　二　直　道
真　关　些　思　男　星　说　经　半

shared part	characters
人	人，大，太，天
田	
目	
二	
月	
纟	

8.   Find the words and phrases

You won't be able to completely understand the following passage, but it contains many characters that we have learned, including more than twenty words composed of two or more characters.

a. Circle fourteen *words* that we have learned that are *composed of two or more characters each* and write them on the answer sheet below.

"今年" is an example of a word that is composed of two or more characters.

"我也" is composed of two characters in a row that we have learned, but it is *not* a word.

今年夏天放暑假的时候，我从中国回美国看我的父母。我有半年多没有看见他们了，很想他们。他们当然也很想我。到了家，我妈妈问我最想吃什么，她可以去买给我做。我说我很想吃的东西，不用去买，家里一定有很多。我跟他们说我刚到中国的时候，最不习惯的就是吃北京的早饭。我觉得北京的早饭油很多，不太健康。我喜欢美国的谷物早餐，加一些牛奶就可以了。又方便，又健康。中国虽然有谷物早餐，可是很贵。爸爸说："对。谷物早餐在宿舍吃就可以了。又可以起得很晚，又可以不去餐厅。"我说："爸爸，你上大学的时候就这样吧。"

Words in this paragraph composed of two or more characters:

1.____   2.____   3.____   4.____   5.____   6.____   7.____

8.____   9.____   10.____   11.____   12.____   13.____   14.____

b. In one sentence in English, state the general topic of this passage.

9. Dictionary skills

Following the instructions in Lesson 17 of the Textbook, look up these characters in a Chinese dictionary and provide the requested information.

a. 相

pronunciation:

meaning:

one two-character word or phrase in which it occurs:

b. 己

pronunciation:

meaning:

one two-character word or phrase in which it occurs:

c. 第

pronunciation:

meaning:

one two-character word or phrase in which it occurs:

10. Find the incorrect characters

Xiao Zhang has written this email to a friend back home, but he has written thirteen different characters incorrectly (some more than once). Read the passage aloud, circle the mistakes, and correct them on the answer sheet below. If the same mistake occurs twice, count it as a single mistake.

> 学期钱天就开学了。我非常忙。这个学期我上了四们课，一们 **yīnyuè** 科，一们法问课，还有两们中文课。**Yīnyuè** 课早上八店中就开 **shǐ**，**suǒ** 以我得早一点七 **chuáng**。我七 **chuáng** 的是候我得 **tóngwū** 还再 **shuì** 觉。我美天上课一前现吃一点东西。

a. ____   b. ____   c. ____   d. ____   e. ____   f. ____   g. ____

h. ____   i. ____   j. ____   k. ____   l. ____   m. ____

11. Scrambled sentences

Rewrite these phrases as sentences, putting the words in the correct order to match the English translations.

a. 会 / **kuài** 子 / 很 / 吃 / 喜欢 / 不 / 用 / 吃饭 / 可是 / **suī** 然 / 她 / 她 / 中国饭

Although she likes to eat Chinese food a lot, she can't use chopsticks to eat.

b. 都 / 的时候 / 忙 / 学生 / 非常 / 刚 / 学期 / 开 **shǐ**

When the semester just begins, the students are all extremely busy.

c. yīnyuè / 一直 / 我 / 有 xìngqu / 对 / 很

I've always been very interested in music.

d. 有意思 / 那本 / 没 / 听说 / 书

I have heard that that book is not interesting.

e. 都 / 学校 / 他们 / 在 / 的 / 吃饭 / cāntīng / 每天

They eat at the school cafeteria every day.

12. Translation

Read the following passage and translate it into English.

明天的明天是后天。"后天"的"后"是"后 biān"的"后"。中文的后天不是在你的后 biān。中文的后天是在你的前 biān。后天还没有到呢。昨天的昨天是前天。"前天"的"前"是"前 biān"的"前"。中文的前天不是在你的前 biān。中文的前天在你的后 biān。前天已经过去了。

13. Pinyin to characters

Rewrite the following sentences in Chinese characters.

a. **Wǒ shì dàxué èr niánjí de xuésheng**。 (Write **jí** in Pinyin.)

b. **Wǒ qiántiān gāng cóng jiā huí xuéxiào**。

c. **Zhè gè xuéqī wǒ yào shàng Zhōngwén kè xué Zhōngwén**。

d. **Wǒ tīngshuō Zhōngwén kè yǒu yīdiǎn nán, kěshì wǒ yīzhí juéde Zhōngwén hěn yǒu yòng**。

e. **Wǒ de xuéxí hěn máng, bùguò wǒ de kè dōu hěn yǒu yìsi**。

Focus on structure

1.   Everyone is busy (Use and Structure note 17.2)

It is Sunday evening. Everyone in the house is so busy concentrating on what they are doing that no one hears the doorbell ringing. Describe what everyone is busy doing, using 忙 **zhe.**

(cooking)	(surfing the internet)
a. 妈妈	b. 爸爸
(doing homework)	(talking on the phone)
c. 小明	d. 小明的 **jiějie**

a.

b.

c.

d.

2.   回来，回去 (Use and Structure note 17.3)

Here are the names of some Chinese students studying at our school. Write a sentence in Mandarin for each one, stating what date they went back to their home country last spring and what date they came back to campus this fall.

	went home in the spring	came back this fall
a. Zhái Yàn	June 9	August 14
b. Wáng Jú	May 29	September 1
c. Chén Wén	July 2	August 31

a.

b.

c.

3.   I haven't done that for a long time (Use and Structure note 17.4)

Xiao Yang has been busy working on a school project for two months now. He finally turned it in today and is complaining about all the fun that he missed. Write each of his complaints in Mandarin, using the example as your guide.

Example:

watching movies, two months   →   我有两个月没有看电 **yǐng** 了。

a. singing Karaoke, one and a half months   →

b. calling my girlfriend, ten days   →

c. going home, one month   →

d. watching television, three weeks   →

e. taking a shower, two days   →

f. sleeping, twenty-five hours   →

4.   Cause and effect (Use and Structure note 17.5)

Here is a list of people, followed by some information about them. Express each line of information in a complete Mandarin sentence, using **yīn** 为 and **suǒ** 以. Then translate your sentences into English.

a. 小王…用功…学得很好
   your sentence:
   English:

b. 陈明…**cōng** 明…学得很快
   your sentence:
   English:

c. 小白的 **tóng** 学…**bèn**…学得很慢
   your sentence:
   English:

d. 美 **lì**…明天有 **kǎoshì**…今天晚上在图书馆 **fù** 习功课
   your sentence:
   English:

e. 小 **Yè**…对 **shù** 学有 **xìngqu**…**xuǎn** 了两门 **shù** 学课。
   your sentence:
   English:

5. Indirect questions and reported questions (Use and Structure note 17.9)

Zhang Dawei asked Xie Guoqiang a lot of questions on the way to the bookstore. Afterward, Xie Guoqiang told his friend Chen Ming what Zhang Dawei had asked. Here are the English versions of the questions. Rewrite them in Mandarin, as in the example.

Example:

He asked me if the bookstore was open. → 张大为问我书店开不开门。

a. He asked me what time the movie begins. →

b. He asked me if the math teacher was strict. →

c. He asked me whether that Chinese book is useful. →

d. He asked me if that Japanese class was hard. →

e. He asked me how many courses I am taking this semester. →

6. Asking indirect questions (Use and Structure note 17.9)

Rewrite the <u>question part</u> of each dialogue exchange as a sentence with an indirect question, as in the example.

Example:

小谢：你这个学期上中文课吗？ → 小谢问小张这个学期<u>上不上</u>中文课。
小张：上。

a. 小 Lǐ：你会开车吗？ →
   小王：不会。

b. 谢太太：你们吃过 jiǎo 子吗？ →
   小高：吃过。我很喜欢。

c. 小马：你昨天看的那个电影有 yìsi 吗？ →
   小钱：非常有 yìsi。

d. 王老师：你觉得中国文 huà 课难不难？ →
   小张：不太难，只是 kǎoshì 很多。

7. What did they say?

Rewrite the <u>reply</u> in each of the dialogue exchanges in Exercise 6 as a sentence, stating what the person said, as in the example. Use the word supplied in parentheses in your sentence.

Example:
小谢：你这个学期上中文课吗？　→　（跟）小张跟<u>小谢说</u>他这个学期上中文课。
小张：上。

a.（**gàosu**）：

b.（说）：

c.（**gàosu**）：

d.（说）：

8.　一点 or 有一点 (Use and Structure note 17.13)

Complete each sentence in Mandarin to match the English translation, using 一点 or 有一点 as appropriate.

a. 这本书太 **guì** 了。　*Can it be a little bit cheaper?*

b. *I've heard that this class is a little hard.* 老师也很 **yán**。

c. *It's already a little late.* 我 **yīnggāi** 回 **sùshè** 了。

d. 明天是星期天。　*You can wake up a little later.*

e. 这个 **jiǎo** 子很好吃。　*You should eat a little more.*

f. *My home is a little far from the subway station.* 我到车站去 **jiē** 你吧。

g. 你说话说得快。　*Please speak a little slower.*

9.　Reporting rumors, gossip, hearsay: I've heard that...

Here are some rumors. Tell Ye Youwen what you heard, as in the example.

Example:
You heard: 张大为 went back home the day before yesterday.
You say: 听说张大为前天回家了。

a. Students are only allowed to take four courses.

b. The Chinese Culture teacher is a little strict.

c. Tomorrow night's movie is very interesting.

d. Xie Guoqiang likes Li Jiazhen.

e. The food in the student cafeteria isn't very tasty.

f. Xiao Ma has a new boyfriend.

10.   Interested or not interested? (Use and Structure note 17.14)

Here is a list of things that Gao Meili is interested in and a list of things that she is not interested in. Ask her if she is interested in each of these things, and write her response to each of your questions.

Gao Meili is interested in:	Gao Meili is not interested in:
a. French culture	b. travel
c. Japanese cinema	d. dancing
e. math	f. German literature （文学）
g. cooking Chinese food	h. singing karaoke
i. listening to music	j. watching television

a. Q:
  A:

b. Q:
  A:

c. Q:
  A:

d. Q:
  A:

e. Q:
  A:

f. Q:
  A:

g. Q:
  A:

h. Q:
  A:

i. Q:
  A:

j. Q:
  A:

11.   Translation challenge I

Translate these passages to English.

a. 妈妈：**Shù** 学很有用。这个学期你 **yīnggāi xuǎn** 一门 **shù** 学课。

   Hái 子：好。我对 **shù** 学很有 **xìngqu**，不过我听说我们学校的 **shù** 学 **lǎoshī** 都 **bǐjiào yán**。

b. 小王：我前天给你打电话你不在。你忙 **zhe** 做什么呢？

   小马：**Xīn** 学期快要开 **shǐ** 了。我忙 **zhe** 买课本呢。

c. 老师：你 **zìjǐ** 的功课得 **zìjǐ** 做。不要请 **bié** 的学生 **bāng** 你做。

12.   Translation challenge II

Translate these sentences to Mandarin. Use characters wherever we have learned them.

a. This semester I'm taking five courses: one music course, one American Culture course, two Japanese language courses, and one Japanese Culture course. I have three classes every day.

b. Xiao Xie: Do you have Chinese homework every day?

   Xiao Zhang: Yes. This Chinese teacher is very strict. We have homework every day. However, we only have two exams each semester.

c. Xiao Xie asked me if Xiao Mei has a boyfriend. I told him that I'm not interested in other people's lives.

Focus on communication

1.   Dialogue comprehension

Study the Lesson 17 Narrative and Dialogue. Then, read the following statements and indicate whether they are true (T) or false (F).

a. (   ) 学校已经开学了。

b. (   ) 这几天很多学生得买课本。

c. (   ) 大为刚回中国，中文说得很好。

d. (   ) 现在学校的书店开门。

e. (　) 中国文 **huà** 课的老师很有意思。

f. (　) 大为早就对中国文 **huà** 课有 **xìngqu** 了。

g. (　) 星期五大为 **bǐjiào** 忙，**yīn** 为他有很多课。

2.　What do you say?

What do you say in each of the following situations? Type your answers, using characters where we have learned them, and email them to your Chinese teacher.

a. You want to find out if the coffee shop is still open right now.

b. You want to express your long-term interest in Chinese music.

c. You want to tell your roommate that you heard that this Chinese teacher is rather strict.

d. You want to find out how many courses your roommate is taking this semester.

e. You want to explain why your Chinese is a bit rusty. (The reason is that you haven't spoken Chinese for two months.)

3.　Complete the mini-dialogues

Use the structure in parentheses to complete each mini-dialogue.

a. A: 这个 **gōngzuò** 钱不多，你为什么喜欢？

　　B: _____。(**yīn** 为)

b. A: 你觉得你的学校怎么样？

　　B: _____。(只是)

c. A: **Zāogāo**，我 **wàng** 了做功课，老师一 **dìng** 会不高 **xìng**。

　　B: _____。(没关系)

d. A: 听说李老师很 **yán**，是不是？你上过他的课，你觉得呢？

　　B: _____。(不过)

4.　Multiple choice questions

Select the best expression to complete each sentence, and then translate your sentences into English.

a. 我喜欢吃家常 **cài**，_____ 我做得不好。

　　1) **suǒ** 以
　　2) **yīn** 为
　　3) 可是

　　English:

b. _____ 星期五早上我有课，_____我不 **néng xuǎn** 这门课。
   1) **Yīn** 为…**suǒ** 以
   2) **Suī** 然…可是
   3) **Yīn** 为…不过

   English:

c. 书店现在没开门，**suǒ** 以 _____。
   1) 今天是星期天
   2) 一会儿就开了
   3) 我不 **néng** 去买课本

   English:

d. **Suī** 然我已经学了三年的中文了，可是_____。
   1) 我一直对中文很有 **xìngqu**
   2) 我还没去过中国
   3) 我每天都有中文课

   English:

e. **Yīn** 为快 **kǎoshì** 了，_____。
   1) 很多人在图书馆学习
   2) 我下个星期有三个 **kǎoshì**
   3) 听说老师 **bǐjiào yán**

   English:

5.   A conversation between Xiao Zhang and Xiao Wang

Part I.   Fill in the blanks with the correct word, choosing from those given below.

只是	**zìjǐ**	一 **dìng**	门	刚
在	没关系	**zhe**	有	早就

小王：小张，我 _____ 几个星期没有看见你了。你 _____ 忙什么？

小张：我忙 _____ 学习呢。这个学期我 **xuǎn** 了几 _____ **bǐjiào** 难的课。每天都有很多
     功课。我常常没有时 **jiān** 想 **bié** 的事。**Zāogāo**！我 **wàng** 了买中文课本。学校书
     店的书都太 **guì**，我真不想 _____ 那儿买。

小王：我听说学友书店的书都很 **piányi**，_____ 有一点 **yuǎn**。你 _____ **xìngqu** 吗？我
     _____ 想去看看了，不过我不想 _____ 一个人去。

小张：真的吗？有点 **yuǎn** _____，我 _____ 买车，我们可以开我的新车去。

Part II. Read the dialogue above. Then, answer the questions about it in Mandarin.

a. 小张忙 **zhe** 作什么？

b. 小张 **wàng** 了作什么？

c. 学友书店怎么样？

d. 小张想去那个书店吗？ 他打 **suan** 怎么去？

6. Sequence of events

Based on the illustrations given, write out the sequence of events. Use 先…再…最后…in each paragraph.

a.

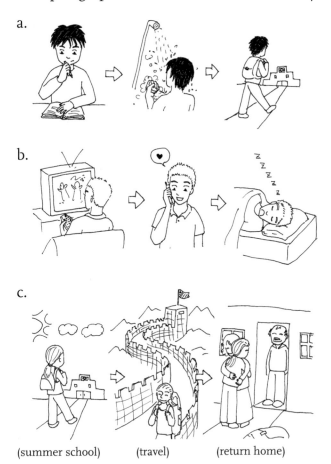

b.

c.

(summer school)　　(travel)　　(return home)

7. Writing I

Write a short paragraph about the classes you are taking this semester. Below is a list of expressions that you can use in your paragraph. Include at least <u>four</u> of them. Your paragraph should be at least 80 characters in length.

yīn 为…suǒ 以	有（一）点	只是	一 dìng	对…有 xìngqu
忙 zhe	不过	bǐjiào	有用	xuǎn

_____

_____

_____

_____

_____

_____

_____

_____

8. Writing II

Write a short paragraph about the classes you decided <u>not</u> to take this semester and explain your decisions. Include in your paragraph at least <u>four</u> of the expressions listed in Exercise 7. Your paragraph should be at least 80 characters in length.

_____

_____

_____

_____

_____

_____

_____

_____

Lesson 18 Workbook

 ## Listening and speaking

Structure drills

1. There is a strong relationship between them (Use and Structure note 18.1)

You will hear two phrases. Say that there is a strong relationship between them, as in the example.

Example:
You will hear: 选 **zhuānyè**，**ài** 好
You will say: 选 **zhuānyè** 跟 **ài** 好有很大的关系。
Click "R" to hear the correct response: 选 **zhuānyè** 跟 **ài** 好有很大的关系。

(a)   (b)   (c)   (d)   (e)   (f)   (g)   (h)

2. There is no connection (Use and Structure note 18.1)

You will hear a question asking if two things are related. Answer each question in a complete sentence saying that they are not related, as in the example.

Example:
You will hear: 这 **jiàn shì** 跟我有关系吗?
You will say: 这 **jiàn shì** 跟你没关系。
Click "R" to hear the correct response: 这 **jiàn shì** 跟你没关系。

(a)   (b)   (c)   (d)   (e)   (f)   (g)   (h)

3. **Rú** 果…就 *if… (then)* (Use and Structure note 18.2)

You will hear two sentences. Restate the sentences using **rú** 果 and 就 to say *if the first one happens, the second one happens,* as in the example.

Example:
You will hear: 你学中文。我也学中文。
You will say: **Rú** 果你学中文，我就学中文。
Click "R" to hear the correct response: **Rú** 果你学中文，我就学中文。

(a)   (b)   (c)   (d)   (e)   (f)   (g)

4. Describing nouns with actions or states, Part I (Use and Structure note 18.3)

You will hear a simple sentence. Restate it as a noun phrase in which the action verb describes the noun, as in the example. English translations are provided for the example.

Example:
You will hear: 我吃饭。 *I eat food (rice).*
You will say: 我吃的饭 *the food (rice) that I eat*
Click "R" to hear the correct response: 我吃的饭

(a)   (b)   (c)   (d)   (e)   (f)   (g)   (h)

5. Describing nouns with actions or states, Part II (Use and Structure note 18.3)

You will hear a simple sentence stating a completed action. Restate it as a noun phrase in which the action verb describes the noun, as in the example. English translations are provided for the example. Remember: do not include completed action 了 in your noun description.

Example:
You will hear: 我昨天买车了。 *I bought a car yesterday.*
You will say: 我昨天买的车 *the car that I bought yesterday*
Click "R" to hear the correct response: 我昨天买的车

(a)   (b)   (c)   (d)   (e)   (f)   (g)   (h)

6.   After doing an action (Use and Structure note 18.7)

You will hear a statement stating two actions that happen in sequence. Restate the information using the structure 在…以后, as in the example.

Example:
You will hear: 你先 **fù** 习功课，再 **cānjiā** 考试。
You will say: 你在 **fù** 习功课以后，再 **cānjiā** 考试。
Click "R" to hear the correct response: 你在 **fù** 习功课以后，再 **cānjiā** 考试。

(a)   (b)   (c)   (d)

7.   Before doing an action (Use and Structure note 18.7)

You will hear a statement stating two actions that happen in sequence. Restate the information using the structure 在…以前, as in the example.

Example:
You will hear: 你先 **fù** 习功课，再 **cānjiā** 考试。
You will say: 你在 **cānjiā** 考试以前，**fù** 习功课。
Click "R" to hear the correct response: 你在 **cānjiā** 考试以前，**fù** 习功课。

(a)   (b)   (c)   (d)   (e)

8.   While doing an action (Use and Structure note 18.7)

You will hear two actions that happen at the same time. Restate the information using the structure 在…时候, as in the example.

Example:
You will hear: 做功课，听 **yīnyuè**
You will say: 我喜欢在做功课的时候听 **yīnyuè**。
Click "R" to hear the correct response: 我喜欢在做功课的时候听 **yīnyuè**。

(a)   (b)   (c)   (d)   (e)   (f)   (g)   (h)

9.   The most (Use and Structure note 18.8)

You will hear a question about the quality of a person, place, or action. Say that it is "the most" in terms of that quality, as in the example.

Example:
You will hear: 那个老师 **yán** 吗？
You will say: 那个老师最 **yán**。
Click "R" to hear the correct response: 那个老师最 **yán**。

(a)   (b)   (c)   (d)   (e)   (f)   (g)   (h)   (i)   (j)

Listening for information

1.   Zhang Wen's siblings

(CD1: 13) You will hear seven questions about the siblings in Zhang Wen's family. Based on the information, answer the questions in Pinyin.

Zhang Wen	Zhang Ping	Zhang Fen	Zhang Ming	Zhang Peng
11th grade	1st year in college	3rd year in college	last semester in college	graduated last year
interested in Math	major undecided	majors in Computer Science and Music	majors in Economics	teaches in a high school

a.

b.

c.

d.

e.

f.

g.

2.   Cai Ting's roommates

(CD1: 14) Cai Ting is describing her roommates. Listen to her description and use it to complete the information in the table.

name	year in college	major
Cai Ting		
Huang An		
Zhang Xin		
Li Qiang		

3. If..., what should you do?

You will hear five different situations. Choose the best solution for each situation.   **(CD1: 15)**

A. take it to the store to be repaired

B. just go to enjoy the others singing

C. find out about study abroad programs

D. call your teacher to explain why

E. ask him to speak slower

F. study harder

a. ( )   b. ( )   c. ( )   d. ( )   e. ( )   f. ( )

4. Huang Licheng's birthday party

Huang Licheng has invited some friends to his twenty-first birthday party. Listen to the **(CD1: 16)** short narrative that describes the people at the party and write each person's name after the appropriate letter on the answer sheet.

A. _____   B. _____   C. _____   D. _____

E. _____   F. _____   G. _____

5.   Grades

(CD1: 17) The 12th grade in Jianguo High School is a small class of seven students. Here is their grade report for Math and English. Students are indicated by number instead of name. You will hear five statements. Indicate whether each statement is true (T) or false (F) based on the information in the grade report.

student number	1/female	2/male	3/male	4/female	5/male	6/female	7/male
Math grade	88	92	88	96	80	75	93
English grade	90	85	82	90	93	77	84

a. ( )   b. ( )   c. ( )   d. ( )   e. ( )

 6.   Interviewing YOU

(CD1: 18) You are having a conversation with your classmate Tan Lun, who is an exchange student from Nanjing, China. He is asking you about your college life. Answer each question in Mandarin, based on your real-life situation, using characters where we have learned them.

a.

b.

c.

d.

e.

f.

g.

 7.   My summer job

(CD1: 19) Listen to the narrative about Ye Chen's summer job and answer the following five questions in English.

a.

b.

c.

d.

e.

8. Dialogue I

Lin Bin, an exchange student from Sichuan, is chatting with Mark about the college (CD1: 20) application process in China and the United States. Answer the following questions based on the information in the conversation.

Note: 高考 is the name of the Chinese college entrance examination.

a. Which statement about the college entrance examination in China is correct?
   1) The entrance examination takes place before summer.
   2) The examination lasts two days.
   3) One can take the examination three times a year.

b. How did Lin Bin do on the exam?
   1) She did well in English, but not in other subjects.
   2) She entered the college that she wanted to attend.
   3) She could study the subject that she planned to major in.

c. How are high school grades considered for college application in China?
   1) Your grades may determine which colleges you can enter.
   2) Grades do not affect one's college application.
   3) Your grades determine which subject you can major in.

9. Dialogue II

Mark is telling Lin Bin about his experience applying for college admission in the United (CD1: 21) States. Answer the following questions based on the information in the conversation.

a. Which statement about Mark is correct?
   1) He took the SAT twice, but he didn't get a good grade either time.
   2) He was tired when taking the SAT the first time.
   3) He took the SAT many times and used his best score to apply to colleges.

b. Why did Mark decide to go to this university?
   1) It is not far away from his family.
   2) He wants to major in Computer Science.
   3) He likes the weather in the east.

c. According to Mark, what are some other advantages of attending this university?
   1) It is not expensive living on campus.
   2) It is a small but diverse school.
   3) It is easier to find a job after graduation.

Reading and writing

1.   Number of strokes

Indicate the number of strokes used in writing each of the following characters.

a. 数 ____   f. 趣 ____

b. 兴 ____   g. 试 ____

c. 作 ____   h. 所 ____

d. 最 ____   i. 因 ____

e. 考 ____   j. 级 ____

2.   Which character?

Circle the character in each line that corresponds to the meaning on the left.

a. **guǒ** (**rúguǒ** *if*)   呆   果

b. **xuǎn** *select*   选   洗

c. **jí** *level in school*   级   极

d. **qù** (**xìngqu** *interest*)   越   趣

e. **xìng** (**xìngqu** *interest*)   兴   应

f. **suǒ** (**suǒyǐ** *therefore, so*)   户   所

g. **háng** (**yínháng** *bank*)   行   街

h. **zuò** *do*   作   昨

i. **shì** (**kǎoshì** *test*)   式   试

j. **zuì** *most*   取   最

k. **shù** (**shùxué** *math*)   数   楼

l. **dìng** (**yīdìng** *certainly*)   定   走

3.   First strokes

Write the first two strokes of each of the following characters.

a. 强 _____   f. 工 _____

b. 定 _____   g. 数 _____

c. 所 _____   h. 选 _____

d. 因 _____   i. 考 _____

e. 最 _____   j. 行 _____

4.   Missing strokes

Complete each character by writing in the missing strokes.

a.   曰   **guǒ** (**rúguǒ** *if*)

b.   走   **qù** (**xìngqu** *interest*)

c.   曰   **zuì** *most*

d.   讠   **shì** (**kǎoshì** *test*)

e.   冂   **yīn** (**yīnwèi** *because*)

f.   纟   **jí** (*level in school*)

g.   弓   **qiáng** *strong*

h.   ⺯   **xuǎn** *select*

i.   彳   **háng** (**yínháng** *bank*), **xíng** *okay*

j.   ⺍   **xìng** (**xìngqu** *interest*)

5.   Total strokes

Rewrite this list of characters, arranging the characters in terms of their total number of strokes. Begin your list with the character with the fewest strokes.

强	试	因	趣	工	作	所	行	兴	果	最	选	定	考	数	级

6.   Radicals

Here are characters that we have learned in this and previous lessons. Rewrite each character in the row next to its radical.

因　　候　　定　　经　　最　　课　　作　　家　　工　　园　　强
趣　　试　　张　　差　　国　　选　　起　　级　　住　　道　　时

宀	
辶	
口	
日	
亻	
走	
讠	
工	
纟	
弓	

7.   Character sleuth

Group the following characters in terms of a part that they share in common. The shared part need not be the radical in each character. Add at least four shared parts to the list, and then write the characters that share the part afterward, as in the example. You can use a character more than once.

考　　期　　数　　在　　作　　最　　定　　坐
趣　　老　　难　　想　　果　　朋　　行　　昨
汉　　本　　做　　往　　起　　前　　怎　　样

shared part	characters
人	人，大，太，天，舍
土	
又	
月	

8.   Skimming for information

Read the following paragraph and provide the requested information. You have not learned all of the characters in the paragraph, but you have learned enough characters and grammatical structures to enable you to identify the main point.

a. Circle the characters that you have not learned.

> 你对哪门课有兴趣，不一定要选那个专业。选专业跟很多方面有关系。第一，那个专业难不难。如果很难，你一定学不好。第二，那个专业有用没有。没有用的东西为什么要学呢？最后，那个专业容易不容易找工作。学了一个专业，可是没有工作有什么用呢？这就是为什么专业跟兴趣有关系，可是关系不大。

b. In one sentence in English, state the general topic of this passage. That is, what is this paragraph about?

9.   Dictionary skills

Following the instructions in Lesson 17 of the Textbook, look up these characters in a Chinese dictionary and provide the requested information:

a. 累
  pronunciation:
  meaning:
  one two-character word or phrase in which it occurs:

b. 业

pronunciation:

meaning:

one two-character word or phrase in which it occurs:

c. 坏

pronunciation:

meaning:

one two-character word or phrase in which it occurs:

10.   Find the incorrect characters

Xiao Zhang has written this email to his older brother, but he has written eleven characters incorrectly. Read the passage aloud, circle the mistakes, and correct them on the answer sheet below.

> 因为我一真对书学很有兴去，所以这个学七我先了两们数学可。可是 **dì** 一个考是以后，我的考是分数不太好。下可以后我去找老师。老师跟我话，**dì** 一个考试的分数好不好没有关西。**Rú** 果你一直很用功，一定 **néng** 字好，一定 **néng** 考好。

a. ____   b. ____   c. ____   d. ____   e. ____   f. ____

g. ____   h. ____   i. ____   j. ____   k. ____

11.   Scrambled sentences

Rewrite these phrases as sentences, putting the words in the correct order to match the English translations.

a. 选 / **bǐjiào** / 我 / 我 / 每个 / 强 / 都 / 数学课 / 所以 / 因为 / 数学 / 学期 / 一门
Since I am relatively strong in math, I take a math class every semester.

b. 兴趣 / 你 / 什么 / 有 / 最 / 对
What are you most interested in?

c. 学生 / 忙 / 一年级 / 每天 / 大学 / 非常 / 都 / 的
First-year college students are extremely busy every day.

d. 以前 / 行 / 功课 / 行 / **fù** 习 / 我们 / 图书馆 / 不 / 考试 / 去
Let's go to the library to review the course work before the test, okay?

e. 工作 / 没 / 那样 / 有 / 的 / 兴趣 / 对 / 我
I am not interested in that kind of job.

12.   Pinyin to characters to English

Rewrite the following sentences in Chinese characters and translate them into English.

a. **Guóqiáng shì xuéxiào yīniánjí de xuésheng。**

English:

b. **Tā měitiān yào qù shàng kè, yě yào qù gōngzuò, suǒyǐ tā hěn máng, yǒu de kǎoshì fēnshù yě bù hǎo。**

English:

c. **Tā yě xiǎng zhǐ shàng kè, bù gōngzuò。**

English:

d. **Zhèyàng tā de kǎoshì fēnshù huì hǎo yīdiǎn。**

English:

e. **Kěshì tā yīdìng děi qù gōngzuò。**

English:

f. **Qù gōngzuò, yǒu le qián, tā cái kěyǐ shàng xué。**

English:

Focus on structure

1.   There is a connection between these things (Use and Structure note 18.1)

Write a sentence for each of the following pairs of situations, saying that there is a relationship between them, as in the example.

Example:

A	B	
选 zhuānyè	你的 ài 好	→ 选 zhuānyè 跟你的 ài 好有关系。

	A	B	
a.	睡 jiào 睡得好	考试分数	→
b.	学生用功不用功	chéngjì 好 huài	→
c.	经 jì	数学	→
d.	老师 yán 不 yán	学生用功不用功	→
e.	你的 ài 好	你的兴趣	→

2.   Is there a connection? (Use and Structure note 18.1)

Rewrite the sentences you wrote in Exercise 1 as questions, and translate your questions into English.

a.

English:

b.

English:

c.

English:

d.

English:

e.

English:

3.   There isn't any connection (Use and Structure note 18.1)

Answer "no" to each of the questions that you wrote in Exercise 2 in complete Mandarin sentences.

a.

b.

c.

d.

e.

4.   What if? (Use and Structure note 18.2)

Answer each of the following questions truthfully in complete Mandarin sentences using **rú** 果 in each of your sentences.

a. **Rú** 果你选的课太难，怎么 **bàn**？

b. **Rú** 果你在看电 **yǐng** 的时候觉得那个电 **yǐng** 没有意思，你会做什么？

c. **Rú** 果你的朋友请你去机 **cháng jiē** 他可是你明天有一个考试，你会做什么？

d. **Rú** 果学校的书店没有你要买的课本，怎么 **bàn**？

e. **Rú** 果你请几个朋友吃饭可是他们今天都太忙，你怎么 **bàn**？

5. Describing nouns, Part I (Use and Structure note 18.3)

Using the pattern <u>description 的 (main) N</u>, translate each of the following noun phrases into Mandarin. The main noun is underlined in each phrase.

Example:
the <u>classes</u> that I selected: 我选的课

a. the <u>cell phone</u> that I bought yesterday   →

b. the <u>Chinese restaurant</u> that we went to   →

c. the <u>movie</u> that I watched   →

d. the <u>students</u> who select a major in economics   →

e. the <u>car</u> that she drives   →

6. Describing nouns, Part II (Use and Structure note 18.3)

Translate the following noun phrases into English

a. 我买的书   →

b. 我昨天看的那本书   →

c. **jiāo** 我中文的老师   →

d. 他昨天 **hē** 的 **jiǔ**   →

e. 我昨天看的电 **yǐng**   →

f. 他上个星期买的中文书   →

g. 我的 **tóngwū** 昨天买的书   →

h. 妈妈给我做的饭   →

i. **cānjiā quán** 国考试的高中生   →

7. Describing nouns, Part III (Use and Structure note 18.3)

The noun phrases that you translated in Exercise 6 above occur as the subject or object of the verb in the following sentences. Translate these sentences into English, referring to your translations in Exercise 6.

a. 我买的书都 **bǐjiào guì**。   →

b. 我昨天看的那本书很好。   →

c. 他是 **jiāo** 我中文的老师。   →

d. 他昨天 **hē** 的 **jiǔ** 是法国 **jiǔ**。   →

e. 我昨天看的电 **yǐng** 没有意思。   →

f. 他上个星期买的中文书非常 **piányi**。   →

g. 我的 **tóngwū** 昨天买的书是一年级的中文书。   →

h. 我最喜欢妈妈给我做的饭。   →

i. **Cānjiā quán** 国考试的高中生都很 **jǐn** 张。   →

8.   Describing nouns, Part IV (Use and Structure note 18.3)

These sentences each contain a noun phrase with a verb description. Translate them into Chinese. The noun phrase and description are underlined.

a. <u>The student who does best on the test</u> does not have to come to class tomorrow.

b. There are a lot of <u>students who plan to apply to college</u>. (Translate it this way: *The students who plan to apply to college are numerous.*)

c. <u>The fruit that you gave me (as a present)</u> is extremely delicious.

d. <u>Students who graduate from college</u> can find somewhat better jobs.

e. <u>The student who returned to her home country this summer</u> is coming back tomorrow.

9.   Describing nouns, Part V (Use and Structure note 18.3)

Put square brackets around the description clauses in each of the following sentences, circle the main verb, and then translate the sentences into English.

a. **Cānjiā** 考试的学生不一定都 **shēn** 请大学。

b. 你 **rènshi** 的高中生 **hē** 不 **hē píjiǔ**?

c. **Bāng** 他学习的那个人已经在中国住了一年了。

d. 你 **néng** 不 **néng** 给我 **jièshào** 昨天晚上跟你吃饭的那个人?

10.   Describing nouns, Part VI (Use and Structure notes 18.3, 18.11)

The following noun phrases each contain a noun that is described by more than one description. Underline each description phrase, and then translate these noun phrases into English.

a. 我昨天买的很 **guì** 的手机   →

b. 我昨天晚上看的很有意思的日本电 **yǐng**   →

c. 这个学期选中文的美国学生   →

d. 那两个 **shēn** 请去中国学习的大学生   →

e. 我觉得最有意思的那些课   →

f. 我们刚 **rènshi** 的学文学的那个人   →

11.   Asking for reasons and giving explanations, Part I (Use and Structure note 18.6)

Translate the following conversations into Mandarin.

a. Lili: Why do you go to sleep so late every night?

Meili: Because I have so much homework in my economics class (*Because my economics class homework is so much.*)

b. Xiao Wang: Why are you so nervous?

Xiao Zhang: Because I'm taking a national college admissions test tomorrow.

Xiao Wang: What happens if you do poorly on the test?

Xiao Zhang: If I do poorly on the test, in the future, I won't be able to attend college.

c. Chen Ming: Why are grades so important?

Teacher: Because your high school grades are related to whether or not you get into college.

12. Asking for reasons and giving explanations, Part II
   (Use and Structure note 18.6)

Translate the following conversations into English.

a. 大为：你昨天为什么没去看电 **yǐng**？
   友文：我去了，可是去晚了。因为昨天的公 **gòng qì** 车非常慢，所以我到的时候电 **yǐng** 已经开 **shǐ** 了。

b. 大为：你的 **zhuānyè** 是经 **jì**，这个学期为什么选了一门 **yīnyuè** 课？
   国强：我选了两门经 **jì** 课。因为经 **jì** 课的功课和考试都很多，我听说 **yīnyuè** 课容易，所以选了一门 **yīnyuè** 课。

c. 美 **lì**：不知道为什么我最 **jìn** 觉得很 **lèi**。
   友文：我想因为快考试了，你 **bǐjiào jǐn** 张。人 **jǐn** 张的时候就容易 **lèi**。

d. **Mài Kè**：这么容易的考试我为什么考得不好呢？我太 **bèn** 了。
   王明：你不 **bèn**。因为你对这门课没有兴趣，学的时候不用功，所以考得不好。

13. From this perspective (Use and Structure note 18.9)

Translate these sentences into English.

a. 我的 **tóngwū** 在学习 **fāngmiàn** 很 **cōng** 明，可是在生 **huó fāngmiàn** 很 **bèn**。我在 **sùshè** 要 **bāng** 他做很多 **shìqing**。

b. 在选 **zhuānyè** 这 **fāngmiàn**，你最好问问你的爸爸妈妈和 **bié** 的 **tóng** 学，不要 **zìjǐ jué** 定。

c. 在中文和中国文 **huà** 这些 **fāngmiàn** 国强 **bāng** 大为，在 **Yīng** 文和 **yīnyuè fāngmiàn** 国强常常请大为 **bāng** 他。

d. **Suī** 然国强常常 **bāng** 大为学中文，可是在中文 **yǔ** 法 **fāngmiàn** 国强也不 **dǒng**。他只知道怎么说。

14.   Translation challenge I

Translate these sentences into English. Begin by identifying the structures used in the sentence, including noun descriptions. The first sentence is outlined for you.

a. 美国的高中生在 **bìyè** 以前，**cānjiā** 不 **cānjiā quán** 国的考试？(___ 以前，___ 的考试)

b. 很多美国的大学生觉得 **hē jiǔ** 跟学习 **chéngjì** 没有关系。最 **zhòng** 要的是 **hē jiǔ** 以后不要开车，学习的时候要用功。

c. 我的 **ài** 好和兴趣是 **yīnyuè** 和 **chàng gē**，可是选 **yīnyuè zhuānyè jiāng** 来不容易找工作。我 **yīnggāi** 怎么 **bàn** 呢？

d. 上大学为什么要选 **zhuānyè** 呢？很多大学生 **bìyè** 以后的工作跟他的 **zhuānyè** 没有一点关系。

e. **Zhuānyè** 没有好 **huài**，可是有的容易，有的难。为什么有很多学生要选很难的 **zhuānyè** 呢？

f. 我快要 **bìyè** 了，开 **shǐ shēn** 请工作。因为现在美国的经 **jì** 很不好，所以大学 **bìyè** 生很难找到 **zìjǐ** 喜欢的工作。我很 **jǐn** 张。我常常想 **rú** 果我可以一直上学就好了。

g. 我昨天在图书馆 **rènshi** 的那个中国学生跟我说 **rú** 果我在学习中文 **fāngmiàn** 有问 **tí** 可以给他打电话问他。

15.   Translation challenge II

Translate these sentences into Mandarin, using the phrase or structure provided.

a. I think this matter is none of your business. (关系)

b. She is the best teacher in our school. (最)

c. If you work very hard (in your studies), in the future, you may become the number one person in your major. Every field produces a leading expert. (Use **rú** 果, also use the Chinese proverb introduced in this lesson.)

d. Before you select your major you should think about your interests. (以前)

e. The strongest students do not necessarily make the most money. (不一定)

f. If you are feeling tired you should go back and go to sleep. (**rú** 果)

g. I've heard that you are interested in Chinese economics. Do you think that in the future you will study in China? (兴趣)

h. Yes. I plan to go to China to study before I graduate college. After I graduate I will go back again and look for work. (以前, 以后)

Focus on communication

1. Dialogue comprehension

Study the Lesson 18 Narrative and Dialogue. Then, read the following statements and indicate whether they are true (T) or false (F).

a. (   ) 选 **zhuānyè** 很 **zhòng** 要，对 **zhuānyè** 没有兴趣，就学不好。

b. (   ) 你的 **jiāng** 来跟你的 **zhuānyè** 有很大的关系。

c. (   ) **Rú** 果学习的时候你很容易 **jǐn** 张，**chéngjì** 也不好，你的 **zhuānyè** 一定选得不好。

d. (   ) 有的 **zhuānyè** 好，有的 **zhuānyè** 很 **zāogāo**。

e. (   ) 美国学生上大学以前先 **jué** 定 **zhuānyè**。

f. (   ) 大为和国强的 **zhuānyè** 都是经 **jì**。

g. (   ) **Rú** 果你经 **jì fāngmiàn** 最强，你就选经 **jì fāngmiàn** 的 **zhuānyè**。

h. (   ) 中国的高中生 **rú** 果不 **cānjiā quán** 国的考试，就不能上大学。

i. (   ) 在中国，你先 **shēn** 请大学和 **zhuānyè** 再考试。

2. What do you say?

What do you say in each of the following situations? Type your answers, using characters where we have learned them, and email them to your Chinese teacher.

a. You want to tell your friend who just did really badly on a test that grades are not the most important thing.

b. You wonder what you should do because economics is not a major that you are interested in.

c. You want your friend to know that you had nothing to do with the situation (matter) that he mentioned.

d. You want to explain to your parents that math is not your strongest subject so you will not pick math as your major.

e. As a father, assure your son that if he begins to earn money right now, he can definitely afford his favorite car in the future.

f. You want to find out why your friend from China already knows her major before she enters college.

g. You express the unlikelihood that you will dive into the job market right after graduation because you first plan to travel in China for three months.

h. You want to encourage your younger brother that if he studies diligently from now on, he can definitely apply to a good college.

i. Tell your roommate that all of the restaurants she picks are great.

j. You were wondering if you could switch to a different teacher if you don't like the one you chose.

3.   Complete the mini-dialogues

Use the structure in parentheses to complete each mini-dialogue. You can respond in any way that makes sense and uses the targeted structure.

a. A: 这个 **jiǎo** 子真好吃！

   B: _____ 当然好吃！(description 的 N)

b. A: 你什么时候可以 **sòng** 我回家？

   B: _____。(以后)

c. A: 你不 **cōng** 明，当然没有女朋友！

   B: _____。(A 跟 B 没有关系)

d. A: 中文、日文和法文哪个难？

   B: _____。(最)

e. A: **Rú** 果书店不卖我要的课本，怎么 **bàn**？

   B: **Bié jǐn** 张，_____。(不会)

4.   Why and how?

Fill in the blanks with 为什么, 这么, 怎么, or 怎么 **bàn** to complete each question. (Use 怎么 only once.) Then answer each question truthfully.

a. 从学校到你家 _____ 走最快？

   Answer: _____

b. 上 **cì** 的中文考试你 _____ 考得不好？

   Answer: _____

c. **Rú** 果你很 **lèi**，没有时 **jiān** 做饭，_____？

   Answer: _____

d. 你 _____ 对中文有兴趣?

    Answer: _____

e. 你想去法国 **lǚyóu**,可是你没有钱,_____?

    Answer: _____

f. 上个学期你的 **chéngjì** 为什么 _____ **zāogāo**(*or* _____ 好)?

    Answer: _____

5.   Multiple choice questions

Select the expression that best completes each sentence and then translate the sentence into English.

a. 中国的高中学生先 **cānjiā quán** 国的考试,_____ **shēn** 请大学和 **zhuānyè**。
    1) 再
    2) 所以
    3) 因为

    English:

b. _____ 星期五早上我没有 **shì**,我 _____ 跟你去那个新的书店。
    1) 因为…所以
    2) **Suī** 然…可是
    3) **Rú** 果…就

    English:

c. 我对数学没有兴趣,所以 _____。
    1) 我的 **zhuānyè** 是数学
    2) 数学 **fāngmiàn** 的课我都不选
    3) 我不 **néng bìyè**

    English:

d. **Suī** 然有的 **zhuānyè jiāng** 来可以 **zhèng bǐjiào** 多的钱,可是 _____。
    1) 我一直对经 **jì** 很有兴趣
    2) **zhuānyè** 和你的 **jiāng** 来有很大的关系
    3) 选一个你最喜欢的 **zhuānyè bǐjiào zhòng** 要

    English:

e. **Rú** 果 _____,就吃一点水果吧。
    1) 你已经吃过饭了
    2) 喝了一点水
    3) 你在吃饭

    English:

6.   小王的 **chéngjì**

Below is Xiao Wang's report card from last semester. He tends to do well in the subjects that he has the most interest in and vice versa. Translate and answer the questions in Mandarin.

Chinese	Chinese Culture	Economics	Mathematics	Chinese Music
A+	A	B+	C−	A−

a. How many courses did Xiao Wang choose last semester?

   Q: _____

   A: _____

b. In which subject did Xiao Wang get the highest grade?

   Q: _____

   A: _____

c. What area was Xiao Wang strongest in?

   Q: _____

   A: _____

d. What factor influences his grades?

   Q: _____

   A: _____

e. What course was Xiao Wang least interested in?

   Q: _____

   A: _____

f. In the future, what area can Xiao Wang look for a job in?

   Q: _____

   A: _____

7.   This is my friend who...

You are showing photos of your college friends to your parents. Follow the example sentence and use <u>description</u> 的 N to complete each sentence.

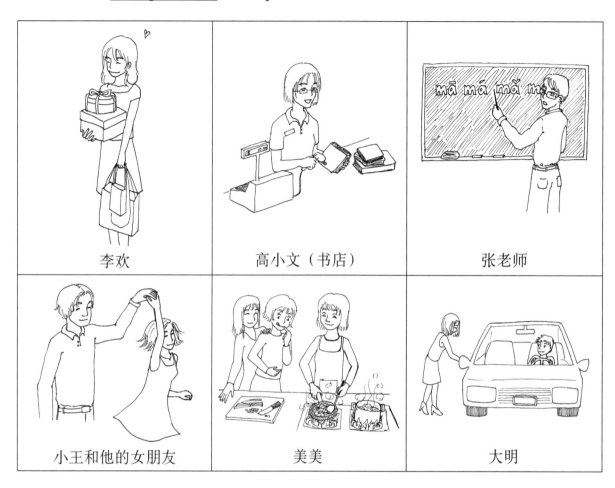

Example:
常常做饭给我们吃的是美美。

a. _____是张老师。

b. _____是大明。

c. _____是小王和他的女朋友。

d. _____是李欢。

e. _____是高小文。

8. Do you agree? Why or why not?

Read each statement and write a simple response stating why you agree or do not agree with it. Start your sentence with 我也觉得 / 我不觉得 + statement, 因为....

a. 选 **zhuānyè** 是大学生最 **zhòng** 要的 **shìqing**。

b. 选 **zhuānyè** 跟 **jiāng** 来的工作有很大的关系。

c. **Rú** 果大家都选这个 **zhuānyè**，这个 **zhuānyè** 一定是最好的。

d. 大学一年级和二年级选的课，可以 **bāng** 你 **jué** 定你的 **zhuānyè**。

e. **Rú** 果选 **bǐjiào** 容易的 **zhuānyè**，大学的生 **huó** 会 **bǐjiào** 快 **lè**。

f. **Rú** 果还没有 **jìn** 大学就选 **zhuānyè**，你不一定会喜欢那个 **zhuānyè**。

9. Writing

Write a paragraph about how you decided on your major and why you chose it. You can use some of the answers you have used in the previous exercise. If you haven't decided on your major, explain what you are interested in and what major you might choose. Below is a list of words/expressions that you can use in your paragraph. Include at least <u>five</u> of them. Your paragraph should be at least 100 characters in length.

因为...所以	A 跟 B 有关系	只是	**jué** 定	对...有兴趣
选	**rú** 果...就	**bǐjiào**	有用	不过

_____

_____

_____

_____

_____

_____

Lesson 19 Workbook

Listening and speaking

(audio online)

Structure drills

1. I've done it already (Use and Structure note 19.2)

You will hear a suggestion that you finish doing some action. Reply that you have already finished, as in the example.

> **Example:**
> *You will hear:* 你要看 **wán** 这本书。
> *You will say:* 这本书我已经看 **wán** 了。
> *Click "R" to hear the correct response:* 这本书我已经看 **wán** 了。

(a)   (b)   (c)   (d)   (e)   (f)   (g)   (h)   (i)   (j)

2. I did it, but I wasn't successful (Use and Structure note 19.2)

You will hear a question asking if you have successfully completed some task. You will say that you did the action, but that you did not successfully complete the task, as in the example.

> **Example:**
> *You will hear:* 那本书你找到了吗?
> *You will say:* 那本书，我找了，可是没找到。
> *Click "R" to hear the correct response:* 那本书，我找了，可是没找到。

(a)   (b)   (c)   (d)   (e)   (f)   (g)   (h)

3. Extremely! (Use and Structure note 19.3)

You will hear a question asking about the characteristic of some person or thing. Say that the person or thing is *extremely* so, as in the example.

> **Example:**
> *You will hear:* 今天的 **kǎoshì** 难吗?
> *You will say:* 今天的 **kǎoshì** 难 **jí** 了。
> *Click "R" to hear the correct response:* 今天的 **kǎoshì** 难 **jí** 了。

(a)   (b)   (c)   (d)   (e)   (f)   (g)   (h)   (i)   (j)

4. Both...and (Use and Structure note 19.6)

You will hear two qualities followed by a noun. Say that the noun has *both* the first quality *and* the second quality, as in the example.

> **Example:**
> *You will hear:* **piányi**、好吃、中国饭
> *You will say:* 中国饭 **yòu piányi yòu** 好吃。
> *Click "R" to hear the correct response:* 中国饭 **yòu piányi yòu** 好吃。

(a)   (b)   (c)   (d)   (e)   (f)   (g)   (h)

5. **Bǎ** with resultative verbs (Use and Structure note 19.7)

You will hear a sentence saying that you should complete some task. Restate the sentence with **bǎ**, as in the example.

> **Example:**
> *You will hear:* 你要看 **wán** 这本书。
> *You will say:* 我 **bǎ** 这本书看 **wán** 了。
> *Click "R" to hear the correct response:* 我 **bǎ** 这本书看 **wán** 了。

(a)   (b)   (c)   (d)   (e)   (f)   (g)   (h)   (i)   (j)

6. Put the object in a location (Use and Structure note 19.7)

You will hear a sentence stating the location of some object. Restate the sentence with **bǎ**, saying that you have put the object in the location.

> **Example:**
> *You will hear:* 书放在书 **jià** 上了。
> *You will say:* 我 **bǎ** 书放在书 **jià** 上了。
> *Click "R" to hear the correct response:* 我 **bǎ** 书放在书 **jià** 上了。

(a)   (b)   (c)   (d)   (e)   (f)   (g)   (h)   (i)   (j)

7.   Negation of **bǎ** sentences (Use and Structure notes 19.7, 19.11)

You will hear a sentence with **bǎ** saying that someone has done some action. Negate the sentence, saying that the person has not done the action, as in the example.

Example:
You will hear: 小谢 **bǎ** 那本书看 **wán** 了。
You will say: 小谢没 **bǎ** 那本书看 **wán**。
Click "R" to hear the correct response: 小谢没 **bǎ** 那本书看 **wán**。

(a)   (b)   (c)   (d)   (e)   (f)   (g)   (h)

8.   Don't do it! (Use and Structure note 19.7)

You will hear a sentence saying that I have put an object in some location. Reply by telling me politely not to put the object in that location, as in the example.

Example:
You will hear: 我 **bǎ** 书放在地上了。
You will say: 请你不要 **bǎ** 书放在地上。
Click "R" to hear the correct response: 请你不要 **bǎ** 书放在地上。

(a)   (b)   (c)   (d)   (e)   (f)   (g)   (h)   (i)   (j)

9.   You have to do it (Use and Structure note 19.8)

You will hear a question asking whether it is necessary to do something. Reply that you have to do it, as in the example.

Example:
You will hear: 那本书你一定要看吗?
You will say: 对，那本书我非看不可。
Click "R" to hear the correct response: 对，那本书我非看不可。

(a)   (b)   (c)   (d)   (e)   (f)   (g)

10.   As soon as I do this, I do that (Use and Structure note 19.10)

You will hear a statement saying that after you do one action, you do another action. Restate the sentence with 一 …就 to say that *as soon as* you do the first action, you do the second one *right afterward*, as in the example.

Example:
You will hear: 我下了课就去图书馆。
You will say: 我一下课，就去图书馆。
Click "R" to hear the correct response: 我一下课，就去图书馆。

(a)   (b)   (c)   (d)   (e)   (f)   (g)   (h)   (i)   (j)

11. Whenever (Use and Structure note 19.10)

You will hear a statement saying that when you do one action, you do another action. Restate the sentence with 一…就 to say that *whenever* you do the first action, you do the second one, as in the example.

Example:
You will hear: 我开车的时候听 **yīnyuè**。
You will say: 我一开车就听 **yīnyuè**。
Click "R" to hear the correct response: 我一开车就听 **yīnyuè**。

(a)   (b)   (c)   (d)   (e)   (f)   (g)   (h)

Listening for information

1.   Moving things around the room

(CD1: 24)

Gaofeng and his roommate are sitting in their dorm room. Gaofeng is telling his roommate to move things to different places in the room. Listen to each of Gaofeng's instructions and draw an arrow from the place where each item is to the place where Gaofeng tells his roommate to put it.

2.   What are they doing?

(CD1: 25) This is the room where Xiao An, Pai Hai, Wen Shan, and Wang Tong live. Their friends Cheng Li, Lao Dong and Xiao Wang are visiting them. Look at the picture to find out what each person is doing and then answer the questions in the recording in English.

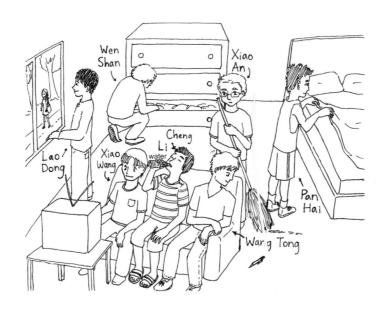

a.

b.

c.

d.

e.

f.

g.

3. Aiping's room

You will hear six statements that describe Aiping's room. Listen to the statements and indicate whether they are true (T) or false (F) based on the drawing.

(CD1: 26)

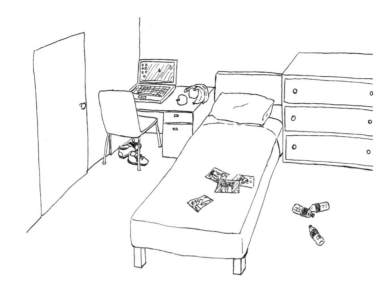

a. ( )   b. ( )   c. ( )   d. ( )   e. ( )   f. ( )

4. Our afternoon

Listen to Xianmin's narration about his afternoon with his girlfriend Xinxin, and write the events in English in chronological order as Xianmin describes them.

(CD1: 27)

a. _____ → b. _____ → c. _____ →

d. _____ → e. _____

5. My girlfriend is visiting

Shucheng is telling his roommate what they need to do before his girlfriend arrives. Listen to his instructions and write the tasks in English in the order in which they are mentioned.

(CD1: 28)

a.

b.

c.

d.

e.

6. Conversation

(CD1: 29) A classmate is asking you about your living situation. Write the answers in complete sentences in Mandarin, based on your situation, writing characters wherever we have learned them. If you live at home, describe your home situation.

a.

b.

c.

d.

e.

f.

7. Listen and reply

(CD1: 30) Xiao Fang has a new roommate. Listen to her description of her new roommate to her mom and answer the questions that follow in English, based on the description.

a.

b.

c.

d.

e.

8. Dialogue I

(CD1: 31) You will hear a dialogue between two classmates who are taking the same course. Answer the questions based on the dialogue.

a. What is the homework?
   1) complete the Lesson 2 workbook
   2) preview the Lesson 3 text
   3) complete the Lesson 3 workbook
   4) preview the Lesson 2 text

b. What is the woman's plan?
   1) She will talk to the teacher.
   2) She will withdraw from the course.
   3) She will do her laundry.
   4) She will get help from the man.

c. Which statement about the woman's clothes is accurate?
  1) She cannot find the clothes that she wants.
  2) She does not have time to wash her clothes now.
  3) All of her clothes are dirty.
  4) She needs to buy some new clothes.

9. Dialogue II

You will hear a dialogue between a brother and sister. Answer the questions based on the **(CD1: 32)** dialogue.

a. Where did the brother last see his cell phone?
  1) at school
  2) in the room
  3) in the restaurant
  4) in the office

b. What did the sister do?
  1) She cleaned his room.
  2) She helped him to remember something.
  3) She scolded him for losing the phone.
  4) She told him where to find the phone.

c. Where is the cell phone?
  1) next to the desk
  2) under a pile of papers
  3) in the office
  4) under the chair

Reading and writing

Focus on Chinese characters

1. Number of strokes

Indicate the number of strokes used in writing each of the following characters.

a. 始 ____   f. 屋 ____

b. 能 ____   g. 间 ____

c. 同 ____   h. 房 ____

d. 洗 ____   i. 舍 ____

e. 虽 ____   j. 床 ____

2. Which character?

Circle the character in each line that corresponds to the meaning on the left.

a. **jiān** (**fángjiān** *room*)   间   问

b. **fāng** (**fángjiān** *room*)   房   放

c. **lǐ** (**lǐbian** *inside*)   里   理

d. **sù** (**sùshè** *dormitory*)   伯   宿

e. **biān** (**lǐbian** *inside*)   边   这

f. **shǐ** (**kāishǐ** *begin*)   始   如

g. **wài** (**wàibian** *outside*)   外   处

h. **chuáng** *bed*   床   庄

i. **shè** (**sùshè** *dormitory*)   含   舍

j. **wū** (**tóngwū** *roommate*)   屋   房

k. **tóng** (**tóngwū** *roommate*)   问   同

l. **suī** (**suīrán** *although*)   虫   虽

3. First strokes

Write the first two strokes of each of the following characters.

a. 虽 ＿＿   f. 屋 ＿＿

b. 放 ＿＿   g. 所 ＿＿

c. 里 ＿＿   h. 房 ＿＿

d. 床 ＿＿   i. 能 ＿＿

e. 边 ＿＿   j. 宿 ＿＿

4.   Missing strokes

Complete each character by writing in the missing strokes.

a.   ㄋ   **biān** (lǐbian *inside*)

b.   丬   **jiān** (fángjiān *room*)

c.   亼   **shè** (sùshè *dormitory*)

d.   宀   **sù** (sùshè *dormitory*)

e.   夕   **wài** (wàibian *outside*)

f.   疒   **fàng** *put*

g.   ㄠ   **néng** *able to, can*

h.   女   **shǐ** (kāishǐ *begin*)

i.   门   **tóng** (tóngwū *roommate*)

j.   口   **suī** (suīrán *although*)

5.   Total strokes

Rewrite this list of characters, arranging the characters in terms of their total number of strokes. Begin your list with the character with the fewest strokes.

舍	虽	屋	同	床	间	放	房	能	始	宿	外	洗	边	里

6.   Radicals

Here are characters that we have learned through this lesson. Rewrite each character in the row next to its radical.

边　定　能　选　外　房　间
始　屋　放　所　床　洗　同

户	
宀	
辶	
口	
月	
夕	
门	
女	
尸	
攵	
广	
氵	

7.   Character sleuth

Group the following characters in terms of a part that they share in common. The shared part need not be the radical in each character.

外　放　洗　多　问　们　能　容　期　选　房
前　妈　用　先　始　馆　朋　宿　好　家　间

shared part	characters
人	人，大，太，天，舍
夕	
门	
月	
方	
先	
女	
宀	

8.   Find the words and phrases

You won't be able to completely understand the following passage, but it contains many characters that we have learned.

a. Circle at least fifteen <u>words</u> that we have learned that are <u>composed of two or more characters each</u> and write them on the answer sheet below.

"今年" is an example of a word that is composed of two or more characters.

"我也" is composed of two characters in a row that we have learned, but it is <u>not</u> a word.

晚上吃晚饭的时候我的手机没有了。我想下午下课以后我去图书馆了。在图书馆一做完作业我就来吃饭了。我一定在图书馆学习的时候把手机放在桌子上了。我回图书馆去找我的手机。找了半天，可是没找到。我不可以没有手机。明天下了课，我非得去买手机不可。我很不高兴地回宿舍了。一打开宿舍的门，我就看见我的手机在宿舍的桌子上。我不用买新的了。我高兴极了。

Words in this paragraph composed of two or more characters:

1. _____   2. _____   3. _____   4. _____   5. _____

6. _____   7. _____   8. _____   9. _____   10. _____

11. _____   12. _____   13. _____   14. _____   15. _____

b. In one sentence in English, state the general topic of this passage.

9.   Dictionary skills

Following the instructions in Lesson 17 of the Textbook, look up these characters in a Chinese dictionary and provide the requested information.

a. 把
   pronunciation:
   meaning:
   one two-character word or phrase in which it occurs:

b. 完
   pronunciation:
   meaning:
   one two-character word or phrase in which it occurs:

c. 衣
   pronunciation:
   meaning:
   one two-character word or phrase in which it occurs:

10. Find the incorrect characters

Xiao Zhang has written this email to his parents but he has written ten characters incorrectly. Read the passage aloud, circle the mistakes, and correct them on the answer sheet below.

> 我这级天非常忙，没友时问去买可本。今天非去不可了，**yīn** 为明天九要开始上课了。一吃 **wán** 早饭，我就到书点去了。**Bié** 的书都卖到了，就是中问课的书卖 **wán** 了，**yīn** 为洗中文课的学生恨多。

a. ____   b. ____   c. ____   d. ____   e. ____

f. ____   g. ____   h. ____   i. ____   j. ____

11. Scrambled sentences

Rewrite these phrases as sentences, putting the words in the correct order to match the English translations.

a. 课本 / 同屋 / 我的 / 的 / 都 / 在 / 他床 / 下边 / 的

My roommate's textbooks are all under his bed.

b. 在 / 可是 / **zhōumò** / 她 / 宿舍 / 她 / 洗 **yīfu** / 虽然 / 住 / 每个 / 回家

Although she lives in a dorm, she goes home every weekend to do laundry (wash clothes).

c. 非常 / 学 / 的时候 / 我 / 开始 / 开车 / 开车 / 慢 / 刚 / 开得 /

When I just started to learn how to drive a car I drove extremely slowly.

d. 能 / 我 / 你 / 不 / **bāng** / 课 / 能 / 选

Can you help me select courses?

e. 的 / 在 / 他 / 都 / 床上 / 东西 / 放

All of his things are on the bed.

12. Translation

Read the following passage and translate it into English.

小 **Yè** 没有同屋，她一个人住。她的宿舍不大，**dàn** 是很 **gānjìng**。房间里的东西不多，一个床、一个 **guì** 子、一个书 **jià**、一张 **zhuō** 子和两 **bǎ yǐ** 子。**Zhuō** 子上有书、**bǐ**、**liàn** 习本，还有一个电 **nǎo**。

13.   Pinyin to characters

Rewrite the following sentences in Chinese characters.

a. **Jīntiān suīrán shì xīngqīliù, bù yòng qù shàng kè, kěshì Dàmíng qǐ chuáng qǐ de hěn zǎo**。

b. **Tā yào gēn tā èr niánjí de jǐ ge péngyou yīqǐ qù tā Zhōngguó tóngwū de jiā**。

c. **Dào Zhōngguó rén de jiā qù kànkan, qù chī fàn, tāmen dōu hěn gāoxìng**。

Focus on structure

1.   He's been doing it a long time (Use and Structure note 19.1)

Here is a list of the things that Meili has done and the amount of time she has spent on each activity. Write a sentence in Mandarin for each activity, describing how long she has done it.

activity	duration
a. washed clothes	more than a half hour
b. watched television	more than three hours
c. studied Chinese	more than one year
d. slept	more than eight hours

a.

b.

c.

d.

2.   Bird watching (Use and Structure note 19.2)

Xie Guoqiang has a new hobby: bird watching. He is keeping a list of birds that can be seen in and around Beijing, and he checks off birds as he sees them. Write a sentence for each bird, saying whether he has seen it or not. The resultative verb that you will use in each sentence is 看到.

bird	sighted
a. golden oriole (**jīn yīng**)	
b. egret (**bái lù**)	✓
c. woodpecker (**zhuó mù niǎo**)	
d. spotted turtle dove (**bān jiū**)	✓

a.

b.

c.

d.

3.   Have you completed the task? (Use and Structure note 19.2)

Here are tasks that Guoqiang has been engaged in. Ask him in complete Mandarin sentences if he has reached the indicated conclusion or result, as in the example.

Example:

看书, finished reading   →   你看 **wán** 书了吗？ or 你看 **wán** 书了没有？

a. 找他的 **shǒujī**, found it   →

b. 买电 **yǐng piào**, bought it   →

c. **shōushi** 房间, finished (and it is now presentable for his guests)   →

d. 写功课, finished   →

e. 选课, finished   →

4.   Done! (Use and Structure note 19.2)

Guoqiang has completed all of the tasks. Answer *yes* to each of the five questions in Exercise 3 using a complete sentence in Mandarin.

a.

b.

c.

d.

e.

5.   When did Guoqiang complete the tasks?

Guoqiang finished some of these tasks a while ago, and some of them just a moment ago. For a few of the tasks, he's almost done. Take your answers in Exercise 4 and rewrite them, adding in the time adverb in the appropriate location. Then translate each of your responses into English.

a. 刚   →
   English:

b. 早就   →
   English:

c. 现在   →
   English:

d. 刚   →
   English:

e. 早就   →
   English:

6.   Not yet done! (Use and Stucture notes 19.2, 19.4, 19.7)

Here are activities that Youwen has been doing, followed by the result or conclusion that she wants to reach. Write a sentence for each of these activities saying that she has been doing it for a long time but she's still not done.

a. **shōushi** 房间 ... **shōushi gānjìng**

b. 做功课 ... 做 **wán**

c. 找她的 **shǒujī** ... 找到

d. 看书 ... 看 **wán**

7.   All except for this (Use and Structure note 19.5, 19.7)

Xiao Chen is getting his dorm ready for a party. For every part of the preparation, he has only one more thing to do. Here is his list of tasks and remaining activities. Complete each sentence in Mandarin and then translate the entire sentence into English. Use the expression 就是 *only, it is only* in each of your Mandarin sentences.

a. 功课都做好了。   *I just haven't finished reviewing the Chinese characters.*
   Mandarin:
   English: _____. *I just haven't finished reviewing the Chinese characters.*

b. 我 **bǎ** 房间 **shōushi** 好了。 *I just haven't put the clothes in the dresser.*
   Mandarin:
   English: _____. *I just haven't put the clothes in the dresser.*

c. 吃的，**hē** 的都买好了。   *I just haven't bought the beer.*
   Mandarin:
   English: _____. *I just haven't bought the beer.*

d. 同学都已经 **gàosu** 了。   *I just haven't invited my teachers.*
   Mandarin:
   English: _____. *I just haven't invited my teachers.*

e. **Bié** 的都好了。   *We just haven't selected the music.*
   Mandarin:
   English: _____. *We just haven't selected the music.*

**8.   What they do in the time before the party
       (Use and Structure notes 19.2, 19.7)**

Xiao Chen and his friends are all going to be busy in the time before the party. Here is what they are doing. Translate their activities into English.

a. 在小 **Chén** 的同学来以前，他得先 **bǎ** 汉字 **fù** 习 **wán**。

b. 在小高去小 **Chén** 家以前，她先给妈妈爸爸打电话。

c. 在大为去晚会以前，他得先 **jiē** 小 **Yè** 和小高。

d. 在小王去小 **Chén** 那儿以前，他先 **bāng** 小 **Chén** 买几 **píng** 可 **lè**。

9.   Both ... and (Use and Structure note 19.6)

Here are comments and observations that Xiao Chen's guests make during the party. Write them in complete Mandarin sentences, using **yòu** AdjV₁ **yòu** AdjV₂.

a. 宿舍（**piàoliang，gānjìng**）　→

b. **cài**（多，好吃）　　　　　→

c. 地 **tiě**（**piányi**，快）　　→

d. 水果（好看，好吃）　　　→

e. 那个日本饭馆（**yuǎn，guì**）→

10.   Have to do it? No need to do it? (Use and Structure notes 19.8, 19.9)

Here is a list of activities. Meili has put a * next to all of the activities she absolutely has to do, and she has put a ☺ next to all of the activities she need not do. Write a Mandarin sentence for each activity saying that she has to do it (非…不可) or need not do it (不用). If the verb phrase consists of a verb + object, state the object before 非…不可.

a. review Chinese *　　　　　　　　　→

b. go to the library ☺　　　　　　　　→

c. finish reading the economics textbook *　→

d. clean up the room ☺　　　　　　　→

e. watch that new Chinese movie *　　　→

f. go downtown to buy a subway map ☺　→

11.   When will you do it? As soon as ... (Use and Structure note 19.10)

Xiao Xie's mother is asking him when he is going to do a number of things. He says he will do them as soon as he finishes another activity. Here is a list of her questions and the activity that he needs to finish first before he does the task that she mentions. Use this information to write Xiao Xie's responses, using 一 VP₁ 就 VP₂ in each response, as in the example.

> **Example:**
> 你什么时候 **shuì** 觉？（看 **wán** 这本书）　→　我一看 **wán** 这本书就 **shuì** 觉。

a. 你什么时候去上课？（吃 **wán** 早饭）　　→

b. 你什么时候做功课？（找到我的课本）　→

c. 你什么时候找工作？（这个学期 **wán** 了）→

d. 你什么时候选 **zhuānyè**？（对课有兴趣）→

e. 你什么时候请你的同屋来家吃饭？（放 **jià**）→

12.   Complete the sentences

Fill in the blanks with one of the following words or phrases to complete each sentence.

就是	半天	非	一定	不用	在

a. 上课的时候不可以 **hē kāfēi**。你得 _____ 上课以前 **hē wán**。

b. 这个店的 **yīfu** 不多，我选了 _____ 也没选到一 **jiàn** 我想买的。

c. 明天 _____ 上课，所以今天晚上可以晚一点 **shuì**。

d. **Rú** 果昨天考试容易一点，我 _____ 会考得 **bǐjiào** 好。

e. 我会说中文、日文、法文、**Dé** 文，_____ 不会说 **Yīng** 文。

f. 功课明天就得给老师，所以今天晚上我 _____ 写 **wán** 不可。

Focus on communication

1.   Dialogue comprehension

Study the Lesson 19 Narrative and Dialogue. Then, read the following statements and indicate whether they are true (T) or false (F).

a. (   ) 小张和小谢这几天忙 **zhe** 选课还有买课本。

b. (   ) 小张和小谢今天晚上请同学来开晚会，所以他们在 **shōushi** 宿舍。

c. (   ) 他们现在都在房间里。

d. (   ) 小张找书找了十二个钟买了。

e. (   ) 他们的房间 **luànjí** 了。这儿、那儿都是书。

f. (   ) 他们 **jué** 定先 **shōushi** 房间，不找课本了。

g. (   ) **Zhuō** 子上和地上的书 **yīnggāi** 放在书 **jià** 上，**yīfu yīnggāi** 放在 **guì** 子里。

h. (   ) 房间 **shōushi** 好以后，小张 **sǎo** 地，小谢 **shōushi xié** 子。

2.   What do you say?

What do you say in each of the following situations? Type your answers, using characters where we have learned them, and email them to your Chinese teacher.

a. You are mad that your younger brother messes up your room. Ask him to straighten it up before you come back tonight.

b. Your hands are full with grocery bags. Ask someone nicely if he can open the door for you.

c. You want to know if your classmate finished selecting his classes.

d. Your friend offers you beer at a party. You decline because you feel sleepy as soon as you drink beer.

e. You wonder if your friend has seen the shoes you purchased yesterday. You've been looking for them for a long time.

f. You tell your friend that he's going to regret it if he does not try this restaurant. (In other words, he must try it!)

g. It's been two weeks since school began. Your teacher wonders why you haven't bought the textbooks yet. What does the teacher say?

h. You are checking out a potential apartment for rent. You don't like it because it's small and expensive.

i. You ask if your roommate can sweep the floor clean because you are busy putting books back on the shelf.

j. You explain to your friend that you've been to France and Germany but you haven't been to China.

k. You brought home from school a bag of dirty clothes. Ask your mom if she can wash them for you.

3. Complete the mini-dialogues

Use the structure in parentheses to complete each mini-dialogue.

a. A: 你不是去买 **xié** 吗？怎么没买到？

　　B: 那些 **xié** ＿＿＿＿＿＿＿＿＿，我都不喜欢。（**yòu**…**yòu**）

b. A: 你打 **suan** 什么时候开始写功课？

　　B: 我 ＿＿＿＿＿＿＿＿＿。（一…就）

c. A: 你看见我的日文课本了吗？我已经找了半天了。

　　B: 没看见。我 ＿＿＿＿＿＿＿＿ 就来 **bāng** 你找。（**bǎ**）

d. A: 你看，这是我昨天买的 **yīfu**，你觉得怎么样？

　　B: ＿＿＿＿＿＿＿＿＿！多少钱？我也想买一 **jiàn**！（**jí** 了）

e. A: ＿＿＿＿＿＿＿＿＿＿＿＿？（不用）

　　B: 你怎么 **wàng** 了？今天是 Veterans Day，放一天 **jià**。

4.   Before and after

Below are two pictures of Xie Weizhong's room, before and after he cleaned it up.

before	after

Part I.   Look at the BEFORE picture. Translate each of the following questions into Mandarin and then answer them in Mandarin.

a. What is in the closet?

  Q:

  A:

b. Where is Xie Weizhong's computer?

  Q:

  A:

c. Where are all the books?

  Q:

  A:

d. What's on the floor?

  Q:

  A:

e. How many pencils are there in Xie Weizhong's room? Where are they?

  Q:

  A:

Part II.   Look at the BEFORE picture and decide whether the following statements are true or false. If a statement is false, please correct it.

Example:

Guì 子里有很多 **xié**.   →   *False:* **Guì** 子里<u>没有</u>xié.

a. 谢为中的电 **nǎo** 在床下边。   →

b. 床上有 **xié**，**yīfu** 还有电 **nǎo**。   →

c. 谢为中的 **bǐ** 都在 **yǐ** 子上。   →

d. 谢为中的床上有 **xié**，地上有 **xié**，**zhuō** 子上也有 **xié**。 →

e. 谢为中的 **guì** 子里没有 **yīfu**。   →

f. 谢为中的书 **jià** 上有一 **píng** 水。   →

Part III.   Look at the AFTER picture. Write <u>four</u> sentences to describe how Xie Weizhong has cleaned up his room. You need to use the **bǎ**-structure.

Example:

谢为中 **bǎ** 水放在书 **jià** 上。

a.

b.

c.

d.

Part IV.   Look at the AFTER picture and write a few sentences to answer this question: 请问，你觉得谢为中 **bǎ** 房间 **shōushi** 好了吗？为什么？

_____

_____

_____

5.   A conversation between Xiao Ye's mother and Xiao Ye

Part I. Fill in the blanks.   Select a word from the following list to complete each sentence.

只是	**wán**	不用	多	没
yīn 为	就是	的	**yòu**	开

Yè太太： 友文，昨天晚上我给你打电话你怎么不在？

小Yè：   妈，昨天小张和小谢在他们的宿舍 ＿＿＿ 晚会，我们都去了。

Yè太太： 晚会有意思吗？

小Yè：   有意思，＿＿＿，他们的宿舍太小，去的人太多，没有 **yǐ** 子坐。

Yè太太： 你们吃什么？

小Yè：   小谢做了很多吃的，很多东西都 ＿＿＿ 吃 **wán**。

Yè太太： 友文，开学已经一个 ＿＿＿ 星期了，忙不忙？

小Yè：   还好。我的课选好了，课本也买好了，＿＿＿ 宿舍还没有 **shōushi** 好。

Yè太太： 没关系，慢慢 **shōushi**。这个 **zhōumò** 回家吃饭吧！我打 **suan** 做你 **zuì** 喜欢 ＿＿＿ **hóngshāo ròu**。

小Yè：   这个 **zhōumò** 不行，＿＿＿ 我下个星期有考试。下个 **zhōumò** 吧！我一考 ＿＿＿ 试就回家。

Yè太太： 要不要爸爸去学校 **jiē** 你？

小Yè：   ＿＿＿，坐地 **tiě** ＿＿＿ 快 **yòu piányi**。

Yè太太： 那也好。那下个星期六见。

小Yè：   妈，再见。

Part II. Q&A.   Read the dialogue above. Then, answer the questions in Mandarin.

a. 昨天晚上小 **Yè** 为什么不在宿舍里？

b. 小 **Yè** 觉得小张和小谢的宿舍怎么样？

c. 他们开学多 **jiǔ** 了？

d. 开学到现在，小 **Yè** 什么 **shì** 还没有做 **wán**？

e. 这个 **zhōumò** 小 **Yè** 会回家吗？为什么？

f. 小 **Yè** 怎么回家？

6.   Writing

Look at this picture and imagine what this mother is saying to her son right now. Use the following structures/words in your paragraph:

luàn	非…不可	yòu…yòu	shōushi	bǎ

_____

_____

_____

_____

_____

_____

_____

Lesson 20 Workbook

 Listening and speaking

Structure drills

1. The whole time (Use and Structure note 20.1)

You will hear a statement followed by a word referring to time. Restate the sentence, saying that the action was true for that whole period of time, as in the example.

> **Example:**
> *You will hear:* 我同屋没睡觉，**yè**
> *You will say:* 我同屋一 **yè** 没睡觉。
> *Click "R" to hear the correct response:* 我同屋一 **yè** 没睡觉。

(a)   (b)   (c)   (d)   (e)   (f)   (g)   (h)   (i)   (j)

2. Are you able to do it? (Use and Structure note 20.6)

You will hear a statement about some action that has reached a result or conclusion. Ask your roommate if she can do this action to the result or conclusion, as in the example.

> **Example:**
> *You will hear:* 看 **dǒng** 中文书
> *You will say:* 中文书你看得 **dǒng** 看不 **dǒng**?
> *Click "R" to hear the correct response:* 中文书你看得 **dǒng** 看不 **dǒng**?

(a)   (b)   (c)   (d)   (e)   (f)   (g)   (h)

3. Focusing on a detail of a past event with 是...的
(Use and Structure note 20.9)

You will hear a sentence about some action. Restate the sentence with 是...的 to focus on some detail of the action, as in the example.

Example:

You will hear: 我昨天去了。
You will say: 我是昨天去的。
Click "R" to hear the correct response: 我是昨天去的。

(a)   (b)   (c)   (d)   (e)   (f)   (g)   (h)   (i)   (j)

4. Asking about a detail of a past event with 是...的
(Use and Structure note 20.9)

You will hear a statement with 是...的 that focuses on some detail of a past event, followed by a question word or phrase. Use that word or phrase to ask the corresponding question with 是...的, as in the example.

Example:

You will hear: 我是在图书馆 **rènshi** 他的。（在哪儿？）
You will say: 你是在哪儿 **rènshi** 他的？
Click "R" to hear the correct response: 你是在哪儿 **rènshi** 他的？

(a)   (b)   (c)   (d)   (e)   (f)   (g)   (h)   (i)   (j)

5. When did it begin? 从 + time + 开始

You will hear an action followed by a time phrase. Say that the action started at that time, as in the example.

Example:

You will hear: **lā dù** 子，昨天晚上
You will say: 我从昨天晚上开始 **lā dù** 子。
Click "R" to hear the correct response: 我从昨天晚上开始 **lā dù** 子。

(a)   (b)   (c)   (d)   (e)   (f)   (g)   (h)   (i)   (j)

6. Focusing on when something began: 是从 + time + 开始的
(Use and Structure note 20.9)

You will hear an action followed by a time expression. Say that the action began at that time, using 是…的 to focus on the starting time, as in the example.

Example:

You will hear: **lā dù** 子，昨天晚上
You will say: 我是从昨天晚上开始 **lā dù** 子的。
Click "R" to hear the correct response: 我是从昨天晚上开始 **lā dù** 子的。

(a)   (b)   (c)   (d)   (e)   (f)   (g)   (h)   (i)   (j)

7. Saying *besides X* with **chú** 了 X 以外，也 VP (Use and Structure note 20.10)

You will hear a statement followed by a statement with additional information on the same topic. Rephrase the information with **chú** 了 X 以外, as in the example.

Example:

You will hear: 你学中文，我们也学中文。
You will say: **chú** 了你以外，我们也学中文。
Click "R" to hear the correct response: **chú** 了你以外，我们也学中文。

(a)   (b)   (c)   (d)   (e)   (f)   (g)   (h)   (i)   (j)

Listening for information

1.   Are you sick?

(CD1: 36) You will hear seven questions asking about the people in the drawings. Answer the questions in English.

| Ke Feng | Mr. Zhang | Ding Ding | Mrs. Huang | Xiao Zheng |

a.

b.

c.

d.

e.

f.

g.

2. We all got sick

(CD1: 37)

Xiao Ping and her three roommates all got sick. Listen to Xiao Ping's narration about everyone's illness. Fill in the missing information in the form, based on the information that she presents.

who	symptoms	action/current status
Yaxin		
		getting better
	headache	
Lingling		

3. Lunch time

(CD1: 38)

Li Tairan is talking about her weekend. Answer the questions that follow, based on the information she provides.

a.

b.

c.

d.

e.

4.   Giving explanations

(CD1: 39) You will hear descriptions of five people. Each description will be followed by a question. Answer each question in English based on the information in the description.

a.

b.

c.

d.

e.

5.   Questions about getting sick

(CD1: 40) Answer the questions you hear in complete sentences in Mandarin, using characters where we have learned them.

a.

b.

c.

d.

e.

f.

6.   Listen and reply

(CD1: 41) Peng Tongda did not feel well, so he went to see a doctor. You will hear what the doctor said to him. Answer the questions in English based on the doctor's diagnosis and instructions.

a.

b.

c.

d.

e.

7. Dialogue I

You will hear a dialogue between a teacher and a student in class. Answer the questions (CD1: 42) based on the dialogue.

a. What symptoms does the student have?
  1) a stomach ache
  2) a sore throat
  3) a fever
  4) a headache

b. What did the teacher suggest the student do first?
  1) take the test
  2) go back to the dorm
  3) see a doctor
  4) take some medicine

c. What will the student do?
  1) drink more water
  2) prepare for the test
  3) go with a classmate to see a doctor
  4) call the teacher when feeling better

8. Dialogue II

You will hear a dialogue between two classmates in the dorm. Answer the questions based (CD1: 43) on the dialogue.

a. What is the main reason why the male student called the female student?
  1) to complain that he cannot fall asleep
  2) to find out if his friend was sleeping
  3) to ask her out
  4) to ask questions about the homework

b. What will they do after the phone call?
  1) go to the library together
  2) do the homework
  3) go to sleep
  4) have some coffee

c. What did the male student do right before he made the phone call?
  1) drank some coffee
  2) tried to go to sleep
  3) called other friends
  4) completed the Chinese homework

Reading and writing

1.   Number of strokes

Indicate the number of strokes used in writing each of the following characters.

a. 惯 _____   f. 别 _____

b. 酒 _____   g. 睡 _____

c. 院 _____   h. 菜 _____

d. 服 _____   i. 喝 _____

e. 次 _____   j. 净 _____

2.   Which character?

Circle the character in each line that corresponds to the meaning on the left.

a. **jìng** (**gānjìng** *clean*)   净   静

b. **huài** *bad*   还   坏

c. **bié** *don't*   别   另

d. **bǎ** *take*   把   吧

e. **tóu** *head*   斗   头

f. **hóng** *red*   江   红

g. **shāo** *simmer* (**fā shāo** *have a fever*)   烧   浇

h. **jiǔ** *alcohol, wine*   酒   西

i. **fú** (**shūfu** *comfortable*)   股   服

j. **yuàn** (**diànyǐngyuàn** *movie theater*) 院   完

k. **gān** (**gānjìng** *clean*)   王   干

l. **guàn** (**xíguàn** *accustomed to*)   惯   愤

3.   First strokes

Write the first two strokes of each of the following characters.

a. 菜 ____   f. 红 ____

b. 惯 ____   g. 坏 ____

c. 睡 ____   h. 喝 ____

d. 次 ____   i. 干 ____

e. 把 ____   j. 烧 ____

4.   Missing strokes

Complete each character by writing in the missing strokes.

a.   月⁷   **fú (shūfu** *comfortable*)

b.   忄甲   **guàn (xíguàn** *accustomed to*)

c.   冫   **cì** *time*

d.   冫勹   **jìng (gānjìng** *clean*)

e.   目⁼   **shuì (shuì jiào** *sleep*)

f.   阝ˋ   **yuàn (yīyuàn** *hospital*)

g.   口冂   **hē** *drink*

h.   火乄   **shāo (fā shāo** *have a fever*)

i.   三口   **tóu** *head*

j.   口   **bié** *don't*

5.   Total strokes

Rewrite this list of characters, arranging the characters in terms of their total number of strokes. Begin your list with the character with the fewest strokes.

服	干	把	院	头	酒	惯	次	菜	烧	红	睡	净	喝	别	坏

6.   Radicals

Here is a list of characters that we have learned through this lesson. Rewrite each character in the row next to its radical.

惯   刚   坏   别   酒   把   洗   忙
汉   坐   到   快   找   地   慢   打

氵	
扌	
刂	
忄	
土	

7.   Character sleuth

Group the following characters in terms of a part that they share in common, as in the example. The shared part need not be the radical in each character. You can use a character more than once.

经   用   些   看   睡   哪   学   宿   服   明   给
容   开   院   都   那   红   字   园   定   能   朋

shared part	characters
人	人，大，太，天
纟	
阝	
二	
月	
宀	
元	
目	

8.   Find the words and phrases

You won't be able to completely understand the following passage, but it contains many characters that we have learned, including at least fifteen words composed of two or more characters.

a. Circle the <u>words</u> we have learned that are <u>composed of two or more characters each</u> and write them on the answer sheet below.

"今年" is an example of a word that is composed of two or more characters.

"我也" is composed of two characters in a row that we have learned, but it is <u>not</u> a word.

我的朋友老李非常喜欢学校旁边的中国饭馆。他每次去都吃他最喜欢的红烧肉。昨天他又跟朋友一起去了那家中国饭馆。他的朋友说你已经吃了好几次红烧肉了。今天别吃了。吃别的菜吧。他没有吃红烧肉，吃了炒白菜，还喝了一点酒。吃完饭他的肚子就不舒服，晚上睡不着。他想这可能是因为没有吃红烧肉。下次还得吃红烧肉。

Words in this paragraph composed of two or more characters:

1. ____   2. ____   3. ____   4. ____   5. ____

6. ____   7. ____   8. ____   9. ____   10. ____

11. ____   12. ____   13. ____   14. ____   15. ____

b. In one sentence in English, state the general topic of this passage.

9.   Dictionary skills

Following the instructions in Lesson 17 of the Textbook, look up these characters in a Chinese dictionary and provide the requested information.

a. 发
pronunciation:
meaning:
one two-character word or phrase in which it occurs:

b. 病
pronunciation:
meaning:
one two-character word or phrase in which it occurs:

c. 包
pronunciation:
meaning:
one two-character word or phrase in which it occurs:

10.   Find the incorrect characters

Xiao Zhang has written this email to a friend back home, but he has written twelve different characters incorrectly (some more than once). Read the passage aloud, circle the mistakes, and correct them on the answer sheet below. If the same mistake occurs twice, count it as a single mistake.

> 这个星斯学小的店 **yǐng** 院有"家"这个店 **yǐng**。我没看过，不只到这个电 **yǐng** 好坏。我文我的同屋看过每有。他说他看过，他很习欢，已红看了好九次了。他还话他可一跟我在看一次。

a. ____   b. ____   c. ____   d. ____   e. ____   f. ____

g. ____   h. ____   i. ____   j. ____   k. ____   l. ____

11.   Scrambled sentences

Rewrite these phrases as sentences, putting the words in the correct order to match the English translations.

a. 东西 / 床 / 在 / 别 / 把 / 的 / 放 / 我的 / 上 /你

Don't put your things on my bed.

b. 饭馆 / 吧 / 去 / 那 / 吃/ 我们 / 下次 / 家 / 饭

Let's eat in that restaurant next time.

c. 酒 / 喜欢 / 为什么 / 喝 / 中国人 / 红

Why do Chinese people like to drink red wine?

d. 把 / 的 / 干净 / 你 / 你 / **yī** 服 / 洗 / 得

You should wash your clothes (clean).

e. 做 / 好 / 妈妈 / 非常 / 你 / 吃 / 菜 / 的

The food that your mother cooks is extremely delicious.

12.   Translate into English

Read the following passage and translate it into English.

小王的女朋友是他在一个一年级的学生晚会上 **rènshi** 的。她是去年从 **Yīng** 国来的。她也是来中国学中文的。她来中国以前在 **Yīng** 国的时候就开始学中文了。她说中文说得非常好。在那个晚会上他们一起 **chàng gē**、**tiào wǔ**、说了很多话、也吃了很多东西。晚上很晚才回宿舍。

13.   Translate into Mandarin

Rewrite the following sentences in Chinese characters.

a. I am not used to using chopsticks (筷子) to eat Chinese food.

b. How come your dorm is so clean?

c. You have a fever. Don't go to class today. (Write **fā** in pinyin.)

d. Don't drink alcohol before going to sleep.

e. My roommate has already been sleeping for ten hours.

Focus on structure

1.   How many times? (Use and Structure note 20.2)

Here is a list of activities that Ye Youwen has done this week and the number of times she has done each one. Rewrite this information in complete Mandarin sentences, using characters where we have learned them.

a. ate Sichuan food (twice)   →

b. cleaned her room (once)   →

c. washed clothes (three times)   →

d. listened to music (many times)   →

e. drank beer (once)   →

f. took the subway (five times)   →

2.   还是 and huòzhě (Use and Structure note 20.5)

Translate these sentences into Mandarin, using 还是 or **huòzhě** in each sentence, as appropriate.

a. Would you like to drink coffee or tea?

b. Tonight we can watch television or listen to music.

c. You can see a doctor tonight or tomorrow morning.

d. Do you prefer to bathe at night or in the morning?

e. Are you going to major in Chinese or Japanese?

3.   Resultative verbs in the potential form
(Use and Structure notes 19.2, 20.6)

Translate each of the following sentences into English.

a. 我打不开这个门。

b. 今天晚上的功课太多了。我做不 **wán**。

c. 这 **jiàn yī** 服太 **zāng**。我洗不干净。

d. 老师说话说得那么快，你听得 **dǒng** 吗？

e. **Hànbǎobāo** (hamburgers) 在中国吃得到吗？

f. 明天是我的生日。今天晚上一定睡不 **zháo**。

g. 这个字写得太小。我看不见是哪个字。

h. 我找不到那个电 **yǐng** 院。请 **gàosu** 我怎么走。

4. Resultative verbs and the potential form (Use and Structure notes 19.2, 20.6)

Complete the following sentences by filling in each blank with one of the following, <u>or leave it empty</u>, to match its English translation:

| 了 | 没 | 不 | 得 |

a. 你这 **jiàn** 衣服 ＿＿ 洗 ＿＿ 干净 ＿＿，你看，这里还有一点儿 **zāng**。
This shirt was not washed clean. Look, there's still a dirty spot here.

b. 我想你大 **gài** 是 ＿＿ 吃 ＿＿ 坏 ＿＿ **dù** 子 ＿＿，所以一直上 **cè** 所。
I think you probably have stomach flu. That's why you keep going to the bathroom.

c. 这么多 **jiǎo** 子，你 ＿＿ 吃 ＿＿ 完 ＿＿ 吗? ＿＿ 吃 ＿＿ 完 ＿＿ 没关系，明天再吃。
So many dumplings! Can you finish them all? It's okay if you can't. We can eat them tomorrow.

d. 我已经找了好几个月的工作，还是 ＿＿ 找 ＿＿ 到 ＿＿ 一个喜欢的 ＿＿。
I have been looking for a job for months but still can't find one that I like.

e. 小张可能是太 **lèi** 了，刚做完功课就在床上 ＿＿ 睡 ＿＿ **zháo** ＿＿。
Xiao Zhang is probably too tired. He fell asleep on his bed right after he finished the homework.

f. 小谢这几天 **yè** 里常 **késou**、有好几天 ＿＿ 睡 ＿＿ 好 ＿＿。
Xiao Xie has been coughing the past few nights. He hasn't slept well for days.

g. 这门课太难了，我上课的时候常常 ＿＿ 听 ＿＿ **dǒng** ＿＿，下课得问同学。
This class is too difficult. A lot of times I couldn't understand in class and had to ask my classmates after class.

h. 王老师，您写的字太小了，我 ＿＿ 看 ＿＿ 见 ＿＿。可以写大一点吗?
Teacher Wang, the characters you wrote are too small, I can't see them. Could you write them a little bigger?

i. 不行，不行，我已经 ＿＿ 吃 ＿＿ **bǎo** ＿＿ 了 ＿＿，不能再吃了。
No way, I'm already full. I can't eat any more.

5.   Details of a past event (Use and Structure note 20.9)

Xiao Xie's father is quizzing him about his activities last weekend. Express each question in Mandarin, using 是...的 in each question.

a. What day did you eat in a restaurant?

b. Who did you have dinner with?

c. Where did you eat?

d. What time did you return to the dorm?

e. What time did you go to sleep?

6.   Your personal information (Use and Structure note 20.9)

Answer questions a.–d. in Mandarin, using 是...的 in each sentence.

a. Where were you born?

b. What month and date were you born?

c. What year were you born?

d. When did you begin to study Chinese?

Translate e.–f. into Mandarin.

e. When did you graduate high school?

f. When did you select your major?

7.   Chú 了 X 以外 (Use and Structure note 20.10)

Rewrite each sentence using the structure **chú** 了 X 以外, as in the example, and translate your new sentences into English.

Example:
我喜欢吃中国菜，也喜欢吃美国菜　→　**Chú** 了中国菜以外，我也喜欢吃美国菜。
English: Besides Chinese food, I also like to eat American food.

a. 我妈妈很会做 **chǎo bái** 菜，还有 **hóng** 烧 **dòufu**　　　→
   English:

b. 我 **fā** 烧，头也很 **téng**　　　　　　　　　　　　→
   English:

c. **Zhuō** 子上有书，地上也有书　　　　　　　　→
   English:

d. 我选了几门 **zhuānyè** 课和一门 **yīnyuè** 课　　　→
   English:

e. 他每天都忙 **zhe** 工作和学习　　　　　　　　→
   English:

f. 你得多喝水，也 **yīnggāi** 去看 **yī** 生，**shēntǐ** 才会好　→
   English:

8.   Complete the sentences

Fill in the blanks with words from the following list to complete each sentence. Then, translate each sentence into English.

次	一	**huòzhě**	马上	大 **gài**	还是	不	没	因为

a. 菜 _____ 就来了，请您再 **děng** 一下。
   English:

b. 他这么不用功，还常常不去上课，**chéngji** _____ 很 **zāogāo**。
   English:

c. 小张 _____ **bìng** 了，所以今天没有来上课。
   English:

d. 你习惯早上 **xǐ zǎo** _____ 晚上 **xǐ zǎo**？
   English:

e. 我不能喝 **kāfēi**，一喝就睡 _____ **zháo**。前天我喝了一小 **bēi kāfēi** 以后，_____

   yè _____ 睡。
   English:

f. **Bìyè** 以后，我想去中国 _____ 去 **Táiwān** 找工作。
   English:

g. 我说了好几 _____，洗好的 **yī** 服得放在 **guì** 子里，你怎么都不听？
   English:

9.   Translation challenge I

Translate these sentences into English.

a. 我今天一天忙 **zhe fù** 习功课，因为明天我有三个考试。

b. **Chú** 了我以外，小 **Yè** 也没 **cānjiā** 今天早上的考试。我们都起晚了。

c. **Chú** 了 **dù** 子不 **shū** 服以外，我不 **fā** 烧，也不头 **téng**。可能是昨天晚上吃得太多了。

d. 今天的中文功课太多了，吃晚饭以前做不 **wán**。

e. 因为我对中国很有兴趣，所以下个学期我要选一门中国文 **huà huòzhě** 中国经 **jì** 的课。

f. 我 **dài** 他到学校的 **yī** 院看 **bìng**。**Yī** 生说他不习惯吃 **là** 的，所以 **dù** 子 **téng**，很快就会好，还给了他一些 **yào**。

g. 这个电 **yǐng** 我很喜欢，已经看了三次了。

h. 美 **lì** 学汉字学得很快，也学得很好。她每天把 **xīn** 学的汉字每个字写三次。

10.   Translation challenge II

Translate these sentences into Mandarin.

a. I was sick all day yesterday and didn't finish my homework.

b. You ate too much. Next time don't eat so much.

c. This is my first time eating spicy food.

d. Q: When you traveled in China could you understand the people?

   A: Except for Sichuan people, I understood everything.

e. I finished reading that book but I didn't understand it.

f. Where did the two of you meet?

g. I'm not interested in music. Whenever I listen to music I fall asleep.

Focus on communication

1. Dialogue comprehension

Study the Lesson 20 Narrative and Dialogue. Then, read the following statements and indicate whether they are true (T) or false (F).

a. (   ) 小张昨天晚上到朋友家去吃饭了。

b. (   ) 小张昨天晚上没有睡觉，因为朋友请他吃饭、喝酒。

c. (   ) 小谢觉得小张大 **gài** 吃坏 **dù** 子了。

d. (   ) 小张吃了晚饭以后开始 **dù** 子 **téng**。

e. (   ) 今天是小谢 **dài** 小张去看 **bìng** 的。

f. (   ) 小张不 **fā** 烧也不 **késou**，就是 **dù** 子有点 **téng**。

g. (   ) **Yī** 生觉得小张昨天晚上吃的东西，可能不太干净，**huòzhě** 四 **chuān** 菜太 **là** 了。

h. (   ) **Yī** 生问了小张以后，给了他一些 **yào**。

2. What do you say?

What do you say in each of the following situations? Type your answers, using characters where we have learned them, and email them to your Chinese teacher.

a. Your roommate looks pale to you. You want to know what's going on.

b. You complain about your sleep problem: you wake up several times in the middle of night.

c. You wonder when your friend started driving because he doesn't seem to be a very experienced driver.

d. You complain about a severe headache and an upset stomach.

e. You need to explain your symptoms to the doctor: you have a fever and have been coughing since last week.

f. You want to let your friend know that you might arrive late, either 3 p.m. or 3:30 p.m.

g. You are telling the hostess that you're too full to eat when she insists that you get a second helping of food.

3.   大家都 **bìng** 了

It's the flu season and everyone in Xiao Zhang's class is sick. Use the information in the pictures to complete each sentence below. Then translate the sentences into English.

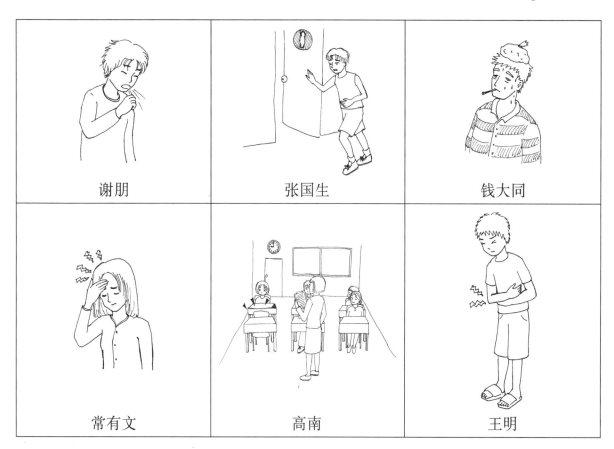

谢朋	张国生	钱大同
常有文	高南	王明

a. _____ **fā** 烧了，**shēntǐ** 很不 **shū** 服。

    English:

b. _____ **bìng** 了好几天了，都没有来上课。

    English:

c. _____ 可能是吃坏 **dù** 子了。昨天一天 **lā** 了好几次 **dù** 子。

    English:

d. _____ 这几天一起床就一直 **késou**。

    English:

e. _____ 头很 **téng**，吃了 **yào** 也没有用。

    English:

f. _____ 的 **dù** 子 **téngjí** 了，已经三天不能吃东西了。她打 **suan** 今天去看 **bìng**。

    English:

4. Complete the mini-dialogues

Use the structure in parentheses to complete each mini-dialogue.

a. A: 你说你选了中文课，还有呢？

   B: _____。（**chú** 了…以外）

b. A: 你 **zhōumò** 做什么？

   B: 我常常 _____。（**huòzhě**）

c. A: 今天回家请写 **dì** 五课、**dì** 六课的功课，明天给我。

   B: 老师，功课太多了，我 _____！（ActV 得/不 + RVE）

d. A: 吃中国饭你怎么不用 **kuài** 子？

   B: _____。（不习惯）

e. A: 明天是你生日，我们去那家日本饭馆吃饭吧。

   B: **Huàn** 一家好不好？那家饭馆我 _____。（好几次）

5. Meet your new teammates

You will be participating in a three-week volunteer program in China this winter break. Today is the orientation and you are meeting the other team members for the first time.

Part I. Write down the questions that you can ask your teammates. Use 是…的 in your questions for c.–f.

Example:

Where are you from?　　　　　　　　→　　你是从哪儿来的？

a. What is your name?　　　　　　　　→

b. Why do you want to go to China?　　→

c. Who did you come with?　　　　　　→

d. When did you begin to study Chinese?　→

e. How did you hear about this job?　　→

f. How did you get here today?　　　　→

g. Write at least one more question:　　→

Part II. Below is information about four other volunteers. Translate the questions into Mandarin and then answer them in Mandarin.

	country	year they began studying Chinese	where they learned Chinese	who they came here with
Zhēnní	France	2006	Paris (**Bālí**)	alone
Tāngmǔ	USA	last September	college	one classmate
Jiékè	Britain	this summer	Beijing	two friends
Mòlì	Japan	last month	Tokyo	her older sister

a. Who came here with her older sister?

Q:

A:

b. Where is **Tāngmǔ** from? (use 是 ... 的)

Q:

A:

c. Did **Jiékè** study Chinese in Tokyo?

Q:

A:

d. How long has **Zhēnní** been learning Chinese?

Q:

A:

Part III.   It's your turn to introduce yourself. Write at least four sentences about yourself.

6. Writing

Xiao Wang is not feeling well.

Part I. This is a story about Xiao Wang. Rearrange the sentences in the right order to form a cohesive paragraph.

a. 虽然没有 **lā dù** 子，可是，头一直很 **téng**，**dù** 子也不太 **shū** 服。

b. 从饭馆回来以后我有点儿不 **shū** 服，就去睡觉了。

c. 早上我的同屋说我大 **gài** 喝太多酒了。

d. **Yè** 里睡不 **zháo**，起来好几次。

e. 我下 **wǔ** 三点才吃 **wǔ** 饭，所以晚饭吃得不多。

f. 我吃了 **yào** 就觉得好一点了。

g. 昨天晚上小张请我们几个人去一家 **xīn** 开的饭馆吃饭，因为他找到工作了。

h. 他给了我一 **piàn** 头 **téng yào**，还叫我多喝一点 **chá**。

i. 不过因为太高兴，喝了好几 **píng pí** 酒。

Part II. Below is a dialogue between Xiao Wang and his roommate. Fill in the roommate's part, based on the paragraph in Part I.

Roommate: 你 _____?
Xiao Wang: 我昨天晚上没睡好，头 **téngjí** 了。

Roommate: **Chú** 了 _____?
Xiao Wang: 我 **dù** 子也不太 **shū** 服。

Roommate: _____?
Xiao Wang: 昨天吃了晚饭以后就开始不 **shū** 服。

Roommate: _____?
Xiao Wang: 我是在一家 **xīn** 开的饭馆吃的晚饭。

Roommate: _____?
Xiao Wang: 我吃得不多，就喝了三 **píng pí** 酒。

Roommate: 三 **píng**? 我想，你 _____。
Xiao Wang: 喝太多了？那怎么 **bàn** 呢？

Roommate: _____。
Xiao Wang: 谢谢。我现在就吃。

Part III. Xiao Wang is feeling sick this morning so he missed his class today. Help him write an email message to his Chinese teacher apologizing for not being at class today. He needs to explain why he missed the class. The email message should be at least 100 characters in length.

李老师，您好：

我是您二年级中文课的学生。对不起，＿＿＿＿＿＿＿＿＿＿＿＿＿＿＿

＿＿＿＿＿＿＿＿＿＿＿＿＿＿＿＿＿＿＿＿＿＿＿＿＿＿＿＿＿＿＿＿

＿＿＿＿＿＿＿＿＿＿＿＿＿＿＿＿＿＿＿＿＿＿＿＿＿＿＿＿＿＿＿＿

＿＿＿＿＿＿＿＿＿＿＿＿＿＿＿＿＿＿＿＿＿＿＿＿＿＿＿＿＿＿＿＿

＿＿＿＿＿＿＿＿＿＿＿＿＿＿＿＿＿＿＿＿＿＿＿＿＿＿＿＿＿＿＿＿

＿＿＿＿＿＿＿＿＿＿＿＿＿＿＿＿＿＿＿＿＿＿＿＿＿＿＿＿＿＿＿＿

明天 **rú** 果您有时间，我可以去找您问几个问 **tí** 吗？谢谢！

王明明

Lesson 21 Workbook

 Listening and speaking

(audio online)

Structure drills

1. More and more (Use and Structure note 21.1)

You will hear a sentence stating the quality of some subject. You will say that the subject
has more and more of that quality, as in the example.

Example:
You will hear: 天 **qì** **lěng** 了。
You will say: 天 **qì yuè** 来 **yuè lěng** 了。
Click "R" to hear the correct response: 天 **qì yuè** 来 **yuè lěng** 了。

(a)   (b)   (c)   (d)   (e)   (f)   (g)   (h)   (i)   (j)

2. Saying that two things are alike (Use and Structure note 21.4)

You will hear two phrases describing different things. Say that they are alike, as in the
example.

Example:
You will hear: 我的中文书，你的中文书
You will say: 我的中文书跟你的中文书一样。
Click "R" to hear the correct response: 我的中文书跟你的中文书一样。

(a)   (b)   (c)   (d)   (e)   (f)   (g)   (h)   (i)   (j)

3.   Saying that two things are not alike (Use and Structure note 21.4)

You will hear two phrases describing different things. Say that they are not alike, as in the example.

> **Example:**
> *You will hear:* 我的中文书，你的中文书
> *You will say:* 我的中文书跟你的中文书不一样。
> *Click "R" to hear the correct response:* 我的中文书跟你的中文书不一样。

(a)   (b)   (c)   (d)   (e)   (f)   (g)   (h)   (i)   (j)

4.   Asking whether two things are alike (Use and Structure note 21.4)

You will hear two phrases describing different things. Ask whether they are alike or not, as in the example.

> **Example:**
> *You will hear:* 你的中文书，我的中文书
> *You will say:* 你的中文书跟我的中文书一样不一样？
> *Click "R" to hear the correct response:* 你的中文书跟我的中文书一样不一样？

(a)   (b)   (c)   (d)   (e)   (f)   (g)   (h)   (i)   (j)

5.   Saying that two things are alike in some way (Use and Structure note 21.4)

You will hear a sentence describing the quality of two things. Restate the sentence, saying that these two things have the same quality, as in the example.

> **Example:**
> *You will hear:* 今天很 **lěng**，昨天也很 **lěng**。
> *You will say:* 今天跟昨天一样 **lěng**。
> *Click "R" to hear the correct response:* 今天跟昨天一样 **lěng**。

(a)   (b)   (c)   (d)   (e)   (f)   (g)   (h)   (i)   (j)

6.   Comparisons with bǐ (Use and Structure note 21.7)

You will hear a sentence describing two noun phrases. Restate the sentence with **bǐ**, as in the example, saying that one has more of some quality than the other.

> **Example:**
> *You will hear:* 我的书三十块钱，他的书三十五块钱。
> *You will say:* 他的书 **bǐ** 我的 **guì**。
> *Click "R" to hear the correct response:* 他的书 **bǐ** 我的 **guì**。

(a)   (b)   (c)   (d)   (e)   (f)   (g)   (h)   (i)   (j)

7. Saying *a lot more* (Use and Structure note 21.7)

You will hear a sentence describing two noun phrases. Restate the sentence with **bǐ**, as in the example, saying that one noun phrase has a lot more of some quality than the other.

Example:
You will hear: 中文课有五个考试，文化课只有一个考试。
You will say: 中文课的考试 **bǐ** 文化课的多得多。
Click "R" to hear the correct response: 中文课的考试 **bǐ** 文化课的多得多。

(a)   (b)   (c)   (d)   (e)   (f)   (g)   (h)

Listening for information

1.   World weather report

The following chart displays the temperatures on January 21 in seven cities around the world. **(CD1: 47)** You will hear seven statements comparing the weather in the cities. Based on the chart, indicate whether each statement is true (T) or false (F).

January 21	
city	temperature
Beijing	28°F/12°F
Shanghai	42°F/33°F
Taipei	62°F/55°F
Paris	48°F/38°F
London	50°F/41°F
New York	43°F/32°F
Houston	74°F/69°F

a. (   )   b. (   )   c. (   )   d. (   )   e. (   )   f. (   )   g. (   )

2.   Today's weather

(CD1: 48) You will hear a short weather forecast for four major US cities: Seattle, Boston, Miami, and Chicago. Complete the following table based on the report, adding in the name of each city and the temperature under the picture that illustrates the weather.

city				
temperature				

3.   Buenos Aires

(CD1: 49) You will hear a short description from a travel agency about the climate of Buenos Aires. Write the answers to the questions in Mandarin, based on the description.

a. **Bùyínuòsī** 最 **lěng** 的天 **qì** 在哪一个月?

b. **Bùyínuòsī** 的 **chūn** 天从哪一个月开始?

c. **Bùyínuòsī** 的 **qiū** 天是哪几个月?

d. **Bùyínuòsī** 的 **dōng** 天有几个月?

e. **Bùyínuòsī**, 二月的天 **qì** 怎么样?

4. Two rooms

The room on the left is Xiao Pan's dorm room. The room on the right belongs to Qi Sheng. **(CD1: 50)**
You will hear six statements comparing their rooms. Based on the pictures indicate whether
each statement is true (T) or false (F).

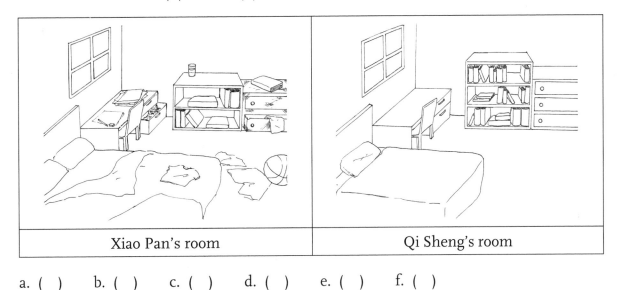

| Xiao Pan's room | Qi Sheng's room |

a. (   )   b. (   )   c. (   )   d. (   )   e. (   )   f. (   )

5. Your hometown

The recording asks you six questions about your hometown. Write down your answers in **(CD1: 51)**
Mandarin, using characters where we have learned them.

a.

b.

c.

d.

e.

f.

6. Telephone message

Your friend Sun Ping left a phone message for you regarding a trip. Listen to the message **(CD1: 52)**
and write a reply to him in Mandarin.

Your reply:

7. Interview

(CD1: 53–54) Zhou Yu and Lanlan are being interviewed by a school newspaper reporter. Listen to their replies and do the following:

a. In English, state the topic of the interview: _____

b. In Mandarin, write a short paragraph comparing the replies of the two students on this topic.

8. Dialogue

(CD1: 55) Two students at a university in the south are talking about the weather. Listen to their conversation and answer the questions based on the dialogue.

a. What is their plan?
  1) to go to the park in the rain
  2) to stay in the dorm
  3) to wait until the rain stops
  4) to eat something first

b. What season is it?
  1) spring
  2) summer
  3) fall
  4) winter

c. How is the weather during the winter in the south?
  1) It only snows a little bit.
  2) It is the longest season.
  3) It is not very cold.
  4) It seldom rains.

d. How is the weather in the north where the male student comes from?
  1) It rains in the spring.
  2) It is hot in the summer.
  3) The winter season is about three months long.
  4) It gets cold in the fall.

e. What is the average temperature in July in the south?
  1) 90–100°
  2) 80–90°
  3) 70–80°
  4) 60–70°

Reading and writing

Focus on Chinese characters

1.   Number of strokes

Indicate the number of strokes used in writing each of the following characters.

a. 亮 _____   f. 化 _____

b. 近 _____   g. 出 _____

c. 衣 _____   h. 夏 _____

d. 概 _____   i. 脏 _____

e. 离 _____   j. 应 _____

2.   Which character?

Circle the character in each line that corresponds to the meaning on the left.

a. **gāi** (**yīnggāi** *should*)   刻   该

b. **jìn** *close*   近   进

c. **piào** (**piàoliang** *pretty, beautiful*)   漂   票

d. **chū** *exit, produce*   山   出

e. **gài** (**dàgài** *probably*)   槩   概

f. **rú** (**rúguǒ** *if*)   如   妇

g. **zāng** *dirty*   脏   肚

h. **shū** (**shūfu** *comfortable*)   舒   舍

i. **yīng** (**yīnggāi** *should*)   広   应

j. **suì** *years of age*   岁   歹

k. **xià** (**xiàtiān** *summer*)   夏   夜

l. **huà** (**wénhuà** *culture*)   华   化

3. First strokes

Write the first two strokes of each of the following characters.

a. 概 _____   f. 应 _____

b. 如 _____   g. 该 _____

c. 岁 _____   h. 近 _____

d. 出 _____   i. 夏 _____

e. 衣 _____   j. 脏 _____

4. Missing strokes

Complete each character by writing in the missing strokes.

a. 讠   **gāi** (**yīnggāi** *should*)

b. 卤   **lí** *separated from*

c. 斤   **jìn** *close*

d. 月   **zāng** *dirty*

e. 百   **xià** (**xiàtiān** *summer*)

f. 舍   **shū** (**shūfu** *comfortable*)

g. 广   **yīng** (**yīnggāi** *should*)

h. 亣   **liàng** (**piàoliang** *pretty, beautiful*)

i. 丿   **huà** (**wénhuà** *culture*)

j. 氵   **piāo** (**piàoliang** *pretty, beautiful*)

5. Total strokes

Rewrite this list of characters, arranging the characters in terms of their total number of strokes. Begin your list with the character with the fewest strokes.

离	近	舒	概	漂	出	脏	衣	化	应	如	亮	夏	岁	该

6.   Radicals

Here is a list of characters that we have learned through this lesson. Rewrite each character in the row next to its radical.

酒　朋　洗　概　法　近　服　能

如　脏　应　始　床　校　漂　选

氵	
木	
女	
广	
辶	
月	

7.   Character sleuth: Look for the phonetic

Group the characters below in terms of their rhyme. Write the characters that rhyme with each other in the column on the right. Write the shared part of each character in the column on the left. For all of these characters, the shared part is the "phonetic," the part of the character that suggests the pronunciation of the character. The first line is completed for you

问，园，跟，吧，放，见，红，钟，马，很，间，现，

块，工，妈，中，们，院，把，吗，房，快，门

'rime'	characters that rhyme and share a common part
女	如

8.   Getting the gist of a paragraph

You won't be able to completely understand the following passage, but you know enough characters and words to be able to identify the topic of the paragraph and some of the supporting details. Read the paragraph for the main ideas and answer the questions that follow in English. Do not look up any characters we have not learned.

> 有的人常常把下雪想得很漂亮，房子上是雪、路上也是雪。我想这些人大概没有看见过下雪。第一，下雪的时候常常很冷。天气太冷让人觉得很不舒服。第二，下雪以后出去、进来、走路、开车都很不方便。第三，下雪以后，很快路上就很脏，鞋、衣服、汽车都很容易脏。下雪的时候可能很漂亮，但是漂亮的时间不长。我真的不喜欢下雪。

This paragraph is about 雪. It is the <u>topic</u> of this paragraph. We have not yet presented the meaning of this character in this book. If you don't recognize it, don't look it up or ask anyone for its meaning.

a. How does the author's opinion about this topic compare with that of other people?

b. How many arguments does the author give to support his opinion?

c. Where in the paragraph does the author directly state his opinion?

d. What do you think 雪 means? What evidence do you have for this meaning?

9.   Dictionary skills

Following the instructions in Lesson 17 of the Textbook, look up these characters in a Chinese dictionary and provide the requested information.

a. 雪
   pronunciation:
   meaning:
   one two-character word or phrase in which it occurs:

b. 长
   pronunciation:
   meaning:
   one two-character word or phrase in which it occurs:

c. 短
   pronunciation:
   meaning:
   one two-character word or phrase in which it occurs:

10.   Find the incorrect characters

Xiao Zhang continues his email correspondence with his classmates back in the USA. He hasn't yet proofread this message, but when he does, he will find that thirteen characters are incorrect. Read the passage aloud, circle the mistakes, and correct them on the answer sheet below.

作天晚上下 **xuě** 了。下了一 **yè**。今天早上我一起床就住 **chuānghu** 外边看。我觉的很票亮。路上没友很多车，可是人非常都。他们都 **chuān** 了很多一服。有的人 **sǎo xuě**，有的人 **wán xuě**。我很我的同屋也到外边去 **wán xuě**。**Wán** 了差不多一个中头。**Wán** 得很高兴，可是国了一回儿我觉得非常 **lěng**。回宿舍我们喝了很多 **rè chá**、吃了一点东酒以后，才觉得书服了。

a. ____   b. ____   c. ____   d. ____   e. ____   f. ____   g. ____

h. ____   i. ____   j. ____   k. ____   l. ____   m. ____

11.   Scrambled sentences

Rewrite these phrases as sentences, putting the words in the correct order to match the English translations.

a. 我 / 我 / 家 / 很近 / 离 / 很早 / 来得 / 学校 / 所以 / 都 / 每天

My home is close to school, so I arrive very early every day.

b. 去 / 夏天 / 中国 / 学习 / 今年 / 要 / 我 / 到 / 中文

I want to go to China this summer to study Chinese.

c. 对 / 真 / 我 / 为什么 / 知道 / 大学生 / 这么 / 有兴趣 / 不 / 很多 / 喝酒

I really don't know why many college students are so interested in drinking.

12.   Pinyin to characters

Rewrite the following sentences in Chinese characters.

a. **Tā de yīfu dōu hěn piàoliang, wǒ xiǎng yīdìng yě dōu hěn guì**。

b. **Zhège xuéqī nǐ yīnggāi xuǎn Zhōngguó wénhuà kè**。

c. **Wǒ de sùshè hěn shūfu yě hěn piàoliang, zhǐ shì yǒu yīdiǎn zāng**。

Focus on structure

1.   State the opposite

Fill in the blanks with the opposite of each word.

Example:

大 ↔ 小。

a. 好 ↔ _____   b. 干净 ↔ _____   c. **bèn** ↔ _____

d. **rè** ↔ _____   e. 多 ↔ _____   f. **duǎn** ↔ _____

g. **guì** ↔ _____   h. 近 ↔ _____   i. 容易 ↔ _____

2.   Getting more and more... (Use and Structure note 21.1)

Describe each situation in a complete sentence that includes **yuè** 来 **yuè**, as in the example.

Example:

| *Monday 11:00 p.m.* | *Tuesday 11:30 p.m.* | *Wednesday 12:30 p.m.* |

小夏睡觉的时间 **yuè** 来 **yuè** 晚。

a. Median house price in California:

November 2007	November 2008	November 2009
$500,000	$450,000	$300,000

b. 天 **qì yùbào**：

今天： 70°F	明天： 73°F	后天： 75°F

c. 北京的 **dōng** 天：

January 2007: −5°C	January 2008: −6°C	January 2009: −7°C

d. 在 **Jiāzhōu** 开车：

e. 张小弟：

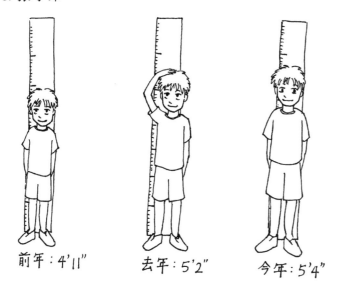

3.   More and more (Use and Structure note 21.1)

Answer each question in a complete sentence that includes the phrase **yuè** 来 **yuè**.

a. 你觉得中文考试怎么样？

b. 如果你吃坏了 **dù** 子，可是你没有吃 **yào**，你的 **dù** 子可能会怎么样？

c. 如果你没有时间 **shōushi** 房间，你的房间可能会怎么样？

4.   真 zāogāo (Use and Structure note 21.3)

Complete each sentence using V + 不了, based on the information in the illustration and the English translation.

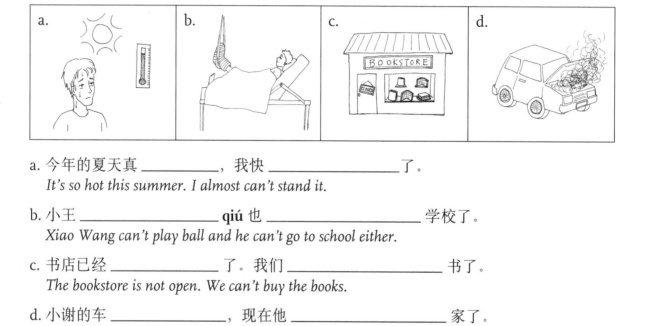

a. 今年的夏天真 _____，我快 _____了。
   It's so hot this summer. I almost can't stand it.

b. 小王 _____ **qiú** 也 _____学校了。
   Xiao Wang can't play ball and he can't go to school either.

c. 书店已经 _____ 了。我们 _____书了。
   The bookstore is not open. We can't buy the books.

d. 小谢的车 _____，现在他 _____家了。
   Xiao Xie's car broke down (it is 'bad'). Now he can't go home.

5.   It can't happen (Use and Structure note 21.3)

Fill in the blank with the appropriate V + 不了 expression, choosing from those given below, to complete each sentence to match the English translation.

> 去不了   走不了   上不了   晚不了   来不了

a. 我现在还有一点 **shì**，＿＿＿＿＿。你们别 **děng** 我了，先走吧。
   I have something to do now and cannot leave. Don't wait for me. Go on ahead.

b. 对不起，这个星期天我得回家。我 ＿＿＿＿＿ 你家了。
   Sorry, I have to go home this Sunday. I can't go to your home.

c. 国强给我打电话说他今天晚上得去工作，＿＿＿＿＿ 了。
   Guoqiang phoned me and said that he has to go to work tonight and he cannot come (here).

d. 电 **yǐng** 八点开始。现在才六点半。我们 ＿＿＿＿＿。
   The movie starts at 8 o'clock. It's only 6:30 right now. We won't be late.

e. 我有点不舒服。请你 **gàosu** 老师今天的课我 ＿＿＿＿＿ 了。
   I'm not feeling well. Please tell the teacher I won't be able to attend today's class.

6.   Saying that two things are the same (Use and Structure note 21.4)

Answer the following questions in complete Mandarin sentences, based on the information given.

month	Jan	Feb	Mar	Apr	May	Jun	Jul	Aug	Sep	Oct	Nov	Dec
temperature (Celsius)	−4.6	−2.7	4.5	13.1	19.8	24.4	25.8	24.4	19.4	12.4	4.1	−2.7

a. Which two months are equally cold?

b. Which two months of the year are equally hot?

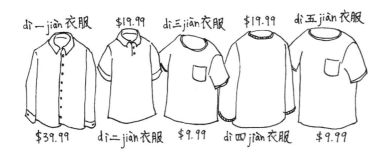

dì 一 jiàn 衣服 $19.99   dì 三 jiàn 衣服 $19.99   dì 五 jiàn 衣服
$39.99   dì 二 jiàn 衣服 $9.99   dì 四 jiàn 衣服 $9.99

c. Which two shirts are equally expensive?

d. Which two shirts are the same?

7. Making comparisons (Use and Structure note 21.7)

Answer each of the following questions in a complete sentence, based on the illustration. Use **bǐ** in each of your answers.

a. 谁的 **guì** 子 **luàn**?

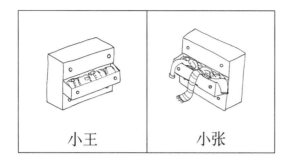

b. 谁的房间干净?

c. 谁的家近?

8. More comparisons (Use and Structure notes 21.4 and 21.7)

Here are some facts about Gao Meili and her roommate Ye Youwen. Answer the questions that follow in complete Mandarin sentences, based on this information.

Gao Meili	Ye Youwen
age: 21 height: 5'4" courses this semester: 4 tests next week: 2 very smart	age: 20 height: 5'5" courses this semester: 5 tests next week: 1 very smart

a. Are Gao Meili and Ye Youwen the same age? (Hint: equally big)

b. Are Gao Meili and Ye Youwen the same height?

c. Who has more classes this semester? (Hint: Whose courses are more numerous?)

d. Who has more tests next week?

e. Who is smarter, Gao Meili or Ye Youwen?

9. Asking about comparisons (Use and Structure notes 21.4 and 21.7)

Translate the questions in Exercise 8 to Mandarin.

a.

b.

c.

d.

e.

10. Rhetorical questions (Use and Structure note 21.5)

Ask the following rhetorical questions in Mandarin.

a. Isn't it the case that Gao Meili and Ye Youwen are the same age (equally big)?

b. Isn't it the case that Gao Meili and Ye Youwen are the same height (equally tall)?

c. Isn't it the case that Gao Meili is smarter than Ye Youwen?

11.   Who made you do it? (Use and Structure note 21.8)

Xiao Zhang is explaining to his parents that different people have made him do certain things. Express each situation in Mandarin, as in the example:

Example:

老师, *put on some more clothes*   →   老师 **ràng** 我多 **chuān** 一点衣服。

a. 我的同屋, put my clothes in the dresser

b. 老师, do homework every day

c. 我的同屋, go to the hospital to see a doctor

d. **Yī** 生, take medicine every day this week (How do you say 'take' medicine in Mandarin? Review Lesson 20.)

12.   That's the difference between A and B (Use and Structure note 21.9)

Sum up each of these sentences by saying "that's the difference between A and B," as in the example.

Example:

Chūn 天常常 **guā fēng**，**qiū** 天不 **guā fēng**。   →   这就是 **chūn** 天和 **qiū** 天的不同。

a. 美国人喜欢早上洗 **zǎo**。中国人喜欢晚上洗 **zǎo**。→

b. 北京一年四 **jì**，南 **Jiāzhōu** 一年一 **jì**。   →

c. 美 **lì** 很用功，她的妹妹太喜欢 **wán**。   →

Focus on communication

1.   Dialogue comprehension

Study the Lesson 21 Narrative and Dialogue. Then, read the following statements and indicate whether they are true (T) or false (F).

a. (   ) 大为是一年多以前来北京的。

b. (   ) 北京 **dōng** 天不下 **xuě**，夏天不下 **yǔ**。

c. (   ) 最近几年北京天 **qì rè** 的时间 **yuè** 来 **yuè** 长也 **yuè** 来 **yuè** 早。

d. (   ) 北京一年四 **jì** 最 **duǎn** 的是 **qiū** 天。

e. (   ) 大为最喜欢北京的 **chūn** 天。

f. ( ) 今天的最高 **wēndù** 只有三、四 **dù**。

g. ( ) 明天很 **lěng**，还会下 **yǔ**。

h. ( ) 后天大概不会下 **yǔ**。

i. ( ) 国强喜欢下 **xuě**，因为下雪的时候可以出去 **wán**。

j. ( ) 下 **xuě** 以后，大为大概不想出去，因为太 **lěng** 了。

k. ( ) 大为是从南 **Jiāzhōu** 来的。

l. ( ) 在 **Jiāzhōu** 的时候，大为如果想去 **hǎi** 边，应该很 **fāngbiàn**。

m. ( ) 大为 **bǐjiào** 喜欢他家 **xiāng** 的天 **qì**。

n. ( ) 小王觉得他的中文老师 **guǎn** 得太多了。

o. ( ) 国强觉得，中文老师只是关 **xīn** 小王。

2. What do you say?

What do you say in each of the following situations? Type your answers, using characters where we have learned them, and email them to your Chinese teacher.

a. Complain about how you can't stand today's high temperature anymore.

b. Advise your little brother to wear more clothes because it's cold outside.

c. Tell your mother that you're already twenty-one, so of course you know how to clean up your room.

d. Remind your roommate that the doctor wanted him to (told him to) finish taking the cold medicine.

e. You wonder why your Chinese teacher cared about what time you go to bed.

f. You brought your friend who just had her wisdom tooth removed some soup. Explain that you made the chicken soup (**jī tāng**) because you were afraid that she'd be unable to eat other food.

g. Comment on the weather in your area these past few days.

h. Explain why you like (or dislike) rain.

i. Compare the winter in your hometown with Beijing's, based on what you have read in this lesson.

j. Complain about the weather these days. The highest temperature has been only 2–3 degrees below zero.

3.   Complete the mini-dialogues

Use the structure in parentheses to complete each mini-dialogue.

a. 小夏： 你们都坐我的车回家吧。小王，我先 **sòng** 你还是先 **sòng** 小张？

    小王： 先 **sòng** 我。我家 _____。（A **bǐ** B…）

b. 小高： 我有一年多没看见你！你 _____ 了！（**yuè** 来 **yuè** AdjV）

    小 **Lín**：哪里，哪里。你也是。

c. 小张： 这个学期你怎么不上中文课了？

    小马： **Yǔ** 法 **yuè** 来 **yuè** 难，我 _____！所以不上了。（V + 不了）

d. 小谢： 你觉得我应该买哪一 **jiàn** 衣服？

    小夏： 都可以。_____。（A 跟 B 一样…）

e. 小高： 你要不要跟我们出去？我们要去买东西。

    小 **Lín**：我不能去。我妈妈 _____。（**ràng**…）

4.   Making connections

Complete the sentences with the clauses given below. For the first part of the sentence, make your choice from the column on the left. For the second part of the sentence, make your choice from the column on the right. Then, translate the sentences into English.

A. 我最喜欢 **qiū** 天   F. 没有时间做功课

B. 这门课很有用，也很有意思   G. 去图书馆做功课

C. **Zhōumò** 我常常在宿舍睡觉   H. 天 **qì** 不 **lěng** 也不 **rè**，非常舒服

D. 昨天我跟小王一起做功课、看电 **shì**   I. 功课 **tè** 别多

E. 我一天都忙 **zhe shōushi** 房间   J. 还一起吃晚饭

a. _____, 因为 _____。

b. _____, **érqiě** _____。

c. _____, **huòzhě** _____。

d. _____, 所以 _____。

e. _____, 只是 _____。

5. 天 qì yùbào

Part I. Six weathermen are presenting weather forecasts for their cities. Identify each weatherman on the basis of their forecast and write their name in the blank space in their forecast. Then translate each forecast into English.

| 王子强 | 谢易南 | 舒国定 |
| 常欢 | 夏如如 | 张明非 |

a. 大家好，我是 _____。明天的天 qì 还是跟这几天一样，非常舒服。虽然有一点儿 fēng，可是不大，是出去 wán 的好天 qì。
   English:

b. 大家好，我是 _____。大家可能觉得，今年的 dōng 天怎么这么 cháng。明天 tè 别 lěng，最高 wēndù 只有 líng 下四、五 dù。最 zāogāo 的是，很可能会下大 xuě，如果没有 shì，就在家里别出去，在路上开车的时候，最好开慢一点。
   English:

c. 大家好，我是 _____。最近这几天又 mēn 又 rè，我想很多人都快 shòu 不了了。明天还是很 rè，不过下 wǔ 会下一点儿 yǔ。应该会 ràng 大家高兴一点。
   English:

d. 大家好，我是 _____。下 **yǔ** 下了一天了，大家今天一定觉得很不 **fāngbiàn**。明天 **chú** 了下 **yǔ** 以外，还会 **guā** 大 **fēng**。这样的天 **qì** 要到 **zhōumò** 才会有一点不同。

English:

e. 大家好，我是 _____。明天会 **bǐ** 今天 **lěng** 得多，**érqiě** 可能会下 **xuě**，出去的时候，别 **wàng** 了多 **chuān** 一点衣服。

English:

f. 大家好，我是 _____。不知道你是不是跟我一样，也觉得 **chūn** 天快到了。最近 **bái** 天 (*daytime*) **yuè** 来 **yuè cháng**。明天也是一个好天 **qì**，不 **lěng** 不 **rè**，舒服 **jí** 了。

English:

_____

Part II. It's your turn to be the weatherman! Check the weather forecast online or on TV, and write about tomorrow's weather in Mandarin. Your weather forecast should be at least 100 characters in length.

_____
_____
_____
_____
_____

6. 一年四 **jì** 我最（不）喜欢…

Part I. Students in Xiao Zhang's class each talked about the season they like or dislike the most. Complete each sentence based on the illustrations.

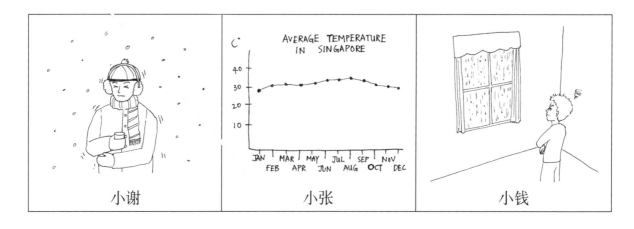

| 小谢 | 小张 | 小钱 |

| 小常 | 小高 | 小王 |

a. 小谢最不喜欢 **dōng** 天，因为 **dōng** 天 _____

_____ 。

b. 小张家 **xiāng** 的天 **qì**，一年四 **jì** 都 _____

_____ 。

c. 小钱不喜欢 **qiū** 天，因为 **qiū** 天 _____

_____ 。

d. 小常最不喜欢夏天，因为夏天 _____

_____ 。

e. 小高最喜欢夏天，因为夏天 _____

_____ 。

f. 小王最喜欢 **dōng** 天，因为 **dōng** 天 _____

_____ 。

Part II.   It's your turn. Tell us your (least) favorite season in your hometown and explain why. Your paragraph should be at least 120 characters in length.

_____

_____

_____

_____

_____

7. 你家 **xiāng** 的天 **qì** 怎么样？

Interview a friend and find out the year-round weather in his/her hometown. Write down the questions you can ask.

Questions about his/her hometown:

a. _____

b. _____

Questions about each season: length, temperature, what s/he likes and dislikes about it:

a. _____

b. _____

c. _____

d. _____

8. Writing

After your Exercise 7 interview, write a short passage about the weather in your friend's hometown. Your passage should be at least 100 characters in length.

_____

_____

_____

_____

_____

_____

_____

9. Form a cohesive paragraph

Rewrite these sentences, putting them in the correct order to form a <u>persuasive paragraph</u> about studying Chinese.

a. **dì** 二，中国和美国是两个很不一样的国家，在学习中文的时候你可知道一些中国文化。

b. **dì** 一，现在中国的经 **jì yuè** 来 **yuè** 好，中国和美国的关系也很好。很多工作都要会说中文的人。

c. 多学一些不同的文化很有意思。

d. 选不选中文 **zhuānyè** 没有关系，但是你在上大学的时候最好学一些中文。为什么呢？

e. 这样，你会 **bǐjiào** 有兴趣，可以学得很快、当然也就可以学得很好。

f. 你会说中文，**bìyè** 以后就容易找工作。

g. 人少的时候，老师和学生的关系，同学和同学的关系都 **bǐjiào** 好。

h. **dì** 三，中文课和数学课、经 **jì** 课很不一样，中文课，每个课的学生 **bǐjiào** 少。

Lesson 22 Workbook

 Listening and speaking

Structure drills

1. Even the object (Use and Structure note 22.7)

Example:
You will hear: 我没有手 **jī**。
You will say: 我 **lián** 手 **jī** 都没有。
Click "R" to hear the correct response: 我 **lián** 手 **jī** 都没有。

(a)   (b)   (c)   (d)   (e)   (f)   (g)

2. Even the subject (Use and Structure note 22.7)

Example:
You will hear: 我妈妈喜欢 **chàng kǎlā OK**。
You will say: **lián** 我妈妈都喜欢 **chàng kǎlā OK**。
Click "R" to hear the correct response: **lián** 我妈妈都喜欢 **chàng kǎlā OK**。

(a)   (b)   (c)   (d)   (e)   (f)   (g)   (h)

3. Even the time (Use and Structure note 22.7)

Example:
You will hear: 他星期天去上课。
You will say: 他 **lián** 星期天都去上课。
Click "R" to hear the correct response: 他 **lián** 星期天都去上课。

(a)   (b)   (c)   (d)   (e)   (f)   (g)   (h)

4. My roommate did the opposite (Use and Structure notes 22.5, 22.6)

Example:

You will hear: 我走进来。

You will say: 我走进来的时候，我的同屋走出去了。

Click "R" to hear the correct response: 我走进来的时候，我的同屋走出去了。

(a)   (b)   (c)   (d)   (e)   (f)

5. Add the object (Use and Structure note 22.6)

Example:

You will hear: 他 **shēn** 出来，手

You will say: 他 **shēn** 出手来。

Click "R" to hear the correct response: 他 **shēn** 出手来。

(a)   (b)   (c)   (d)   (e)   (f)   (g)   (h)   (i)   (j)

6. Not as much as (Use and Structure note 22.9)

Example:

You will hear: 昨天比今天冷。

You will say: 今天没有昨天冷。

Click "R" to hear the correct response: 今天没有昨天冷。

(a)   (b)   (c)   (d)   (e)   (f)   (g)   (h)   (i)   (j)

7 It has that quality all right, but… (Use and Structure note 22.8)

Example:

You will hear: 昨天比今天冷。

You will say: 今天冷是冷，可是没有昨天那么冷。

Click "R" to hear the correct response: 今天冷是冷，可是没有昨天那么冷。

(a)   (b)   (c)   (d)   (e)   (f)   (g)   (h)   (i)   (j)

Listening for information

1.   生 mìng 在 yú yùndòng

(CD1: 58)   You will hear six statements, each of which describes a person's sport preference. Listen to the statements and match each statement with the appropriate person. The statements include one word that we have not presented in the textbook, but you should be able to figure out its meaning as you do this exercise.

person	sport
Mèng Píng	American football
Yè Àiyún	baseball
Qín Fēng	rowing
Lín Yīchén	volleyball
Lǐ Shìchéng	skiing
Sòng Zhèng	soccer

2.   Exercise schedule

(CD1: 59)   You will hear five statements, each of which describes a person's exercise schedule and sports participation. Listen to the statements and fill in the correct information for each person. The statements include one word that has not been introduced in the textbook, but you should be able to work around it.

name	what kind of sport or exercise they do	how often they practice	when the competitions are
Huáng Dézhèng			
Língling			
Hú Zǔwén			
Luó Yǔ			
Jì Wénfāng			

3.   Where are they going?

You will hear five directional phrases, each describing the action in one of the drawings. **(CD1: 60)** Circle the correct directional arrow in each drawing, based on the information that you hear.

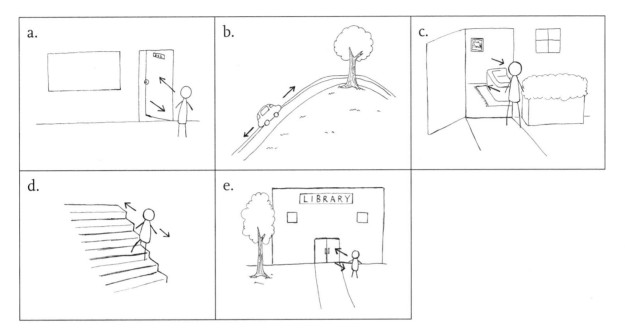

4.   Who goes where?

You will hear five statements, each describing the situation in one of the following pictures. **(CD1: 61)** Based on the information in the recordings, provide the names of the people involved in each situation, and draw an arrow indicating the direction of movement for the person who changes location.

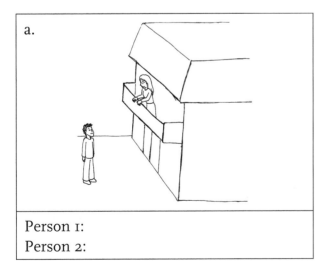

Person 1:
Person 2:

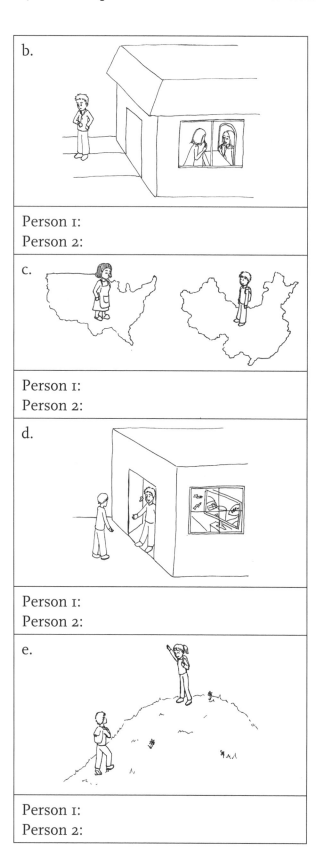

b.

Person 1:

Person 2:

c.

Person 1:

Person 2:

d.

Person 1:

Person 2:

e.

Person 1:

Person 2:

5.   Colder or warmer?

You will hear five statements, each describing today's weather in one of five cities in China. **(CD1: 62)**
Based on this information, write the names of the cities over the temperatures listed below.
The five cities are: Hángzhōu, Chéngdū, Lìjiāng, Tiānjīn, and Wǔhàn.

city					
temperature	65°F	60°F	54°F	48°F	32°F

6.   Even…

You will hear five statements using the sentence pattern **lián**…也/都. In the right-hand **(CD1: 63)**
column of the table below, there are five inferences. In the statement column, write in the
number of the statement that leads to each inference.

statement	inference
	→ 他不怕冷。
	→ 她下个星期有三个考试。
	→ 他很会打 **qiú**。
	→ 她没有时间去看电 **yǐng**。
	→ 他一定很会做饭。

7.   What about you?

Your friend is asking you about sports and exercise. Answer each question truthfully in a **(CD1: 64)**
complete sentence in Mandarin, using Chinese characters where we have learned them.

a.

b.

c.

d.

e.

f.

8. Interview

(CD1: 65) You will hear an interview between a campus newspaper reporter and Zheng Ming, who just returned to Shanghai after studying English for a year in Los Angeles. Summarize Zheng Ming's responses in English on the following three topics:

Summary

1. taking courses

2. campus life

3. studying

9. Dialogue

(CD1: 66) You will hear a conversation between Pan Li and Luo De, who have just met in a building on campus. The conversation contains a word we have not introduced, but you should be able to follow the conversation even if you do not know what this word means.

a. How do you get to the gym?
1) You take the elevator.
2) You just turn left.
3) You enter the gate.
4) You go up to the third floor.

b. Where can you play ping-pong?
1) You go into the room on the right.
2) You go down to the first floor.
3) You leave this building and go someplace else.
4) You go up one floor.

c. What did Luo De tell Pan Li?
1) He does not play tennis well, but he likes it.
2) He plays tennis four times a week.
3) He has a hard time finding a tennis court here.
4) He has not played tennis for years.

d. What do Pan Li and Luo De plan to do?
1) They will watch a game on Saturday.
2) They will meet on Saturday to play ping-pong.
3) They will go to the gym together.
4) They will take a look at the ping-pong room.

Reading and writing

Focus on Chinese characters

1.   Number of strokes

Indicate the number of strokes used in writing each of the following characters.

a. 或 _____   f. 怕 _____

b. 教 _____   g. 进 _____

c. 冷 _____   h. 自 _____

d. 玩 _____   i. 周 _____

e. 比 _____   j. 而 _____

2.   Which character?

Circle the character in each line that corresponds to the meaning on the left.

a. **huò** (**huòzhě** *or, perhaps*)   或   咸

b. **jìn** *enter*   近   进

c. **wán** *play*   完   玩

d. **jiā** *add* (**cānjiā** *participate*)   加   力

e. **fāng** (**dìfang** *place*)   房   方

f. **shǒu** *hand*   手   毛

g. **zì** (**zìjǐ** *self*)   白   自

h. **ràng** *make, let, tell*   让   址

i. **pà** *fear, afraid*   怕   自

j. **mò** (**zhōumò** *weekend*)   末   木

k. **bǐ** *compared to*   北   比

l. **ér** *and*   而   两

3.   First strokes

Write the first two strokes of each of the following characters.

a. 而 _____   f. 且 _____

b. 教 _____   g. 手 _____

c. 者 _____   h. 末 _____

d. 冷 _____   i. 方 _____

e. 或 _____   j. 让 _____

4.   Missing strokes

Complete each character by writing in the missing strokes.

a.   丬   **pà** *fear, afraid*

b.   千   **wán** *play*

c.   ヒ   **bǐ** *compared to*

d.   フ   **jiā** *add* (**cānjiā** *participate*)

e.   豆   **huò** (**huòzhě**) *or, perhaps*

f.   ⺈   **zì** (**zìxíngchě** *bicycle*)

g.   土   **jiào** *teach*

h.   月   **zhōu** (**zhōumò** *weekend*)

i.   冫   **lěng** *cold*

j.   二   **jìn** *enter*

5.   Total strokes

Rewrite this list of characters, arranging the characters in terms of their total number of strokes. Begin your list with the character with the fewest strokes.

周	进	教	或	者	冷	自	手	怕	末	加	比	让	方	玩	而	且

6.   Radicals

Here is a list of characters that we have learned through this lesson. Rewrite each character in the row next to its radical.

进   冷   怕   让   玩   放   选   惯
教   房   课   数   试   近   净   现

冫	
忄	
讠	
户	
辶	
攵	
王	

7.   Character sleuth: Look for the phonetic

Group the characters below in terms of their rhymes or near-rhymes. Write the characters that rhyme with each other in the column on the right. Write the shared part of each character in the column on the left. For all of these characters, the shared part is the "phonetic," the part of the character that provides a clue to its pronunciation. The first set of rhymes is completed for you. There are thirteen additional sets of characters that rhyme or partially rhyme and share a phonetic component among these characters.

块   房   跟   让   快   完   妈   作
女   红   爸   门   放   工   现   吧
把   功   很   间   们   方   问   中
吗   玩   钟   上   见   如   昨   马

phonetic	characters that rhyme or almost rhyme and share a phonetic component
女	如，女

8. Getting the gist of a paragraph

You won't be able to completely understand the following passage, but you know enough characters and words to be able to identify the topic of the paragraph and some of the supporting details. Read the paragraph for the main ideas and answer the questions that follow in English. Do not look up any characters we have not learned.

学习中文和学习数学有相同的地方，也有不同的地方。相同的是要去上课、看书、做功课。不同的是第一，学数学，懂了就可以了，你就可以做数学题了。学中文就很不一样。你可能懂了，但是你还是不会说。所以学中文的时候你要多听录音、多练习说。第二，学数学的时候，你可以不用每天都去上课。周末多用一些时间自己看看书，也可以懂。但是学中文每天都要去上课。一天不去上课你就不知道别的同学在说什么了。

a. What is the general purpose of this paragraph?

b. What are the main expressions used in the paragraph that identify its purpose?

c. The author presents two facts to support one side of the argument. Which side of the argument do these facts support?

9. Dictionary skills

Following the instructions in Lesson 17 of the Textbook, look up these characters in a Chinese dictionary and provide the requested information.

a. 相

pronunciation:

meaning:

one two-character word or phrase in which it occurs:

b. 己

pronunciation:

meaning:

one two-character word or phrase in which it occurs:

c. 第

pronunciation:

meaning:

one two-character word or phrase in which it occurs:

10. Find the incorrect characters

Xiao Zhang has written this email to his parents back in the USA, telling them about his recent basketball game with Xiao Wang and Guoqiang. He hasn't yet proofread this message, but when he does, he will find that eleven different characters are incorrect, several more than once. Read the passage aloud, circle the mistakes, and correct them on the answer sheet below.

> 巴巴妈妈你们好，
>
> 这个周来小王让我和国强跟他一起去大 **lánqiú**。虽然是 **dōng** 天，可是我们还再外边打。开始国强不想去，可是我们非上他去不可。那天 **tè** 别冷。他话 **lián** 手都 **shēn** 不出来，怎么能打 **qiú** 呢？可是我 **gàosu** 他一开是打 **qiú**，一开是 **pǎo bù**，他就不觉的冷了。我们打了一回儿，不 **dàn** 不觉得冷，而且觉得很 **rè**，很舒服。我想下个周末我们还会一走去打 **qiú**。
>
> 你们最进怎么样？

a. _____   b. _____   c. _____   d. _____   e. _____   f. _____

g. _____   h. _____   i. _____   j. _____   k. _____

11.   Scrambled sentences

Rewrite these phrases as sentences, putting the words in the correct order to match the English translations.

a. 得 / 我 / 高 / 王 / 老师 / 多 / 比

I'm a lot taller than Professor Wang.

b. 去 / 我们 / 个 / 吧 / 周末 / 玩 / 下 / 公园

Let's go to the park and have some fun next weekend.

c. 外边 / 很 / 有 /宿舍 / 自行车 / 的 / 多

There are a lot of bicycles outside of the dorm.

12.   Comprehension

Read the following paragraph and indicate whether the statements below are true (T) or false (F), based on the information in the passage.

中文的"自行车"是"自 jǐ 走的车"的意思。"行"就是"走"。我刚来美国的时候，看见可以过马路的地方都有"Xing"这个字。我想可能是现在在美国学中文的人很多，但是因为汉字很难写，所以他们不写汉字。或者是因为"Xing"很不容易说，所以写在马路上，让他们每天都看。

a. (   ) The narrator has just arrived in the USA.

b. (   ) The narrator thinks that few Americans study Chinese.

c. (   ) The narrator thinks that perhaps the character 行 is hard for Americans to write.

d. (   ) There is an overlap in meaning between the word 行 in Chinese and the use of "Xing" in English.

e. (   ) The narrator thinks that "Xing" means *bicycles* in English.

Focus on structure

1.   Similarities and differences (Use and Structure notes 22.1, 22.2)

Write a sentence for each of the following lines, stating that A and B have similarities and differences when it comes to C, as in the example, and translate your sentence into English.

Example:
A: 美国的大学生   B: 中国的大学生   C: **duànliàn shēntǐ**

美国的大学生跟中国的大学生在 **duànliàn shēntǐ** 上有 **xiāng** 同的地方，也有不同的地方。
When it comes to exercising, American students and Chinese students have similarities and differences.

a. A: 北京   B: **Tái** 北   C: 天 **qi**

Your sentence: _____

English: _____

b. A: 美国   B: 中国   C: 文化

Your sentence: _____

English: _____

c. A: 美国大学生   B: 中国大学生   C: 学习

Your sentence: _____

English: _____

d. A: 日本人   B: 中国人   C: 吃饭

Your sentence: _____

English: _____

e. A: **Yīng** 文   B: 中文   C: **yǔ** 法

Your sentence: _____

English: _____

2.   Stating similarities (Use and Structure note 22.2)

Continuing the comparisons you introduced in Exercise 1, write a Mandarin sentence stating that *the similarity is that:*

a. the summer is very hot

b. American students and Chinese students are hardworking

c. before students graduate they have to select a major

d. both use chopsticks to eat

e. the subject (**zhǔyǔ**) is before the verb (**dòngcí**), and the object (**bīnyǔ**) is after the verb

3. Stating differences and linking information with 而 (Use and Structure notes 22.2, 22.4)

Continuing the comparisons you introduced in Exercise 1, write a Mandarin sentence for each pair that you are comparing, stating that *the differences are....* Link the differences with 而.

a. Beijing has four seasons and Taipei doesn't have winter.

b. American people use given names to call (叫) their friends and Chinese people use family name + given name (**xìngmíng**) to call their friends.

c. American students select their major when they are in their third year, and Chinese students select their major before they begin to attend college. (Use 才 and 就 in this sentence.)

d. Chinese people like to eat hot and spicy food and Japanese people do not.

e. English has 'the' and 'a' and Chinese does not.

4. Directional complements (Use and Structure notes 22.5 and 22.6)

Write a sentence using a verb of motion with a directional complement describing the motion in each of the following pictures from Xiao Wang's perspective. Do not include the phrases "toward Xiao Wang" or "away from Xiao Wang" in your sentences.

| a. | ride down, toward Xiao Wang |

b.		ride up, away from Xiao Wang
c.		jump down, toward Xiao Wang (**tiào** *jump*)
d.		drive up, away from Xiao Wang
e.		ride across, toward Xiao Wang
f.		run in, toward Xiao Wang
g.		ride out, away from Xiao Wang

h.		run out, toward Xiao Wang
i.		walk in, away from Xiao Wang
j.		walk up, toward Xiao Wang

5.   They can't do it (Use and Structure note 22.6)

Rewrite each of your sentences in Exercise 4 from Xiao Wang's perspective, saying that the subject is unable to do the action.

a.

b.

c.

d.

e.

f.

g.

h.

i.

j.

6.   Walk out of the park

Rewrite each of your sentences in Exercise 4 from Xiao Wang's perspective, adding in the location that serves as the reference point of the action. As an example, (a) has been completed for you.

a. 他 **qí** 下山来。

b.

c.

d.

e.

f.

g.

h.

i.

j.

7.   Even they can do these activities (Use and Structure note 22.7)

Translate a.–d. to English, and translate e.–h. to Mandarin, using characters where we have learned them. Complete i.–k. with the phrases provided in parentheses.

a. 自行车容易 **qí**。**Lián** 我 **mèimei** 都能 **qí**。

b. 我 **dìdi** 很喜欢打 **qiú**。**Lián páiqiú** 也喜欢（打）。

c. 他不 **dǒng** 中文。**Lián** "你好" 也不 **dǒng**。

d. 我的同屋每天都去 **jiàn shēn**房 **duànliàn shēntǐ**。她 **lián** 周末都去。

e. In my hometown, it is cold in the spring. It is even very cold in April.

f. My older sister is very hardworking. She even studies on Friday night.

g. In my school, a lot of students participate in school sports teams. Even the first year students participate.

h. Yesterday's test was too long. Even the smartest students didn't finish it.

i. 大为每天都去 **pǎo bù**，_____。（下 **xuě** 的时候）

j. 国强的房间 **luànjí** 了，_____。（坐的地方）

k. 小张昨天很不舒服。一吃东西就 **lā dù** 子，_____。（水）

8. Comparisons with 没有 (Use and Structure note 22.9)

Write a complete Mandarin sentence for each line, saying that NP₁ is *not as* AdjV as NP₂.

NP₁	NP₂	AdjV
a. American football	soccer	interesting
b. June	August	hot
c. my older sister	my older brother	hardworking
d. taking a bus	driving a car	convenient
e. my room	your room	messy
f. my hobbies	my roommate's hobbies	many

9. It is AdjV all right, but… (Use and Structure note 22.8)

Using the information in Exercise 8, say that NP₁ has the quality of the adjectival verb, but that it doesn't have as much as NP₂, following the example below.

Example:

NP₁	NP₂	AdjV
movie tickets	*football game tickets*	*expensive*

电 **yǐng piào guì** 是 **guì**，可是没有 **zúqiú** 比 **sài piào** 那么 **guì**。

Movie tickets are expensive all right, but they are not as expensive as football game tickets.

a.

b.

c.

d.

e.

f.

10.   Scrambled sentences

Rewrite these phrases into sentences, putting them in the right order to match the English translations.

a. 做 / 没有 / 开始 / 忙 **zhe** / 玩 **qiú** / 功课 / 学期 / 时间 / 学生 / 一 / 都 / 而

Once the semester begins, the students are all busy doing their course work and do not have time to play ball.

b. 喜欢 / **shēntǐ** / 喜欢 / **duànliàn** / 到 **dǐ** / 你 / 不

Do you really like to work out or not?

c. 吗 / 了 / **pǎo** 上 / 你 / 他 / 小张 / 去 / 看得见 / 山 (2 sentences)

Xiao Zhang ran up the mountain. Can you see him?

d. 真 / 冷 / 下 **xuě** / 可是 / 冷 / 漂亮 / 北京 / 是 / 的时候 / **dōng** 天

Winter in Beijing is indeed cold, but it's really beautiful when it snows.

e. **xiāng** 同 / 在 / 和 / 习惯 / 她 / 生 **huó** / 很不 / 上 / 她 **mèimei**

When it comes to daily habits, she and her younger sister are very different.

Focus on communication

1.   Dialogue comprehension

Study the Lesson 22 Narrative and Dialogue. Then, read the following statements and indicate whether they are true (T) or false (F).

a. (   ) 美国的大学生和中国的大学生都喜欢 **duànliàn shēntǐ**，只是他们喜欢的 **yùndòng** 不太一样。

b. (   ) **Pīngpāng qiú** 和 **páiqiú** 是美国大学生和中国大学生都喜欢的 **yùndòng**。

c. (   ) 美国大学周末常常有校 **duì** 的比 **sài**。

d. (   ) 小王跟大为要去打 **lánqiú**。

e. (   ) 国强不想去，因为他手 **téng**，**shēn** 不出来。

f. (   ) 前两天比这几天冷。

g. (   ) 大为觉得自 **jǐ duànliàn** 得比国强多。

h. (   ) 国强的 **yùndòng** 就是打 **qiú**、**qí** 自行车和坐电 **tī**。

i. (   ) 国强最后 **jué** 定跟他们一起去打 **qiú**。

2. What do you say?

What do you say in each of the following situations? Type your answers, using characters where we have learned them, and email them to your Chinese teacher.

a. State at least three kinds of sports that you like.

b. Ask someone how frequently s/he works out at the gym.

c. Advise your friend that s/he should exercise more.

d. Argue that you exercise by walking to school every day and never taking the elevator.

e. Tell people not to jump (**tiào** in **tiàowǔ** *dance*) down.

f. You are competing with your sibling/roommate/friend. Brag about two things that you do much better than s/he does.

g. You are arguing with your friend about winter in your city. You agree that he has a point, but you have a different opinion about winter.

3. Complete the mini-dialogues

Use the structure in parentheses to complete each mini-dialogue.

a. A: 王老师，中文和 **Yīng** 文最大的不同是什么？

　 B: ＿＿＿＿＿＿＿＿＿＿＿＿＿＿＿＿＿＿＿＿＿。（…而…）

b. A: 你最近在忙什么？怎么都没看见你？

　 B: 我每天都忙 **zhe** ＿＿＿＿＿＿＿＿＿＿＿＿＿＿。（**lián**…都…）

c. A: 你昨天说 **dù** 子 **téng**，现在呢？还 **téng** 不 **téng**？

　 B: 现在好多了。＿＿＿＿＿＿＿＿＿＿＿＿＿＿。（没有…那么…）

d. A: 四 **chuān** 菜真好吃！

　 B: ＿＿＿＿＿＿＿＿＿＿＿＿＿＿＿＿。（A 是 A, 可是…）

e. A: 我问了你那么多次，你 ＿＿＿＿＿＿＿＿＿＿＿＿？（到 **dǐ**）

　 B: 我怎么会不喜欢你呢！你想太多了。

4. Multiple choice

Select the appropriate line to complete each sentence, and then translate the sentence into English.

a. 我和我 **mèimei** 很不一样。我很喜欢走路 **duànliàn shēntǐ**，而 _____。
   1) 我昨天走路走了一个 **zhōngtou**
   2) 她只喜欢坐车、坐电 **tī**
   3) 她今年是一年 **jí** 的学生

   English:

b. 小美的 **shēntǐ** 很好，她每天 **yùndòng**，**lìng** 外，_____。
   1) 她还 **cān** 加学校的校 **duì**
   2) 小美这个学期选了四门课
   3) 小张不喜欢 **yùndòng**

   English:

c. 加 **zhōu** 漂亮是漂亮，可是 _____。
   1) 天 **qì** 真好
   2) 我比 **jiào** 喜欢 **Niǔyuē**
   3) 在加 **zhōu** 开车很方 **biàn**

   English:

d. **Yùndòng** 对 **shēntǐ** 很好，而且 _____。
   1) 今天这么冷，我就不出去 **yùndòng** 了
   2) 美国大学生跟中国大学生在 **yùndòng** 上有 **xiāng** 同的地方，也有不同的地方
   3) 我觉得 **yùndòng** 以后 **tè** 别舒服

   English:

e. 下 **xuě** 的时候，我喜欢在家睡觉或者 _____。
   1) 喝一 **bēi rè chá**，看外边的 **xuě**
   2) 路上很脏，不能出去玩儿
   3) 冷得手都 **shēn** 不出来

   English:

5.   Sports event schedule

Here is a sports schedule at a college in California. Answer the questions that follow in Mandarin, based on this schedule.

team	date	opponent
soccer	2/18	UC Irvine
basketball	2/18	UC Davis
basketball	2/19	UC Santa Barbara
sailing	2/22	UC Berkeley
volleyball	3/1	CSU Long Beach
sailing	3/2	UC Santa Cruz
cycling	3/2	UC Davis
cycling	3/4	Caltech
volleyball	3/5	UC Riverside
volleyball	3/9	UCLA

a. 这个学校有什么校 **duì**？

b. 小周 **tè** 别喜欢看 **zúqiú** 比 **sài**，你想他哪天一定会去看比 **sài**？

c. 二月二十二号这个学校跟哪个学校比 **sài**？比什么？

d. 小王 **cān** 加学校的 **lánqiú duì**，你想他哪几天大概不能去上课？

e. **Lánqiú** 比 **sài** 早还是自行车比 **sài** 早？

f. 今天是二月二十八号，你觉得我还能买到 **páiqiú** 比 **sài** 的票吗？为什么？

26

6.   Read and retell

Part I.   Read the paragraph and fill in the blanks with a verb + directional complement based on the English translation.

今天是小 **Yè** 的生日。小张让小 **Yè** 下了课以后就在 **kāfēi** 馆 **děng** 他。小张 _____

_____ (walked into the coffee shop) 的时候，看见小谢和小高 _____

(run out)。小 **Yè** 说，小谢和小高听说今天是她的生日，他们要让她高兴一下。小张

让小 **Yè** 把手 _____ (extend out)，他给小 **Yè** 买了一 **jiàn** 漂亮的衣服。小 **Yè**

非常高兴。他们两个人一起 _____ (walk out of the coffee

shop)，看见小谢的车 _____ (drive over)，小高让他们 _____

_____ (enter in)，小谢打 **suan dài** 他们去吃晚饭。

Part II.   Read the paragraph again. Imagine what was said during those situations:

a. Xiao Xie wonders what Xiao Ye is doing in the coffee shop and Xiao Ye explains.

b. Xiao Zhang is surprised to see Xiao Xie, and Xiao Gao rushing out and asks them where exactly (到 **dǐ**) they are going and why they are running so fast.

c. Xiao Zhang tells Xiao Ye that he heard it was her birthday today and he bought her a little something.

d. Xiao Ye gushes about the beautiful gift and thanks Xiao Zhang.

e. Xiao Gao suggests to Xiao Xie that they drive over to the coffee shop to take Xiao Zhang and Xiao Ye to the mountain top.

f. Xiao Gao tells Xiao Zhang and Xiao Ye to hurry and get into the car.

g. Xiao Xie tells them that he is driving them up to the mountain for dinner.

7. Talk about your favorite sports/workout

Part I.   Answer the following questions truthfully.

a. 你喜欢 **yùndòng** 吗？你最喜欢什么 **yùndòng**？

b. 你是什么时候开始做这个 **yùndòng** 的？

c. 你为什么喜欢这个 **yùndòng**？

d. **Yùndòng** 以后，你觉得怎么样？

e. 这个 **yùndòng** 有什么好的地方？有没有不方 **biàn** 的地方？是什么？

f. 你一个星期做几次这个 **yùndòng**？

g. 你在哪儿做这个 **yùndòng**？

h. 下 **yǔ** 或者天 **qì** 不好的时候，如果不能 **yùndòng**，你怎么 **duànliàn shēntǐ**？

i. **Chú** 了你最喜欢的这个 **yùndòng** 以外，你还想试试什么 **yùndòng**，为什么？

Part II.   Use your answers above to write a paragraph about your favorite sports. Your paragraph should be at least 120 characters in length.

_____

_____

_____

_____

_____

_____

_____

_____

_____

_____

8.   Writing a comparison paragraph

Part I.   Form a cohesive paragraph. Rearrange these sentences so that they become a cohesive paragraph that compares college life in the past with life nowadays.

a. 还可以跟朋友一起出去玩，很晚才回宿舍也没有关系。

b. 不同的是，以前的大学生跟朋友在宿舍、**cāntīng**、**kāfěi** 馆 **tán** 话，去图书馆找上课要用的书。

c. 虽然很多 **shì** 都得自 **jǐ** 做，**lián** 衣服都得自 **jǐ** 洗。

d. **Lìng** 外，有了电 **nǎo** 以后，选课、买书，都比以前方 **biàn**。

e. 以前的大学生跟现在的大学生在生 **huó** 上有 **xiāng** 同的地方，也有不同的地方。

f. 可是在学校住可以自 **jǐ jué** 定吃饭、睡觉的时间。

g. 而现在的大学生上 **wǎng** 跟朋友 **tán** 话、找上课要用的东西。

h. **Xiāng** 同的是年 **qīng** 人都喜欢住校的生 **huó**。

Part II.   Write your own comparison paragraph: Following the structure of the above paragraph, write a similar paragraph to compare high school life and college life from your own experience. Your paragraph should be at least 120 characters in length.

_____

_____

_____

_____

_____

_____

_____

_____

_____

_____

Lesson 23 Workbook

 Listening and speaking

(audio online)

Structure drills

1. Even more (Use and Structure note 23.2)

You will hear a comparison between two people, places, or things, followed by a new person, place, or thing. Say that the new item has *even more* of some quality than the first item, as in the example.

Example:
You will hear: 中文比 **Yīng** 文难。（日文）
You will say: 日文比中文 **gèng** 难。
Click "R" to hear the correct response: 日文比中文 **gèng** 难。

(a)   (b)   (c)   (d)   (e)   (f)   (g)   (h)   (i)   (j)

2. 只要 S/VP₁ 就 VP₂ *as long as*, Part I (Use and Structure note 23.4)

You will hear two statements. Rephrase them using 只要 to say that as long as the first statement is true, the second one is true.

Example:
You will hear: 你喜欢，你就可以买。
You will say: 只要你喜欢，就可以买。
Click "R" to hear the correct response: 只要你喜欢，就可以买。

(a)   (b)   (c)   (d)   (e)   (f)   (g)   (h)   (i)   (j)

3. 只要 S/VP₁ 就 VP₂ *as long as*, Part II (Use and Structure note 23.4)

Restate each sentence with 只要 S/VP₁ 就 VP₂, as in the example.

> **Example:**
> *You will hear:* 你去看电 **yǐng**，我也去。
> *You will say:* 只要你去看电 **yǐng**，我就去。
> *Click "R" to hear the correct response:* 只要你去看电 **yǐng**，我就去。

(a)   (b)   (c)   (d)   (e)   (f)   (g)   (h)   (i)   (j)

4. 一点儿都 NEG V *not even a little*, Part I (Use and Structure note 23.5)

You will hear a sentence describing the quality of some person, place, or thing. Restate the sentence to say that it has none of that quality, as in the example.

> **Example:**
> *You will hear:* 你不 **pàng**。
> *You will say:* 你一点儿都不 **pàng**。
> *Click "R" to hear the correct response:* 你一点儿都不 **pàng**。

(a)   (b)   (c)   (d)   (e)   (f)   (g)   (h)

5. 一点儿 NP 都 NEG V *not even a little* NP, Part II
(Use and Structure note 23.5)

You will hear a sentence talking about something that I have not done. Rephrase the sentence to say that I didn't even do a little of the action.

> **Example:**
> *You will hear:* 我没喝酒。
> *You will say:* 我一点儿酒都没喝。
> *Click "R" to hear the correct response:* 我一点儿酒都没喝。

(a)   (b)   (c)   (d)   (e)   (f)   (g)

Listening for information

1.   Listen and draw

You will hear five statements, each of which mentions an object with a certain color. Listen (CD1: 69) to the sentences and draw each item, indicating its color, in the corresponding box.

a.	b.	c.	d.	e.

2.   Shopping spree

(CD1: 70) Xiao Ping, Jia Ting, and Lai Xinxin went shopping last weekend. Listen to what they bought and write in the information on the following form.

name	item	size	price	color
Xiao Ping				
Jia Ting				
Lai Xinxin				

3.   What is the condition?

(CD1: 71) You will hear five statements, each describing a condition that leads to some result. In the "condition" column of the following table, write down the letter of the condition that leads to each of the results in the "result" column.

condition	result
	→ **dù** 子就不 **téng** 了。 *no stomach ~*
	→ 就可以买这条 **lán qún** 子。
	→ 身体一定会很好。
	→ 妈妈就让他出去玩。 *~*
	→ 就可以选这门课。 *course*

4.   My sisters and I

(CD1: 72) Listen to the passage about me and my sisters, and write down each of our clothing sizes.

person	3rd younger sister (xiǎo mèi)	2nd younger sister (èr mèi)	1st younger sister (dà mèi)	me
size				

5. Not at all

You will hear five statements, each describing a different situation. In the "conclusion" column of the following table, write the letter of the statement that can be used to sum up or conclude each of the following situations.

situation	conclusion
我两点才吃 **wǔ** 饭。	
我昨天晚上睡了十个钟头。	
这个考试只要十分钟就写完了。	
那家新 **cāntīng** 又贵，服务又慢。	
这条 **qún** 子太 **duǎn** 了。	

6. Conversation

Answer the questions you hear truthfully, based on your personal experience and interests.

a.

b.

c.

d.

e.

f.

7. Listen and write

You will hear a phone message from Aunt Lin. Write an email to answer her questions in Mandarin, using characters where we have learned them.

Email to Aunt Lin

8. Meizhen's shopping experience

(CD1: 76) Meizhen is talking about her shopping experience. Based on her narrative, indicate whether each of the following statements is true (T) or false (F).

a. (   ) Meizhen wears a size 5.

b. (   ) The skirt is 50% off.

c. (   ) Meizhen likes the color red.

d. (   ) Meizhen bought some things, but she didn't buy a skirt.

e. (   ) Meizhen went shopping last weekend.

 9. Dialogue

(CD1: 77) Zhijie is phoning Wenna to invite her to an event. Listen to their conversation and select the correct answer to each of the following questions.

a. What event will they attend tomorrow night?
　1) an evening party
　2) a dance party
　3) a singing performance
　4) a musical

b. How did the woman learn about the event?
　1) from the campus newspaper
　2) from her friend
　3) from a radio broadcast
　4) from some school posters

c. What will the woman probably wear tomorrow night?
　1) a long skirt
　2) a short skirt
　3) a pair of red pants
　4) a traditional dress

d. Why does the man want to go to the event?
　1) His friends organized the event.
　2) He was asked to buy the tickets.
　3) He is going on a date with the female speaker.
　4) His sister is singing at the event.

e. What is their plan for tomorrow?
　1) They will take the subway.
　2) They will meet at the auditorium.
　3) They will drive there.
　4) They will walk together.

Reading and writing

Focus on Chinese characters

1. Number of strokes

Indicate the number of strokes used in writing each of the following characters.

a. 新 _____   f. 贵 _____

b. 员 _____   g. 绿 _____

c. 特 _____   h. 连 _____

d. 铁 _____   i. 穿 _____

e. 事 _____   j. 球 _____

2. Which character?

Circle the character in each line that corresponds to the meaning on the left.

a. **shì (shìyàng** *style*)   式   试

b. **yùn** *move* (**yùndòng** *movement*)   动   运

c. **xīn** *heart*   心   新

d. **wán** *finish, end*   院   完

e. **yòu** *also, both*   友   又

f. **lián** *even*   车   连

g. **tiě** *iron* (**dìtiě** *subway*)   钦   铁

h. **tiáo** (*classifier for streets, skirts*)   冬   条

i. **tǐ** (**shēntǐ** *body*)   体   本

j. **shēn** (**shēntǐ** *body*)   身   夏

k. **yuán** (**fúwùyuán** *server, clerk*)   员   贵

l. **qì** (**tiānqì** *weather*)   汽   气

3. First strokes

Write the first two strokes of each of the following characters.

a. 春 _____   f. 累 _____

b. 山 _____   g. 绿 _____

c. 市 _____   h. 条 _____

d. 务 _____   i. 心 _____

e. 叶 _____   j. 动 _____

4. Missing strokes

Complete each character by writing in the missing strokes.

a.   勹   **shēn** (**shēntǐ** *body*)

b.   丁   **shì** (**shìyàng** *style*)

c.   宀   **wán** *finish, end*

d.   冂   **lèi** *tired*

e.   宀   **chuān** *wear, put on*

f.   干   **qiú** *ball*

g.   广   **guì** *expensive*

h.   人   **qì** (**tiānqì** *weather*)

i.   二   **chūn** *spring*

j.   亠   **shì** (**shì zhōngxīn** *city center*)

5. Total strokes

Rewrite this list of characters, arranging the characters in terms of their total number of strokes. Begin your list with the character with the fewest strokes.

动	特	叶	事	绿	穿	式	新	身	完	员	体	心	累	气	铁	贵	又	运	条

6.   Radicals

Here is a list of characters that we have learned through this lesson. Rewrite each character in the row next to its radical.

完　员　叶　春　经　运　绿　连
进　玩　边　定　喝　岁　球　周

口	
日	
宀	
山	
辶	
纟	
王	

7.   Character sleuth: Look for the phonetic

Group the characters below in terms of their rhymes or near-rhymes. Write the characters that rhyme with each other in the column on the right. Write the shared part of each character in the column on the left. For all of these characters, the shared part is the "phonetic," the part of the character that provides a clue to its pronunciation. The first set of rhymes is completed for you. There are nine additional sets of characters that rhyme or partially rhyme and share a phonetic component among these characters.

女　如　现　玩　把　门　放　红
房　先　工　式　选　完　让　爸
见　试　跟　院　上　方　问　很

phonetic	characters that rhyme or almost rhyme and share a phonetic component
女	如

8.   Getting the gist of a paragraph

You won't be able to completely understand the following passage, but you know enough characters and words to be able to identify the topic of the paragraph and some of the supporting details. Read the paragraph for the main ideas and answer the questions that follow in English. Do not look up any characters we have not learned.

我真的不知道为什么有这么多的人喜欢打球。打球到底有什么意思呢？很多人在一起，跑来、跑去。不是把球踢出去，就是把球抢过来，又脏、又热、又累。有的时候还会伤了身体，不得不去看医生。如果真的那么喜欢球，每个人自己买一个拿回家不是很好吗？

---

a. What is the general topic of this paragraph?

b. What is the narrator's opinion about this topic?

c. Circle one or two sections of the passage that reveal the narrator's opinion.

9.   Dictionary skills

Following the instructions in Lesson 17 of the Textbook, look up these characters in a Chinese dictionary and provide the requested information.

a. 街
   pronunciation:
   meaning:
   one two-character word or phrase in which it occurs:

b. 花
   pronunciation:
   meaning:
   one two-character word or phrase in which it occurs:

c. 种
   pronunciation:
   meaning:
   one two-character word or phrase in which it occurs:

10.   Find the incorrect characters

Xiao Zhang has written this email to his parents back in the USA, telling them about one of his classmates, but he has typed ten characters incorrectly. Read the passage aloud, circle the mistakes, and correct them on the answer sheet below.

> 爸爸，妈妈，你们好！
>
> 你们身体好吗？北京的天汽 **yuè** 来 **yuè** 冷。宿舍，叫 **shì** 都很舒朋，可是去外力得多穿衣服。**Guā fēng** 的时候觉得 **gèng** 冷。我有一个同学非常怕冷。因为怕冷，所以他很少跟我们至宿舍外边去云动。团为很少运动，所以他也很容以累。如果有人请他出去吃反，看电 **yǐng**，买东四，他说如果坐地铁去，他就去。如果走路去，他就不去。

a. _____   b. _____   c. _____   d. _____   e. _____

f. _____   g. _____   h. _____   i. _____   j. _____

11.   Scrambled sentences

Rewrite these phrases as sentences, putting the words in the correct order to match the English translations.

a. 以后 / 去 / 晚饭 / 男朋友 / 新 / 市中心 / 买 / 她 / 衣服 / 和 / 的 / 的 / 吃完 / 小叶

After finishing dinner, Xiao Ye and her boyfriend went downtown to buy new clothes.

b. 的 / 天气 / 春天 / 好 / 舒服 / 好 / 没有 / 的 / 那么 / 夏天 / 是 / 可是

The weather in the summer is good all right, but it is not as comfortable as the spring.

c. 都 / 打球 / 周末 / 没有 / 时间 / 我们 / 连

We don't even have time to play ball on the weekend.

12.   Comprehension

Read the following paragraph and indicate whether the statements below are true (T) or false (F), based on the information in the passage.

> 有的人很喜欢买东西。有用的东西也买，没有用的也买。只要看见他喜欢的东西，他就非买不可。我就 **rènshi** 一个这样的人。他最喜欢买不同式样的衣服。虽然买了很多，但是没有时间穿。以前差不多每个周末他都出去买衣服，最近不买了。因为他买了很多，所以现在他连一点钱都没有了。他的房间虽然很大，但是连再放一 **jiàn** 衣服的地方都没有了。他说以后有了钱，他还会买。你说这样的人有意思吗？

a. (　) The narrator's friend only likes to buy one style of clothing.

b. (　) The narrator's friend buys clothes that he doesn't wear.

c. (　) The narrator's friend can't buy any more clothes because his house isn't big enough
to store more clothes.

d. (　) The narrator's friend only buys clothes if they are on sale.

e. (　) The narrator thinks that buying clothes is interesting.

Focus on structure

1.   Even more (Use and Structure note 23.2)

Translate a.–c. into English and d.–f. into Mandarin.

a. 天气 **yùbào** 说明天比今天还冷。

b. 我觉得这 **shuāng xié** 子比那 **shuāng xié** 子 **gèng** 舒服一点。

c. **Qí** 自行车比走路快。坐出 **zū** 车 **gèng** 快。

d. Japanese is hard all right, but Chinese is even harder. (Use **gèng**.)

e. The red skirt is even prettier than the blue one. (Use 还.)

f. She is even smarter than her older sister. (Use 还.)

2.   I have no alternative (Use and Structure note 23.3)

Your roommate is wondering about your choice of action. Explain to her why this is your
only option.

a. 你的同屋：你今天怎么穿这 **jiàn** 衣服？

你说：_____，所以我不得不穿这 **jiàn** 衣服。

b. 你的同屋：你不是不喜欢吃中国饭吗？为什么你会去那个饭馆吃饭？

你说：_____，所以我不得不去。

c. 你的同屋：周末要不要跟我一起去看 **lán** 球比 **sài**？

你说：我不能去。_____

d. 你的同屋：天气这么冷你还要出去运动？

你说：**Yī** 生说 _____，所以我 _____。

3.   Giving your opinion (Use and Structure note 23.4)

Xiao Zhang is expressing his concerns to Xiao Xie. Translate each of Xiao Zhang's sentences into English, and translate Xiao Xie's responses into Mandarin, using the expression 只要…就 in each of the responses.

a. 小张：我对我的 **zhuānyè** 没有兴趣了。

   Xiao Xie: Whether you are interested or not is not important. As long as your grades are good, it's okay.

b. 小张：天气 **yùbào** 说明天会很冷。

   Xiao Xie: As long as it doesn't snow, it's okay.

c. 小张：我们的房间又 **luàn** 又脏！

   Xiao Xie: It doesn't matter whether it's clean or not. As long as we have a place to sleep, it's okay.

d. 小张：明天是小叶的生日。你说我应该给她买什么东西？

   Xiao Xie: It's not important what you buy. As long as you buy her something, she will be happy.

e. 小张：我看书看得太慢了。

   Xiao Xie: It doesn't matter if you read slowly. As long as you <u>understand what you are reading</u>, its okay. *(Use a resultative verb in the potential form for the underlined expression.)*

4.   Not even a little (Use and Structure note 23.5)

Answer each of the following questions in complete Mandarin sentences, using the expression 一点都 NEG VP, and then translate your answers into English.

a. 你觉得这 **jiàn** 衣服 **liú** 行吗？
   Your reply in Mandarin:
   English:

b. 你觉得春天穿这 **jiàn** 衣服 **héshì** 吗？
   Your reply in Mandarin:
   English:

c. 你觉得昨天的考试难不难？
Your reply in Mandarin:
English:

d. 你对美式 **zú** 球有兴趣吗？
Your reply in Mandarin:
English:

e. 你 **pīngpāng** 球打得怎么样？
Your reply in Mandarin:
English:

5. Scrambled sentences

Rewrite these phrases into sentences, putting them in the right order to match the English translations.

a. 是 / **gù** 客 / 看起来 / 这个 / 年 **qīng** 人 / **shāng** 店 / 的 / 都

It looks like the customers for this store are all young people.

b. **héshì** / 不 / 很 / 可是 / 式样 / 都 / **liú** 行 / 大小 / 一点

The size is right, but the style isn't very current.

c. 是 / 那本 / 一点 / 看完了 / 可是 / 我 / 不 / **dǒng** / 书 / 看完了 / 都

I finished that book all right, but I didn't understand it at all.

d. **jiǎn jià** / **shāng** 店 / 都 / **gù** 客 / 让 / 春 **jié** / 多 / 点 / 东西 / 到了 / 打 **zhé** / 买

When the Chinese New Year is approaching, the stores all give discounts and reduce prices to get the customers to buy more things.

e. 一点 / 觉得 / **huángsè** 的 / 绿 **sè** / 我 / 的 / **liú** 行 / 还 / 比

I think the yellow one is a little more stylish than the green one.

Focus on communication

1. Dialogue comprehension

Study the Lesson 23 Narrative and Dialogue. Then, read the following statements and indicate whether they are true (T) or false (F).

a. (   ) 最近去买东西特别好，因为很多 **shāng** 店都在打 **zhé**。

b. (   ) 小叶喜欢 **guàng jiē**，而小张和小高不喜欢。

c. (　) 小张觉得 **pá** 山、打球没有 **guàng shāng** 店那么累。

d. (　) 小叶喜欢的 **qún** 子 **yánsè** 和式样都好，就是比 **jiào** 贵。

e. (　) 小叶觉得自己 **pàng** 了，所以不想买 **qún** 子了。

f. (　) 小高觉得自己太 **shòu** 了，小叶 **zhèng héshì**。

g. (　) 小叶特别喜欢穿 **lánsè** 的衣服。

h. (　) 小高觉得小叶穿 **lánsè** 的不好看，所以让她试一下别的 **yánsè** 的。

i. (　) 小叶试穿的这条 **qún** 子很多人买，因为今年 **liú** 行这个式样。

j. (　) 红色的 **qún** 子小叶穿起来 **shòu** 一点，**gèng** 好看，所以小叶就买了。

2.　What do you say?

What do you say in each of the following situations? Type your answers, using characters where we have learned them, and email them to your Chinese teacher.

a. Talk about one language that's even more difficult than Chinese.

b. Explain that you are obliged to do something so you can't come to the party tomorrow.

c. You gained a few pounds over the holiday break. Find some excuses to explain it.

d. Request a different size item of clothing from what you are trying on.

e. Suggest your friend try a pair of shoes in a different color because the green shoes don't look good.

f. Say something nice about what your friend is wearing right now. (For example, you look good in xxx color, etc.)

3.　Complete the mini-dialogues

Use the structure in parentheses to complete each mini-dialogue.

a. A: 你今天为什么出来买衣服？你不是最不喜欢 **guàng jiē** 吗？

　 B: ＿＿＿＿＿＿＿＿＿＿＿＿＿＿＿＿＿＿＿＿＿＿＿。（不得不）

b. A: 真 **zāogāo**，这么多 **yánsè**，我到 **dǐ** 要选哪一个？

　 B: ＿＿＿＿＿＿＿＿＿＿＿＿＿＿＿＿＿＿＿＿。（只要…就…）

c. A: 那门课不是很难吗？你为什么要选？

　 B: ＿＿＿＿＿＿＿＿＿＿＿＿＿＿＿＿＿＿＿。（一点儿都不）

d. A: 我穿这条红 **qún** 子怎么样，还可以吗？

   B: _____。（看起来）

e. A: 这 **shuāng xié** 你穿特别好看，你一定要买！

   B: 好看是好看，可是_____。（**gèng**）

4. Multiple-choice

Choose the correct answer based on the context, and then translate the sentence into English.

a. 这么冷的天，我真不想出去，可是 _____，我不得不去。
   1) 天气太冷
   2) 我不怕冷
   3) 小张的球 **duì** 少一个人

   English:

b. 我觉得一门课难一点儿没关系，只要 _____。
   1) 有用就好
   2) 有一点难
   3) 老师也很 **yán**

   English:

c. 她最近忙 **zhe** 学习、考试，_____
   1) 到 **dǐ** 去不去晚会？
   2) 连吃饭的时间都没有。
   3) 可是真的没有时间。

   English:

d. 这 **jiàn** 衣服穿在你身上真漂亮，而且 _____。
   1) 一点儿都不 **piányi**
   2) 买一 **jiàn** 吧
   3) 打完 **zhé** 以后就 **gèng piányi** 了

   English:

e. 打 **zhé jiǎn jià** 的时候好是好，可是 _____。
   1) 人太多了
   2) 我可以买到很 **piányi** 的东西
   3) 你喜欢就好

   English:

5. Customer or clerk?

Identify each statement as something the **gù** 客 or the 服务员 would say.

a. 这条 **qún** 子太大了，有没有小一号的？　　　　　[　] **gù** 客　　[　] 服务员

b. 您这么高，这条长 **qún** 子 **zhèng héshì**。　　　　[　] **gù** 客　　[　] 服务员

c. 您想买什么 **yánsè** 的？　　　　　　　　　　　　[　] **gù** 客　　[　] 服务员

d. 我不穿 **huángsè** 的，还有别的 **yánsè** 的吗？　　[　] **gù** 客　　[　] 服务员

e. 这是今年最 **liú** 行的 **yánsè**，您试一试，一定好看。　[　] **gù** 客　　[　] 服务员

f. 买一 **jiàn** 给女朋友吧？她一定会很高兴的。　　[　] **gù** 客　　[　] 服务员

g. 这 **shuāng xié** 好看是好看，可是我已经有太多 **xié** 了。　[　] **gù** 客　　[　] 服务员

h. 这就是我要的，谢谢！　　　　　　　　　　　　[　] **gù** 客　　[　] 服务员

i. 这 **shuāng xié** 打完 **zhé** 以后一点都不贵，想买要快！　[　] **gù** 客　　[　] 服务员

6. What are your preferences?

Use the following questions as the basis for an interview with one of your classmates. Write a paragraph about her based on her answers. Your paragraph should be at least 120 characters in length.

a. 你最喜欢什么 **yánsè**？

b. 你常常穿什么 **yánsè** 的衣服？

c. 你的 **guì** 子里没有什么 **yánsè** 的衣服？

d. 红 **sè** 让你想到什么？

e. 你会买绿 **sè** 的车还是 **lánsè** 的车？为什么？

f. 你觉得 **lánsè** 的房间看起来舒服，还是红 **sè** 的？

g. 你现在用的 **bǐ** 是什么 **yánsè** 的？

h. 你喝过绿 **chá** 吗？你喜欢喝红 **chá** 还是喜欢喝绿 **chá**？

_____

_____

_____

_____

_____

_____

7. Shopping experience

As a customer, explain why you are hesitant about buying a certain item (size, color, price, etc.). As a salesperson, try your best to talk your customer into making a purchase.

Example:

A mini-skirt.

Customer: 这条 **qún** 子很好看，就是太 **duǎn** 了。

Salesperson: 怎么会太 **duǎn**？今年就 **liú** 行 **duǎn qún**，穿在你身上 **zhèng héshì**。

a. A blue shirt (size small, $59.99)

Customer: _____

_____

Salesperson: _____

_____

b. A pair of yellow shoes (size 11, $35.00)

Customer: _____

_____

Salesperson: _____

_____

c. A long red skirt (size medium, $34.99)

Customer: _____

_____

Salesperson: _____

_____

d. A refurbished iPhone 3GS (16GB, $199.00)

Customer: _____

_____

Salesperson: _____

e. A brand new IBM laptop ($1,200)

Customer: _____

_____

Salesperson: _____

_____

8.　Xiao Ye's weight loss plan

Part I.　Read the paragraph and select the expressions that best complete the story.

叶小文最近每天 ＿＿＿＿（①都 ②也）走路去上课，在学校也不 ＿＿＿＿（①走 ②坐）电梯，都走 ＿＿＿＿（①上去 ②出去），走下来。每天晚上去 **jiàn** 身房 **duànliàn** 三个小时。＿＿＿＿（① **chú** 了 ② **lìng** 外）运动以外，小文也吃得很少。两个月以后，小文 **shòu** ＿＿＿＿（①得 ②了）很多，她自己觉得很高兴，因为她现在可以穿二号的衣服了。可是她的朋友都说，小文以前一点都 ＿＿＿＿（①没 ②不） **pàng**，现在 **shòu** ＿＿＿＿（①是 ②一） **shòu**，可是 ＿＿＿＿（①比 ②没有）以前那么好看了。＿＿＿＿（①不过 ②连）她的男朋友都觉得她看 ＿＿＿＿（①起来 ②出来）太 **shòu** 了，＿＿＿＿（①让 ②对）她多吃一点。

Part II.　Read the above paragraph again and decide whether the statements below are true (T) or false (F). If a statement is false, explain why in the space below the statement.

a. (　) 小文有时候开车，有时候走路去学校。

_____

b. (　) 小文每天的运动是去 **jiàn** 身房的两个小时。

_____

c. (　) 小文每天都运动因为她觉得自己太 **pàng** 了。

_____

d. (　) 小文以前穿不下二号的衣服。

_____

e. (　) 小文的朋友和她的男朋友都觉得她现在 **shòu** 一点，所以比以前好看。

_____

f. (　) 小文的男朋友觉得她吃得太少了。

_____

9.　Talk about your favorite store

Part I.　Answer the following questions truthfully.

a. 你喜欢去哪个 **shāng** 店买东西？

b. 那个 **shāng** 店在哪儿？你怎么去？

c. 你多 **jiǔ** 去一次那个 **shāng** 店？

d. 你去那个 **shāng** 店都买什么？为什么？

e. 那个 **shāng** 店跟别的 **shāng** 店有什么不同的地方？

f. 你最近是什么时候去的？你买了什么？

g. 下次你想去买什么？

Part II. Write a paragraph. Use your answers above to write a paragraph about your favorite store. Your paragraph should be at least 120 characters in length.

_____

_____

_____

_____

_____

_____

_____

_____

_____

_____

10. Writing about shopping

Part I. Form a cohesive paragraph. Rearrange these sentences so that they form a cohesive paragraph about shopping.

a. 现在我都上 **wǎng** 买东西。上 **wǎng** 比去 **shāng** 店方 **biàn** 得多。

b. 想 **děng** 打 **zhé** 的时候再买吗？打 **zhé** 的时候 **gù** 客那么多，你想要的东西，可能早就卖完了。

c. 你走进一个 **shāng** 店去，不一定找得到你想要的东西。

d. 我最不喜欢的事就是 **guàng jiē**，因为 **guàng jiē** 真的太 **huā** 时间了。

e. 我觉得，这样的"**guàng jiē**"特别舒服。

f. 你只要坐在电 **nǎo** 前面，就可以慢慢地找你要的 **yánsè**、大小和式样。

g. 而且，**xiāng** 同的东西，常常可以找到最 **piányi** 的。

h. 有时候找到了，可是 **yánsè** 或者大小不 **héshì**。有的时候东西好是好，可是太贵了。

Part II.   Write about your own shopping habits. Following the structure of the paragraph above, write a similar paragraph talking about whether you like to shop online or in an actual store. Your paragraph should be at least 120 characters in length.

_____

_____

_____

_____

_____

_____

_____

_____

_____

_____

_____

_____

Lesson 24 Workbook

 Listening and speaking

(audio online)

Structure drills

1.   What color clothing? (Use and Structure note 23.7)

You will hear a phrase describing clothing of a certain color. Restate the phrase to say *one* article of that color clothing, as in the example.

> **Example:**
> *You will hear:* **lán kù** 子
> *You will say:* 一条 **lán** 颜色的 **kù** 子
> *Click "R" to hear the correct response:* 一条 **lán** 颜色的 **kù** 子

(a)   (b)   (c)   (d)   (e)   (f)   (g)   (h)   (i)

2.   I didn't do anything (Use and Structure note 24.1)

You will hear a question asking about something that you did. Reply that you didn't do anything at all, as in the example.

> **Example:**
> *You will hear:* 你买什么了？
> *You will say:* 我什么都没买。
> *Click "R" to hear the correct response:* 我什么都没买。

(a)   (b)   (c)   (d)   (e)   (f)   (g)

3. So AdjV that VP/sentence (Use and Structure note 24.5)

You will hear a statement that includes a description, followed by a result. Restate the information using AdjV 得 VP/sentence, as in the example.

Example:
You will hear: 我很忙，没时间吃饭。
You will say: 我忙得没时间吃饭。
Click "R" to hear the correct response: 我忙得没时间吃饭。

(a)   (b)   (c)   (d)   (e)   (f)   (g)   (h)

4. Not only this but also that (Use and Structure note 24.7)

You will hear a statement describing some noun. Restate it with 不但 and 而且, as in the example.

Example:
You will hear: 这双鞋颜色好，也很便宜。
You will say: 这双鞋不但颜色好，而且很便宜。
Click "R" to hear the correct response: 这双鞋不但颜色好，而且很便宜。

(a)   (b)   (c)   (d)   (e)   (f)   (g)   (h)   (i)   (j)

5. If it isn't one thing, it is another (Use and Structure note 24.11)

You will hear a statement presenting two alternatives. Restate the sentence using 不是 A, 就是 B, as in the example.

Example:
You will hear: 这本书是你的，或者是你同屋的。
You will say: 这本书不是你的就是你同屋的。
Click "R" to hear the correct response: 这本书不是你的就是你同屋的。

(a)   (b)   (c)   (d)   (e)   (f)   (g)

6. Not even one (Use and Structure note 24.12)

You will hear a statement about something that someone did not do or does not have. Restate it, to say *not even one,* as in the example. Be careful to use the right classifier.

Example:
You will hear: 我没买书。
You will say: 我连一本书都没买。
Click "R" to hear the correct response: 我连一本书都没买。

(a)   (b)   (c)   (d)   (e)   (f)   (g)   (h)   (i)   (j)

Listening for information

1.   Let's go shopping

(CD1: 81)   Listen to the five questions and answer them based on the information below.

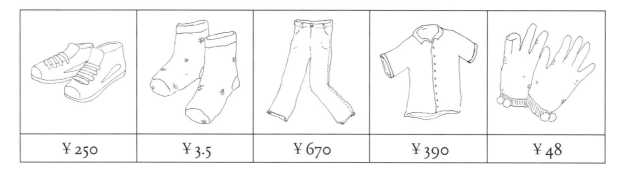

| ¥250 | ¥3.5 | ¥670 | ¥390 | ¥48 |

a.

b.

c.

d.

e.

2.   What will she wear today?

(CD1: 82)   Chen Fang and Wenwen are discussing what Chen Fang will wear to the party today. Based on Chen Fang's description, draw Chen Fang's outfit and indicate the color of each item.

Draw and color Chen Fang's outfit

3.   A hectic week (Use and Structure note 24.5)

Gao Ming is complaining about her life last week. Complete each description in English (CD1: 83) based on her narrative.

a. She had so much homework that...

b. Her stomach was so painful that...

c. She was so tired that...

d. She was so busy that...

4.   Big sale

The following items in a store are on sale. You will hear five questions asking about the (CD1: 84) prices of these items. Answer each question in English.

original price	¥ 50	¥ 1,200	¥ 88	¥ 105
discount	15%	25%	10%	not on sale

a.

b.

c.

d.

e.

5.   An afternoon at Tom's

Tom invited me to his house to watch a football game. Listen to my experience and write in (CD1: 85) English the items that Tom does not have in his room.

Tom does not have...

a. _____   b. _____   c. _____   d. _____

6.   A conversation

(CD1: 86)   An exchange student from China just came to your campus. She is asking you some questions about clothing and shopping. Answer her questions in Mandarin, based on your own experience. Use characters where we have learned them.

a.

b.

c.

d.

e.

f.

7.   Phone message

(CD1: 87)   Youmei has just left you a phone message. Listen to her message and write an email to her in Mandarin, responding to each of her questions. Use characters where we have learned them.

```

```

8.   Mali's shopping experience

(CD1: 88)   Mali is talking about her shopping experience in China. Based on her narrative, indicate whether the following statements are true (T) or false (F).

a. (   ) Mali spent ￥320 in that store.

b. (   ) The salesperson encouraged Mali to buy more things.

c. (   ) According to Mali, you can bargain in any store in China.

d. (   ) Mali walked out of the store without buying anything.

e. (   ) Mali bought a trendy, brightly colored shirt.

9. Dialogue

Listen to the conversation between a husband and wife, and then select the appropriate (CD1: 89) answer to each of the following questions.

a. What will they do after the conversation?
   1) They will make a list of the clothing items they need to buy.
   2) They will check to see which stores have sales.
   3) They will head downtown to go shopping.
   4) They will buy some new spring clothes.

b. What did the wife tell her husband?
   1) The spring collection is on sale.
   2) It is a good time to buy winter clothing.
   3) The spring fashions just came out.
   4) They need warm clothes for the coming cold front.

c. What does the husband need?
   1) shoes
   2) a jacket
   3) gloves
   4) shirts

d. What did they say about style and color?
   1) The husband is worried that the new styles and colors will not suit him.
   2) The wife promises that the stores have the most recent fashions.
   3) The husband does not care about the style or color of his clothes.
   4) The wife suggests that men's fashion does not vary much from year to year.

Reading and writing

Focus on Chinese characters

1. Number of strokes

Indicate the number of strokes used in writing each of the following characters.

a. 麻 _____   f. 姐 _____

b. 算 _____   g. 帮 _____

c. 颜 _____   h. 丽 _____

d. 诉 _____   i. 流 _____

e. 折 _____   j. 鞋 _____

2.   Which character?

Circle the character in each line that corresponds to the meaning on the left.

a. **sù** (**gàosu** *inform*)   诉   折

b. **yí** (**piányi** *cheap*)   宜   直

c. **shāng** (**shāngdiàn** *shop*)   周   商

d. **lìng** (**lìngwài** *in addition, furthermore*)   另   别

e. **sè** (**yánsè** *color*)   爸   色

f. **fēi** (**kāfēi** *coffee*)   非   啡

g. **jī** (**shǒujī** *cell phone*)   机   几

h. **wǎng** (**shàng wǎng** *use the internet*)   网   冈

i. **dàn** (**bùdàn** *not only*)   但   胆

j. **huā** (**huā qián** *spend money*)   花   化

k. **jiù** *old*   日   旧

l. **qì** (**qìchē** *car*)   汽   气

3.   First strokes

Write the first two strokes of each of the following characters.

a. 帮 _____   f. 啡 _____

b. 位 _____   g. 颜 _____

c. 告 _____   h. 花 _____

d. 色 _____   i. 姐 _____

e. 宜 _____   j. 烦 _____

4.   Missing strokes

Complete each character by writing in the missing strokes.

a.   氵   **liú** *flow*

b.   又   **shuāng** *pair*

c.   革   **xié** *shoe*

d.   丷   **gào** (**gàosu** *inform*)

e. ⺮   **suàn** *calculate, count*

f. 扌   **zhé** (**dǎ zhé** *give a discount*)

g. 火   **fán** (**máfan** *trouble, bother*)

h. 讠   **sù** (**gàosu** *inform*)

i. 亠   **shāng** (**shāngdiàn** *shop*)

j. 亻   **pián** (**piányi** *cheap*)

5. Total strokes

Rewrite this list of characters, arranging the characters in terms of their total number of strokes. Begin your list with the character with the fewest strokes.

咖	色	帮	商	姐	但	位	宜	丽	网	花	麻	便	鞋	件	百	算	颜

6. Radicals

Here is a list of characters that we have learned in this lesson. Rewrite each character in the row next to its radical.

诉   流   折   颜   便   旧   啡   另
位   咖   但   告   商   件   员   汽

口	
日	
氵	
亻	
扌	
讠	
页	

7. Character sleuth: Look for the phonetic

Group the characters below in terms of their rhymes or near-rhymes. Write the characters that rhyme with each other in the column on the right. Write the shared part of each character in the column on the left. For all of these characters, the shared part is the "phonetic," the part of the character that provides a clue to its pronunciation. The first set of rhymes is completed for you. There are twelve additional sets of characters that rhyme or partially rhyme and share a phonetic component among these characters.

马	吗	妈	现	子	花	非	加	几
玩	块	式	坏	机	跟	让	见	试
啡	上	咖	还	快	字	化	完	很

phonetic	characters that rhyme or almost rhyme and share a phonetic component
马	吗，妈

8. Scrambled sentences

Rewrite these phrases as sentences, putting the words in the correct order to match the English translations.

a. 这 / 贵 / 我 / 不 / 双 / 一点 / 觉得 / 鞋子 / 都

I think this pair of shoes isn't expensive at all.

b. 衣服 / 红 / 喜欢 / 姐姐 / 我 / 颜色 / 最 / 穿 /的

My older sister likes to wear red clothes the best.

c. 流行 / 没 / 打 / 流行 / 折 / 我 / 买 / 只要是 / 不 / 关系 / 就

Whether or not it is stylish isn't important. As long as it's on sale, I'll buy it.

9.   Dictionary skills

Following the instructions in Lesson 17 of the Textbook, look up these characters in a Chinese dictionary and provide the requested information.

a. 拿
   pronunciation:
   meaning:
   one two-character word or phrase in which it occurs:

b. 千
   pronunciation:
   meaning:
   one two-character word or phrase in which it occurs:

c. 死
   pronunciation:
   meaning:
   one two-character word or phrase in which it occurs:

10.   Find the incorrect characters

Xiao Zhang has written this email to his parents back in the USA telling them about one of his classmates, but he has typed ten characters incorrectly. Read the passage aloud, circle the mistakes, and correct them on the answer sheet below.

> 昨天我和小张和我的同屋友文到市中心去 **guàng** 商点。因为天汽 **yuè** 来 **yuè** 冷，所以我卖了手 **tào** 和 **ěrzhào**。 也买了心的大衣和一双红色的 **pí** 谢。春 **jié** 以前大大小小的商店都在大折，所以我买的东西都很便以。一 **gòng** 化了一 **qiān** 多块钱。小张什么都没买，只 **péi** 我们去 **guàng jiē**，帮我们 **ná** 东西。到了晚上，我们是在外边吃了饭才做出 **zū** 车会宿舍的。

a. ＿＿＿   b. ＿＿＿   c. ＿＿＿   d. ＿＿＿   e. ＿＿＿

f. ＿＿＿   g. ＿＿＿   h. ＿＿＿   i. ＿＿＿   j. ＿＿＿

11. Reading for information I

Read the paragraph for the main ideas and answer the questions that follow in English. You have learned almost all of the characters and words used in this paragraph, so you should be able to answer the questions without looking up any characters we have not learned. If you are stumbling over more than five characters in the passage, you need to review the characters from this and previous lessons.

什么样的衣服最流行，我就最不喜欢。流行的衣服很多人都有，很多人都穿，我为什么要跟他们穿一样的衣服呢？不流行没关系，只要我自己喜欢就好。我不管别人怎么想。我给我自己穿衣服，不是给别人穿衣服。另外，流行的衣服，很多人都想买，所以也就会比较贵。本来一件衣服不会那么贵，就是因为很多人都想买才会那么贵。这就是我为什么不喜欢流行的衣服。

a. What is the general topic of this paragraph?

b. What is the narrator's opinion about this topic?

c. What arguments does the narrator give to explain why he holds this opinion?

d. Circle the phrase that the narrator uses to sum up his opinion.

12. Reading for information II

Read the following from a mother to her son, and answer the questions that follow in English.

虽然这件衣服穿在你身上很 **héshì**，但是我觉得你应该买再大一号的。**Dì** 一，穿大一点的衣服，你看起来比 **jiào shòu**。**Dì** 二，衣服大一号，夏天穿你不觉得很 **rè**，**dōng** 天你里边还可以再穿别的衣服。**Dì** 三，这件和大一号的一样贵。最后，如果你以后高了呢，大一号的还可以穿，而现在 **héshì** 的就不能穿了。

a. What is the purpose of this paragraph?

b. How does the mother's opinion differ from the opinion of her son?

c. How many reasons does the mother provide to support her opinion?

d. What is the mother's final argument?

Focus on structure

1.   Anyone, anywhere, any time (Use and Structure note 24.1)

Xiao Zhang is a talented, agreeable person. Here are sentences that describe him. Translate a.–d. into English and e.–g. into Mandarin, using the phrases in parentheses in your translations.

a. 谁都喜欢他。

b. 他觉得什么电 **yǐng** 都很有意思。

c. 他什么 **gē** 都能 **chàng**。

d. 他比谁都 **pǎo** 得快。

e. He understands everything. (什么)

f. He likes to go everywhere. (哪儿)

g. He helps everyone. (谁)

2.   No one, nowhere, never (Use and Structure note 24.1)

Xiao Gao was feeling sick yesterday. Here is how she described her day. Translate a.–c. into English, and d.–f. into Mandarin, using the phrases in parentheses in your translations.

a. 我什么东西都没吃。

b. 我谁都没看。

c. 我哪儿都没去。

d. I didn't do any homework. (什么)

e. I didn't watch any television. (什么)

f. I didn't read any books. (什么)

3. On sale! (Use and Structure note 24.2)

Indicate these discounts as percentages off the price.

a. 打三折   →

b. 打4.5折   →

c. 打九折   →

d. 打四折   →

4. Do it again! (Use and Structure note 24.3)

Translate these sentences into Mandarin, using 再 ActV or 又 ActV 了 *again*, as appropriate.

a. Can you please help me again?

b. I've forgotten her name again. How embarrassing!

c. It's raining again today. When is it going to get warm?

d. The prices in that store are really cheap. I'm definitely going to shop there again.

e. Don't wear those slacks again. They are too old.

f. He accompanied his girlfriend shopping again.

5. So AdjV that... Part I (Use and Structure note 24.5, 24.12)

It is the end of the fall semester and everyone is cold, tired, and ready for vacation. This is how some of the students describe how they feel. Translate their descriptions into English.

a. 小王：我忙得连早饭都没有时间吃。

b. 小马：我冷得早上都不想起床了。

c. 小高：我累得连自行车也 **qí** 不了。

d. 小叶：我忙得连电 **shì** 都不能看。

e. 小谢：今天冷得我穿了两双 **wà** 子。

6. So AdjV that…Part II (Use and Structure note 24.1, 24.5)

Translate these sentences into Mandarin.

a. The test was so difficult that no one could finish it. (谁)

b. The price of those shoes is so cheap that everyone wants to buy a pair. (谁)

c. My hands are so cold that they are numb.

d. The book was so long that I couldn't finish reading it.

e. There were so many people that I couldn't find him. (Hint: *The people were so numerous that…*)

7. What are they wearing? (Use and Structure note 24.6)

Translate these descriptions into Mandarin in complete sentences, using characters where we have learned them.

a. Xiao Gao is wearing a new red skirt.

b. Xiao Xie is wearing his old black slacks.

c. Xiao Ye is wearing a pair of white gym shoes.

d. Xiao Lin is wearing a blue coat and a pair of cute blue earmuffs.

e. Xiao Ma is wearing a stylish yellow shirt.

8. Not only…but also (Use and Structure note 24.7)

Here is a list of nouns and descriptions. Rewrite each line in a complete Mandarin sentence, saying that the noun is *not only* A *but also* B, using 不但 VP₁/sentence 而且 VP₂/sentence.

	noun	A	B
a.	this skirt	stylish	cheap
b.	leather shoes	appropriate	nice looking
c.	my roommate	has diarrhea	has a fever
d.	this fitness center	convenient	clean
e.	today's weather	cold	windy

a.

b.

c.

d.

e.

9.   Take it (Use and Structure note 24.8)

Xiao Zhang and Xiao Xie are cleaning up their room again. Translate each of Xiao Xie's directions into Mandarin, using the words in parentheses.

a. Put all of the sneakers under the bed. (把, 放)

b. Bring that pair of slacks over to me. (把, **ná**, 过来)

c. Take all of those books back to the library. (把, **ná**)

d. Take the dirty socks into the bathroom and wash them. (把, **ná**, 把, 洗干净)

e. Bring all of the basketballs and soccer balls inside and put them in the closet. (把, **ná**, 放)

10.   If it isn't one thing, it's the other thing (Use and Structure note 24.11)

Xiao Gao is very predictable. These sentences describe her behavior. Translate a.–b. into English and c.–e. into Mandarin, using characters where we have learned them.

a. 小高每天不是喝咖啡就是喝 **chá**。

b. 小高每天不是穿红色的 **qún** 子就是穿红色的 **chènshān**。

c. When Xiao Gao goes to school, if she doesn't take the bus she takes the subway.

d. After Xiao Gao gets out of class, she either phones her mother or she phones her older sister.

e. On the weekends, Xiao Gao and her friends either go window shopping or they go see a movie.

11.   Scrambled sentences

Rewrite these phrases into sentences, putting them in the right order to match the English translations.

a. **chènshān** / 这 / 那 / 跟 / **huáng** 色 / **qún** 子 / **pèi** / 条 / 的 / 件 / 很

This skirt really matches that yellow blouse.

b. 不 / 家 / 的 / **jià** 钱 / **shāng** 店 / 贵 / 那 / 本来 / 太

The prices in that store were not too expensive to begin with.

c. 便宜 / 算 / 就 / 的 / 是 / 一点 / 意思 / 打折

"Give a discount" means "figure the price a little cheaper."

d. 会 / 位 / 那 / **tǎo jià huán jià** / 小姐 / 真

That young lady certainly knows how to bargain.

e. **rè** / 天气 / 家 **xiāng** / 不是 / 冷 / 非常 / 的 / 舒服 / 我 / 不 / 太 / 太 / 就是

The weather in my hometown is either too hot or it's too cold, it's extremely uncomfortable.

Focus on communication

1. Dialogue comprehension

Study the Lesson 24 Narrative and Dialogue. Then, read the following statements and indicate whether they are true (T) or false (F).

a. ( ) 小叶和小高买的 **qún** 子，一件三百块。

b. ( ) 小高买了 **qún** 子、**pí** 鞋、**ěrzhào** 和手 **tào**，可是没有买 **kù** 子。

c. ( ) 因为地铁人太多，所以他们坐出 **zū** 车回学校。

d. ( ) 小高想买的 **qún** 子，本来一条一百五十二块，服务员说可以打八折。

e. ( ) 小高想买 **ěrzhào**，因为北京太冷了，她的 **ěrduǒ** 冷得没有 **gǎn** 觉了。

f. ( ) 小高喜欢的 **ěrzhào pèi** 她的咖啡色大衣，一定很好看。

g. ( ) 服务员想让小高试一 **fù** 手 **tào**。

h. ( ) 小叶觉得大为应该买新 **kù** 子，因为他的 **kù** 子看起来太旧了。

i. ( ) 大为什么都不买，因为他今天 **wàng** 了 **dài** 钱了。

j. ( ) 今天运动鞋和 **wà** 子都特别便宜。

k. ( ) 他们买的东西太多了，所以小谢来帮小张 **ná**。

l. ( ) 小张、小叶和小高三个人一起回小张的宿舍。

m. ( ) 小张累 **sǐ** 了，因为他买了太多东西。

2. What do you say?

What do you say in each of the following situations? Type your answers, using characters where we have learned them, and email them to your Chinese teacher.

a. Ask the salesperson to bring you that black shirt.

b. Explain to your friend why you absolutely have to go shopping today. (Use the structure 非…不可. Here are some possible reasons: there is a huge sale, you need a jacket because of the cold weather, you are upset over something, etc.)

c. Offer to buy more than one item and ask for a discount.

d. Agree to give the customer a discount, but ask them to keep it quiet and come back next time.

e. Complain that you are tired to death today because you've been cleaning up your room.

f. Comment on how well the skirt matches the blouse that your friend is wearing right now.

g. Ask your friend to go shopping with you.

h. Name three things that you can do with your cell phone.

i. Explain to your friend that you are so tired that you don't feel like eating at all.

j. Persuade your friend to purchase the brown earmuffs because you've never seen any earmuffs cheaper than this pair.

3.   Complete the mini-dialogues

Use the structures in parentheses to complete each mini-dialogue.

a. A: 春 **jià** 快到了，你打算做什么？

   B: _____。（不是…就是…）

b. A: 你看这件大衣怎么样？我还没 **jué** 定我到 **dǐ** 要不要买。

   B: _____，你一定要买。（不但…而且…）

c. A: 这么好的 **cháng** 周末，你上哪儿去了？

   B: 周末那么冷，我 _____。（冷得 VP）

d. A: 你来北京三个月了，去过什么地方？

   B: 我每天都忙 **zhe** 学习，_____。（QW + 都 NEG VP）

4.   Multiple-choice

Using the context as your guide, choose the correct expression to complete each sentence, and then translate the sentences into English.

a. 我 _____ 只想去中国 **lǚyóu**，可是太喜欢那儿，所以 **jué** 定在那儿找工作。
   1) 因为
   2) 本来
   3) 不但

   English:

b. 你 _____ 很累，昨天晚上没有睡好吗？
   1) 看起来
   2) 看
   3) 觉得

   English:

c. 我家 **xiāng** 的 **dōng** 天，不但很少下 **xuě** 而且 _____。

   1) 每天都下 **yǔ**

   2) 冷 **sǐ** 了

   3) 比很多地方都 **nuǎn** 和多了

English:

d. 我从昨天晚上开始头 **téng**，**téng** 得 _____。

   1) 我 **bìng** 了

   2) 大概是因为太冷了

   3) 我什么都做不了

English:

5.   Reading comprehension

Look at the following two sale flyers and answer the questions.

A)

大减价 SALE	春季服饰 3折起

a. What does "3折起" mean?

b. What season does this sale occur in?

B)

大减价 10 元 任选1件	大减价 15 元 任选2件

a. This promotion is about a discount. How does the discount work?

6.   Sale promotions

Match each sale promotion sign with its description below, writing the letter of the description above the matching sign. The descriptions include a few words that we have not yet learned, but that should not affect your comprehension of the main points.

A) _____   B) _____   C) _____

| Buy One Get One **FREE!** | Spend $50, **get $20**

Now through December 3ʳᵈ | Now through Sunday!

Buy any regular-priced item & take

50% off

any second regular-priced item |

D) _____   E) _____   F) _____

| **20% OFF** when

purchasing 3 or more items | 4 DAYS ONLY
TAKE AN EXTRA
30% OFF
ALL SALE ITEMS | WINTER CLEARANCE
SALE
Up to **70% OFF** |

a. 只有四天！已经打折的东西再打七折。

b. 买一 **sòng** 一。

c. 从现在开始到星期天，买一件，第二件就打五折。

d. 买三件以上就打八折。

e. 冬季大 **jiǎn** 价：三折起。

f. 现在起到十二月三号，你每花五十块我们就 **sòng** 你二十块。

7. Tǎo jià huán jià

Imagine you're the customer. Try your best to bargain with the salesperson to get a discount. Do not use the same tactic twice.

a. 服务员：这条 **kù** 子是今年最流行的，只要六十四块。

Customer: _____

_____

b. 服务员：这 **fù** 手 **tào** 在我们这儿卖得特别好，跟你的大衣的颜色很 **pèi**。

Customer: _____

_____

c. 服务员：如果你要买这件，我可以给你打八折。

Customer: _____

_____

d. 服务员：　七十块真的不贵，因为这件 **chènshān pèi qún** 子或者 **kù** 子都好看，什么时候都可以穿。

Customer: _____

_____

8. Writing about the shopping experience

Part I. Form a cohesive paragraph   Rearrange these sentences so that they form a cohesive paragraph that explains how to bargain for the best price. (Note: 谢春美 is a person's name.)

a. 谁都喜欢跟春美一起去买东西，因为不但可以买到便宜的衣服，而且还可以 **rènshi** 不少商店的服务员。

b. 或者，如果衣服的 **jià** 钱太高，但是春美很喜欢，她一定能让服务员给她打折。

c. 她觉得，**guàng jiē** 不一定每次都要买东西。

d. 谢春美跟每一个女 **hái** 子一样，很喜欢 **guàng jiē**。

e. **Rènshi** 了以后，下次再去，就可以请他们打折了。

f. 不过，大 **jiǎnjià** 的时候，就非买不可了。

g. 春美很会跟服务员 **tǎojià huánjià**，如果一件衣服已经打折了，她一定会说，买两件再算她便宜一点。

h. 有的时候虽然不买，看看商店卖的新衣服，可以知道今年流行什么，自 **jǐ** 在家穿衣服的时候就知道怎么 **pèi** 比 **jiào** 好看。

Part II. Shopping: love it or hate it   Follow the structure of the paragraph above, write a similar paragraph talking about a shopaholic friend (or yourself), or someone who hates shopping. Your paragraph should be at least 120 characters in length.

_____

_____

_____

_____

_____

_____

_____

_____

_____

_____

_____

Lesson 25 Workbook

 Listening and speaking

(audio online)

Structure drills

1. Noun phrases with the main noun omitted (Use and Structure 25.2)

You will hear a sentence in which the subject includes a description and a main noun. Rephrase the sentence, leaving out the main noun, as in the example.

Example:
You will hear: 我买的衣服很便宜。
You will say: 我买的很便宜。
Click "R" to hear the correct response: 我买的很便宜。

(a)   (b)   (c)   (d)   (e)   (f)   (g)   (h)   (i)   (j)

2. I've never done it before (Use and Structure note 25.11)

You will hear a question asking about your general behavior, or whether you have done something before. Answer that you do not have that behavior, or that you have never done that action before, as in the example.

Example:
You will hear: 你吃过这么好吃的 **yú** 吗?
You will say: 我从来没吃过这么好吃的 **yú**。
Click "R" to hear the correct response: 我从来没吃过这么好吃的 **yú**。

(a)   (b)   (c)   (d)   (e)   (f)   (g)   (h)   (i)   (j)

3. Ongoing situations at a location (Use and Structure note 25.3)

You will hear a sentence about a situation at a location. Restate the sentence, using 着 to indicate that the situation is ongoing, as in the example.

Example:

You will hear: 他 **tǎng** 在地上。

You will say: 他在地上 **tǎng** 着。

Click "R" to hear the correct response: 他在地上 **tǎng** 着。

(a)   (b)   (c)   (d)   (e)   (f)   (g)   (h)   (i)   (j)

4. Two ways to indicate duration (Use and Structure note 25.5)

You will hear a sentence about the duration of some activity. Restate the sentence, indicating duration with the structure V duration 的 N, as in the example.

Example:

You will hear: 他们坐火车坐了八个钟头。

You will say: 他们坐了八个钟头的火车。

Click "R" to hear the correct response: 他们坐了八个钟头的火车。

(a)   (b)   (c)   (d)   (e)   (f)   (g)   (h)   (i)   (j)

5. Talking about two actions happening at the same time
   (Use and Structure note 25.7)

You will hear a sentence talking about two actions that happen at the same time. Restate the sentence with 一边 action₁ 一边 action₂, as in the example.

Example:

You will hear: 我吃饭的时候看电 **shì**。

You will say: 我一边吃饭一边看电 **shì**。

Click "R" to hear the correct response: 我一边吃饭一边看电 **shì**。

(a)   (b)   (c)   (d)   (e)   (f)   (g)   (h)   (i)   (j)

6. Two ways to indicate that situations occur at the same time
   (Use and Structure notes 25.3, 25.7)

You will hear a sentence saying that two actions occur at the same time. Restate the sentence using V₁ 着 V₂, as in the example.

Example:

You will hear: 我们一边 **liáo** 天，一边吃饭。

You will say: 我们 **liáo** 着天吃饭。

Click "R" to hear the correct response: 我们 **liáo** 着天吃饭。

(a)   (b)   (c)   (d)   (e)   (f)   (g)   (h)   (i)   (j)

Listening for information

1. 过春节

(CD1: 92) You will hear a short narration about a Chinese family celebrating the New Year. Listen to the passage to find out who is doing each activity and write their name in English under the corresponding activity.

2. A dorm room scene

You will hear Liu Xun introducing his roommates. Listen to his introduction and identify **(CD1: 93)** each roommate by name (in Pinyin) in the following picture.

A.

B.

C.

D.

E.

3. Four sisters

Here is a picture of four sisters: Lanlan, Tingting, Meimei, and Xinxin. Listen to the description **(CD1: 94)** and identify each sister, writing each person's name under her picture.

4. Eating out

(CD1: 95) Listen to Wang Shan talking about her experience eating out tonight. Based on her narrative, indicate whether each of the following statements is true (T) or false (F).

a. ( ) 小张没有来日本饭馆。

b. ( ) 小张 **wàng** 了怎么去那个日本饭馆。

c. ( ) 我自己一个人先去那个饭馆。

d. ( ) 我打电话给小张的时候，他刚到家。

e. ( ) 这家日本饭馆一点也不贵。

5. An oral quiz

(CD1: 96) Teacher Zhou is asking you several questions about the Chinese New Year. Answer the questions in Mandarin, using characters where we have learned them.

a.

b.

c.

d.

e.

f.

6. Responding to a phone message

(CD1: 97) Listen to this phone message from Jiajia, an exchange student from China, and prepare an email in Mandarin in reply to her questions.

7.   Preparations for the New Year

Língling is telling her foreign friends about how Chinese people prepare for the New Year. **(CD1: 98)** Based on the information she provides, indicate whether the following statements are true (T) or false (F).

a. (   ) **Niángāo** is easy to make, so it is usually made on New Year's Eve.

b. (   ) Chinese people eat **niángāo** during the Chinese New Year because it is very nutritious.

c. (   ) A lot of house-cleaning has to be done before New Year's Eve.

d. (   ) Dirty clothes need to be washed so that they can be worn on the first day of the New Year.

e. (   ) It is difficult to buy groceries during the Chinese New Year.

8.   Traveling in China

Two foreign students in China are discussing their recent travel experiences. Based on the **(CD2: 1)** information in the conversation, select the appropriate answers to each of the following questions.

a. How does the **ruǎnwò** seat differ from the **yìngwò** seat?
   1) They are about ¥ 200 different in price on a trip from Beijing to Hankou.
   2 Six people share a **ruǎnwò** room.
   3) **Ruǎnwò** seats have private rooms.
   4) If you travel by **ruǎnwò**, it takes less time to get to the destination.

b. What does the woman think about taking a train in China?
   1) She prefers using other forms of transportation.
   2) She is very excited about it.
   3) She thinks it is uncomfortable traveling by train.
   4) She worries that trains are too crowded.

c. What does the man think about taking a train in China?
   1) It takes a lot of time to travel by train.
   2) One may meet new people on trains.
   3) One has to be cautious when taking trains.
   4) It is better to buy **ruǎnwò** seats when taking trains.

d. How long will it take to go from Beijing to Hankou by train?
   1) eleven hours by express train
   2) one day by regular train
   3) fifteen hours by **ruǎnwò**
   4) twenty hours by **yìngwò**

Reading and writing

Focus on Chinese characters

1.   Number of strokes

Indicate the number of strokes used in writing each of the following characters.

a. 绍 ＿＿＿   f. 茶 ＿＿＿

b. 音 ＿＿＿   g. 假 ＿＿＿

c. 黄 ＿＿＿   h. 越 ＿＿＿

d. 蓝 ＿＿＿   i. 等 ＿＿＿

e. 弟 ＿＿＿   j. 乐 ＿＿＿

2.   Which character?

Circle the character in each line that corresponds to the meaning on the left.

a. **jiǎo** (**jiǎozi** *dumplings*)   饺   较

b. **huó** *live*   活   话

c. **gèng** *even more*   更   便

d. **lè** (**kuàilè** *happy*)   乐   东

e. **yuǎn** *far*   元   远

f. **mǔ** *mother*   母   每

g. **quán** *entire*   全   金

h. **rèn** (**rènshi** *know*)   订   认

i. **jiè** (**jièshào** *introduce*)   介   父

j. **shào** (**jièshào** *introduce*)   绍   邵

k. **dì** (**dìdi** *younger brother*)   弟   第

l. **jià** (**fàng jià** *begin vacation*)   假   佳

3.   First strokes

Write the first two strokes of each of the following characters.

a. 等 ＿＿＿   f. 着 ＿＿＿

b. 越 ＿＿＿   g. 谈 ＿＿＿

c. 蓝 ＿＿＿   h. 较 ＿＿＿

d. 除 ＿＿＿   i. 正 ＿＿＿

e. 极 ＿＿＿   j. 火 ＿＿＿

4.   Missing strokes

Complete each character by writing in the missing strokes.

a.   苂   **chá** *tea*

b.   艹   **jié** *holiday*

c.   八   **fù** (**fùmǔ** *father and mother*)

d.   讠   **shí** (**rènshi** *know, recognize, meet*)

e.   氵   **huó** (**shēnghuó** *life*)

f.   亠   **yè** (**yèlǐ** *in the middle of the night*)

g.   立   **yīn** (**shēngyīn** *sound*)

h.   乚   **lè** (**kuàilè** *happy*), **yuè** (**yīnyuè** *music*)

i.   艹   **huáng** *yellow*

j.   走   **yuè** *more*

5.   Total strokes

Rewrite this list of characters, arranging the characters in terms of their total number of strokes. Begin your list with the character with the fewest strokes.

更	着	父	夜	远	识	茶	全	较	介	音	弟	假	母	认	等	谈	正	除

6.   Radicals

Here is a list of characters that we have learned in this lesson. Rewrite each character in the row next to its radical.

节   认   看   馆   着   谈   茶   起   远   饭   边
近   话   蓝   饱   识   花   越   菜   趣   活   睡

辶	
目	
氵	
饣	
走	
讠	
艹	

7.   Character sleuth: Look for the phonetic

Group the characters below in terms of their rhymes or near-rhymes. Write the characters that rhyme with each other in the column on the right. Write the shared part of each character in the column on the left. For all of these characters, the shared part is the "phonetic," the part of the character that provides a clue to its pronunciation. The first set of rhymes is completed for you. There are twelve additional sets of characters that rhyme or partially rhyme and share a phonetic component among these characters.

选   级   人   上   识   气   饺   红   远   房   花
式   放   非   把   加   化   方   咖   汽   让   认
啡   爸   园   活   极   工   较   试   只   话   先

phonetic	characters that rhyme or almost rhyme and share a phonetic component
工	工红

8. Scrambled sentences

Rewrite these phrases as sentences, putting the words in the correct order to match the English translations.

a. 半夜 / 吃 / 十二点 / **bāo** 饺子 / 等到 / 我们 / 以前 / 的时候

We wrap dumplings before midnight, and when it is midnight we eat them.

b. 可以 / 我 / 你 / 弟弟 / 如果 / 我 / 你们 / 认识 / 介绍 / 不 / 给

If you don't know my younger brother, I can introduce you.

c. 可乐 / 茶 / 喝 / 喝 / 你 / 呢 / 想 / 还是

Do you want to drink cola or tea?

d. 一 / 都 / 学生 / 回家 / 放假 / 父母 / 看 / 学校

As soon as the school begins vacation, the students return home to see their parents.

e. 更 / 觉得 / 蓝色的 / 黄色的 / 好看 / 我 / 比

I think that the blue one is even nicer looking than the yellow one.

9. Dictionary skills

Following the instructions in Lesson 17 of the Textbook, look up these characters in a Chinese dictionary and provide the requested information.

a. 准
pronunciation:
meaning:
one two-character word or phrase in which it occurs:

b. 鱼
pronunciation:
meaning:
one two-character word or phrase in which it occurs:

c. 热
   pronunciation:
   meaning:
   one two-character word or phrase in which it occurs:

10. Find the incorrect characters

Zhang Dawei is preparing a short talk that he will give in class tomorrow. His ideas are all set but he has written ten characters incorrectly. (Two of them are written incorrectly twice.) Read the passage aloud, circle the mistakes, and correct them on the answer sheet below.

> 我给你节绍节绍我刚人识的朋友。他 **xìng** 黄。他的父每都是中国人，可是他在美国生活了十多年了。他说 **Yīng** 文说得很好，可是他说中文说得便好，因为方假的时候他常常跟他的父母会中国。跟他谈活的时候，我比饺喜难说中文，因为这羊可以让我的中文走来走好。

a. _____   b. _____   c. _____   d. _____   e. _____

f. _____   g. _____   h. _____   i. _____   j. _____

11. Reading for information

Read the paragraph for the main ideas and answer the questions that follow in English. You have learned almost all of the characters and words used in this paragraph, so you should be able to answer the questions without looking up any characters we have not learned. If you are stumbling over more than five characters in the passage, you need to review the characters from this and previous lessons.

> 小孩子都非常喜欢过年。过年的时候可以吃很多好吃的东西，穿新衣服，跟别的小朋友一起放鞭炮，还会得到很多红包。红包就是红颜色的信封。信封里边是钱。过年的时候，除了父母会给孩子们红包，家里来的叔叔阿姨也会给。在短短的几天里，有的小孩子可以得到很多钱，所以他们都特别喜欢过年。他们觉得过年是他们一年里最高兴的日子。

a. What is the general topic of this paragraph?

b. The narrator mentions a number of reasons why children like this topic. List them here.

c. What does the narrator present as the most important reason? How can you tell?

Focus on structure

1. AdjV 不得了 (Use and Structure note 25.1)

Describe each of these people or objects in complete sentences using AdjV 不得了.

a.	小王	
b.	小马	
c.	**Chén** 先生	
d.	120 mph	
e.	$$$$	

2.   What can you do lying down? (Use and Structure note 25.3)

Here are things that Xiao Zhang likes to do lying down, sitting, and standing. Write a sentence stating each situation using V 着 in each sentence.

Lying down

a. read   →

b. listen to music   →

c. watch television   →

Standing up

d. sing   →

e. make phone calls   →

Sitting down

f. sleep   →

g. drink coffee   →

3.   Don't do these while driving! (Use and Structure note 25.3)

Here are some things that you should not do while driving. Translate them into English, and then add two more of your own (in Mandarin).

a. 别看着电 **shì** 开车。 →

b. 别打着电话开车。   →

c.

d.

4.   How long did she do these activities? (Use and Structure note 25.5)

Here is a list of things that Meili did yesterday and the amount of time she spent on each of them. Write a complete sentence in Mandarin for each activity using the structure <u>V duration 的 O</u>.

a. listened to music (one hour)   →

b. used the internet (one and a half hours) →

c. watched television (a half hour)   →

d. slept (seven hours)   →

e. rode a bicycle (forty-five minutes)   →

5. Multi-tasking (Use and Structure note 25.7)

Describe what the people are doing in each of the following pictures in complete sentences, using the structure 一边…一边….

Example:

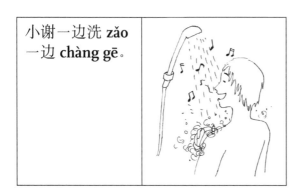

小谢一边洗 **zǎo** 一边 **chàng gē**。

a. 张友蓝	b. 王刚	c. 谢子真
d. 常学音	e. 高大南	f. 钱家明和她的朋友

a.

b.

c.

d.

e.

f.

6.   Never did it, never do it (Use and Structure note 25.11)

Xiao Wang has invited his roommate home to Xi'an for the New Year and is going over some of the things that they will do. He wants to know if his roommate has ever done these things before. Help him ask these questions by translating them into Mandarin. His roommate has never done any of these things before. Provide his answers here, using 从来 + NEG in each of his replies.

a. Have you been to Xi'an before?

   Q:

   A:

b. Have you eaten hot and spicy food before?

   Q:

   A:

c. Have you set off fireworks before?

   Q:

   A:

d. Have you made dumplings before?

   Q:

   A:

7.   Translation into English

Translate these sentences into English.

a. 刚才来找你的那个人是谁？

b. 真没想到用中文跟中国人 **liáo** 天这么容易。

c. 我刚学 **bāo** 饺子，所以 **bāo** 得不好。

d. 在床上 **tǎng** 着看书是非常不好的习惯。

e. 你怎么连 **kuài** 子都不会用。你从来没吃过中国饭吧。

f. 因为你刚学会开车，所以你一定不可以一边开车一边打电话。

g. 我的同屋每天晚上都 **fù** 习好几个钟头的中文，常常一直到半夜。

h. 友文把美丽介绍给她的父母以后，美丽就把她 **sòng** 给友文父母的东西 **ná** 出来了。

8.   Translation into Mandarin

Translate these sentences into Mandarin, using characters where we have learned them.

a. Yesterday's test was unbelievably difficult.

b. What is that noise outside? Can you hear it?

c. I have never set off fireworks before.

d. I didn't expect that the Spring Festival would be this lively.

e. I found the book that you were just looking for. It was under the bed.

f. You were born in January of 1990. Are you (do you belong to) a snake (**shé**) or a horse?

g. I just got home and I'm dead tired. Help me prepare dinner.

h. I ate until I was full. (Use 吃 and a resultative ending.) I never expected that at midnight we would begin eating dumplings.

9.   Scrambled sentences

Rewrite these phrases into sentences, putting them in the right order to match the English translations.

a. 喝 / 一 **píng** / 他 / 回家 / 可乐 / 走路 / **ná** 着 / 一边/ 一边

   Holding a bottle of cola, he drank and walked home.

b. 穿 / 出去 / 先 / 你 / 等到 / 大衣 / 再 / **ná** 着/ 的時候

   Take your coat. Put it on when we go out.

c. **bāo** / **bāo** / 我 / 好 / 你 / 饺子/ 这么 / 没想到 / 得

   I didn't know that you could wrap dumplings so well.

d. 的时候 / 放 / 孩子 / **pǎo** / 看 / 刚才 / **biānpào** / 出来 / 都

   Just before when you were setting off the fireworks, the children all ran outside to watch.

e. 火車 / 我 / 人 / 坐 / 会 / 这么 / 多 / 没想到 / 回家 / 春节 / 的

   I had no idea that there would be this many people taking the train home for the Spring Festival.

Focus on communication

1.   Dialogue comprehension

Study the Lesson 25 Narrative and Dialogue. Then, read the following statements and indicate whether they are true (T) or false (F).

a. (   ) 今年的春节跟学校放 **hán** 假在 **xiāng** 同的时间。

b. (   ) 友文 **dài** 美丽坐火车回家过年。

c. (   ) 火车非常 **jǐ**，因为放 **hán** 假的时候，火车 **piào tè** 别便宜。

d. (   ) **Shūshu** 就是你爸爸的弟弟。

e. (   ) 友文和美丽刚到，年夜饭已经 **zhǔnbèi** 好了。

f. (   ) 叶家的年夜饭很 **fēngfù**，有饺子还有很多菜。

g. (   ) 全家一起 **bāo** 饺子、吃饺子，是中国人过年的习惯。

h. (   ) 友文不知道是谁把她家门口的 "春" 字 **tiē dào** 了。

i. (   ) **Tiē dào** 的 "春" 字跟年夜饭的 **yú** 都有特别的意思。

2.   What do you say?

What do you say in each of the following situations? Type your answers, using characters where we have learned them, and email them to your Chinese teacher.

a. You want to find out your friend's Chinese zodiac sign.

b. You want to greet people during the Chinese New Year holidays.

c. You want to find out how long it takes your friend to walk from his place to school.

d. You want to learn about your friend's breakfast ritual: does s/he eat standing (by the table), or sitting down.

e. You want to tell your little cousin that he has to wait until the happy birthday song ends before he eats the cake (**dàngāo**).

f. You want to announce your New Year's resolutions (that is, what you definitely will do this year).

g. You want to apologize to your friend that you didn't answer the phone when he called, and you want to explain that you didn't hear the phone ring because you were in the shower just a moment ago.

h. You want to complain about the movie that you just saw. You want to say that it's the worst movie you've ever seen.

i. You want to express your surprise about the subway and say that you did not expect the subway to be this crowded.

3. Complete the mini-dialogues

Use the structure in parentheses to complete each mini-dialogue.

a. A: 你每天吃饭的时候看电 **shì** 吗?

   B: 对, _____。（一边…一边…）

b. A: 你知道"好年春"这个饭馆吗?

   B: _____。（从来 + NEG V…）

c. A: 我妈妈 **bāo** 的饺子怎么样? 好吃吗?

   B: _____。（AdjV 得不得了）

d. A: 妈妈, 我什么时候才能买那双蓝色的 **pí** 鞋?

   B: _____。（等到…）

e. A: 你看起来很累, 是不是昨天晚上睡得太少?

   B: _____。（V + duration 的 O）

f. A: 对不起, 我刚下课, 所以晚了几分钟。电 **yǐng** 开始多 **jiǔ** 了?

   B: 没问 **tí**, _____。（刚刚）

4. 同音字

You have learned how 同音字 can carry symbolic significance in Chinese. Read the following sentences and choose the best answer. Then translate each sentence into English.

a. 过年的时候, 除了吃饺子以外, 中国人也喜欢吃"**fà** 菜"(literally "hair weed"), 因为吃 **fà** 菜就是说你会 _____。
   1) 吃很多饭
   2) **fā cái**
   3) 有长头 **fa**

   English:

b. "**Sòng zhōng**"的意思就是"**péi** 着快要 **sǐ** 了的父母"。所以中国人过生日的时候最不喜欢 **sòng** 别人 _____。
   1) **zhuō** 子
   2) 钟 (*clock*)
   3) 床

   English:

c. 在中国, 很多 **yī** 院没有四 **lóu** (*fourth floor*), 因为"四"的 **shēng** 音跟 _____ 差不多。
   1) "冷 **sǐ** 了"的"**sǐ**"
   2) "有事"的"事"
   3) "认识"的"识"

   English:

5.   Describe the pictures

Look at the following pictures and write a few sentences to describe each situation.

a. Use V 着 in your sentence.

_____

_____

_____

_____

b. Use 一边…一边…in your sentence.

叶大明

_____

_____

_____

_____

c. Use V 着 in your sentence.

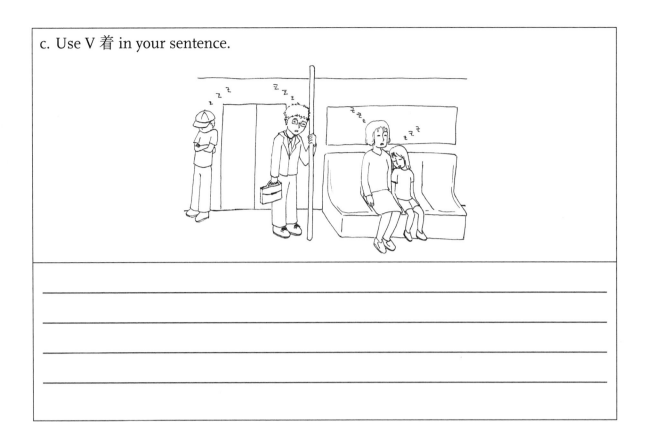

_____

_____

_____

_____

_____

6.   Chinese New Year celebration

Match each picture with its description by writing the letter for the description in the line above the appropriate picture.

A. **Bāo** 饺子，等到半夜再吃。

B. 到外边去放 **biānpào**。

C. 全家人在一起吃 **fēngfù** 的年夜饭，一边吃饭，一边 **liáo** 天。

D. 把家里 **shōushi** 干净。

E. 门上的"春"字 **dào** 着 **tiē**。不是 **tiē** 得不对，是"春到了"。

F. 小 **hái** 子最高兴的，就是可以 **ná** 到红 **bāo**。

7. 我最喜欢过春节

Part I.   The following paragraph talks about traditions of the Chinese New Year celebration. Fill in the blanks with the sentences (A.–F.) from Exercise 6.

一年里我最喜欢的就是春节，因为不但有好吃的，而且有好玩的。中国新年不是在一月就是在二月。每年春节，在别的地方工作、学习的人都一定会回到自己的家 **xiāng** 过节。所以那时候的火车票特别难买。春节的前几天，我妈妈就 ＿＿＿＿，等着大姐回来过节。而爸爸忙着写春 **lián** (*spring couplets*, matching lines of poetry hung on either side of the door)，**tiē** 在门上。小时候爸爸就告诉我，我家 ＿＿＿＿。

除 **xī** 的早上，我们就开始做饭，晚上 ＿＿＿＿，是我最快乐的时候。晚饭以后我和大姐帮 **zhù** 妈妈 ＿＿＿＿。**Bāo** 好饺子爸爸就 **dài** 着我们 ＿＿＿＿。半夜除了吃饺子以外，＿＿＿＿。因为我们可以 **ná** 着爸爸妈妈给我们的红 **bāo**，去买自 **jǐ** 喜欢的东西。每年爸爸妈妈给我们 **sòng** 红 **bāo**，等着买自己喜欢的东西。**Dì** 二天早上是新年，我们不是一家人开车出去玩，就是去看朋友。每个人一看到朋友就说：**Gōng** 喜 **fācái**，新年快乐！过年那几天，每天我都高兴得不得了。

Part II.   Complete the following table in Mandarin. In Column A, provide your answers based on the information in the passage in Part I. In Column B, provide information about your favorite holiday. Here are the names of two holidays in Mandarin that you might want to write about:

Gǎn ēn 节 *Thanksgiving*, **Shèngdàn** 节 *Christmas*.

	A: 中国新年	B: Your favorite holiday _____
time		
significance		
preparation		
things that people do		
favorite part of this holiday as a kid		
why it's my favorite holiday		

8. What is your favorite holiday?

Following the structure of the paragraph in Exercise 7, Part I, and using the information you wrote in Part II, write a paragraph talking about your fondest memories of your favorite holiday. If we have not learned a word in Mandarin, write it in English. Your paragraph should be at least 120 characters in length. When you revise this essay you can look these words up in a dictionary and add them in Mandarin.

_____

_____

_____

_____

_____

_____

_____

_____

_____

_____

_____

_____

Lesson 26 Workbook

 Listening and speaking

(audio online)

Structure drills

1. 把 NP (PP) V 一下 (Use and Structure note 26.1)

You will hear a statement asking you to do something. Rephrase the statement with 把 NP V 一下, as in the example.

> **Example:**
> *You will hear:* **Tián** 这张 **biǎo**。
> *You will say:* 请你把这张 **biǎo tián** 一下。
> *Click "R" to hear the correct response:* 请你把这张 **biǎo tián** 一下。

(a)   (b)   (c)   (d)   (e)   (f)   (g)   (h)   (i)   (j)

2. Expressing the passive with **bèi** (Use and Structure note 26.4)

You will hear a sentence stating an action. Rephrase the sentence with **bèi**, as in the example.

> **Example:**
> *You will hear:* 他拿走了我的书。
> *You will say:* 我的书 **bèi** 他给拿走了。
> *Click "R" to hear the correct response:* 我的书 **bèi** 他给拿走了。

(a)   (b)   (c)   (d)   (e)   (f)   (g)

3. Expressing events from different perspectives with 把 and **bèi**
(Use and Structure notes 19.7, 26.1, and 26.4)

You will hear a sentence that includes 把 describing an event. Restate the sentence with **bèi** to change the perspective of the description, as in the example.

Example:
You will hear: 他把我的书拿走了。
You will say: 我的书 **bèi** 他拿走了。
Click "R" to hear the correct response: 我的书 **bèi** 他拿走了。

(a)　　(b)　　(c)　　(d)　　(e)

4. Talking about hypothetical situations involving the same subject in both clauses: 要是…就 (Use and Structure note 26.7)

You will hear a statement about two situations in which the subject is the same for both situations. Restate it to say that if the first situation occurs, the second one should or will follow, using 要是…就, as in the example.

Example:
You will hear: 你把 **hù** 照 **diū** 了很麻烦。
You will say: 你要是把 **hù** 照 **diū** 了，就很麻烦。
Click "R" to hear the correct response: 你要是把 **hù** 照 **diū** 了，就很麻烦。

(a)　　(b)　　(c)　　(d)　　(e)　　(f)　　(g)　　(h)

5. Talking about hypothetical situations involving two different subjects: 要是…就 (Use and Structure note 26.7)

You will hear a statement about two situations in which there is a different subject for each situation. Restate it to say that if the first situation occurs, the second one should or will follow, using 要是…就, as in the example.

Example:
You will hear: 你不喜欢吃中国饭，我们去吃日本饭。
You will say: 你要是不喜欢吃中国饭，我们就去吃日本饭。
Click "R" to hear the correct response: 你要是不喜欢吃中国饭，我们就去吃日本饭。

(a)　　(b)　　(c)　　(d)　　(e)　　(f)　　(g)　　(h)　　(i)　　(j)

6. 从 time 起 *from this time on* (Use and Structure note 26.12)

You will hear a statement about some action that you do, followed by a time phrase. Say that beginning with that time, you will do or have done the action.

Example:
You will hear: 我要看好自己的东西。（现在）
You will say: 从现在起，我要看好自己的东西。
Click "R" to hear the correct response: 从现在起，我要看好自己的东西。

(a)   (b)   (c)   (d)   (e)   (f)   (g)   (h)

Listening for information

1.   What to do?

(CD2: 5)   You will hear four different situations. Respond to each situation in a complete Mandarin sentence, using Pinyin or a mix of characters and Pinyin, as instructed by your teacher.

a.

b.

c.

d.

2.   Equal to

(CD2: 6)   Listen to the five questions and provide appropriate responses. You may want to have your calculator handy!

(¥1 = US$0.17, US$1 = ¥6.8)

a. _____   d. _____

b. _____   e. _____

c. _____

3. The population of major cities

You will hear five announcements stating the current population of five cities in China, the United States, and Taiwan. Listen to the announcement and write the population of each city on the following form.

(CD2: 7)

city	population (人口)
Shanghai	
New York	
Beijing	
Taipei	
Houston	

4. Mother's instructions

Yòuwén is reporting what her mother has told her to do. Listen to her report and fill in the tasks in the order in which her mother wants her to do them.

(CD2: 8)

first task   →   second task   →   third task   →   last task

_____   _____   _____   _____

5. Test information

Zhang Ping needs to take the Chinese placement test. However, he left the information sheet on his desk at home. He called his mother to check the information. Based on the details stated by his mother, fill in the information in the following form.

(CD2: 9)

中文考试	
date	
time	
location	
address	

6.   Where is the purse?

(CD2: 10–11) Listen to Wang Lili tell us what happened to her purse. Then, listen to each of the questions that follow, and answer them in English.

a.

b.

c.

d.

e.

7.   Train station announcement

(CD2: 12) Listen to the announcement at a train station and choose an appropriate answer for each of the two questions below.

a. When does this train leave for Xi'an?
1) 11:00 p.m.
2) 2:00 p.m.
3) 3:00 p.m.
4) 4:00 p.m.

b. What should the passengers do after hearing the announcement?
1) check their luggage
2) get off the train in five minutes
3) turn off any electronic devices
4) show their tickets

8.   Listen and write

(CD2: 13) Chen Wen left a phone message for Maliya, an exchange student from Spain who is going on a trip soon. Listen to Chen Wen's message and write down the main points in English.

The main points of Chen Wen's phone message:

9.   Dialogue

Shibo is telling his friend about his computer. Listen to the conversation and answer the (CD2: 14) following questions.

a. What did the library administrators do when Shibo told them about his computer?
1) They called the school policemen.
2) They checked the students sitting around Shibo.
3) They searched the library.
4) They did not do anything.

b. Who stole Shibo's computer, according to a female student?
1) someone who said that he was Shibo's friend
2) a man with black hair
3) a tall, thin man
4) a student wearing a pair of shorts

c. What was Shibo doing when his computer got stolen?
1) talking to a girl
2) checking out some books
3) drinking water
4) going to the restroom

Reading and writing

Focus on Chinese characters

1.   Number of strokes

Indicate the number of strokes used in writing each of the following characters.

a. 哥 _____   f. 椅 _____

b. 旁 _____   g. 妹 _____

c. 爬 _____   h. 码 _____

d. 厕 _____   i. 拿 _____

e. 寒 _____   j. 长 _____

2.   Which character?

Circle the character in each line that corresponds to the meaning on the left.

a. **qíng** (**shìqing** *situation, matter*)   请   情

b. **xìng** *family name*   姓   虹

c. **xiāng** (**xiāngjī** *camera*)   相   想

d. **jǐ** (**zìjǐ** *self*)   己   已

e. **xuě** *snow*   雷   雪

f. **yòu** *right*   右   友

g. **míng** (**míngzi** *name*)   各   名

h. **gē** (**gēge** *older brother*)   哥   歌

i. **lǔ** (**lǔxíng** *travel, journey*)   放   旅

j. **sòng** *give as a gift*   关   送

k. **qiān** *thousand*   干   千

l. **dì** (**dì'yī** *first*)   弟   第

3.   First strokes

Write the first two strokes of each of the following characters.

a. 包 _____   f. 元 _____

b. 妹 _____   g. 爬 _____

c. 照 _____   h. 名 _____

d. 第 _____   i. 送 _____

e. 长 _____   j. 情 _____

4. Missing strokes

Complete each character by writing in the missing strokes.

a. 人   **ná** *take*

b. 冂   **zhù** (**bāngzhù** *help*)

c. 忄   **qíng** (**shìqing** *situation, matter*)

d. 厂   **cè** (**cèsuǒ** *toilet*)

e. 𠂇   **zuǒ** *left*

f. 女   **xìng** (**xìngmíng** *family name and given name*)

g. 𠂊   **dì** (**dì'yī** *first*)

h. 勹   **bāo** *bag*

i. 𠂇   **yòu** *right*

j. 亠   **páng** (**pángbiān** *beside*)

5. Total strokes

Rewrite this list of characters, arranging the characters in terms of their total number of strokes. Begin your list with the character with the fewest strokes.

第	旅	寒	姓	己	名	爬	助	码	情	右	拿	送	妹	照	长	哥	于	椅	英	旁	雪	包

6. Radicals

Here is a list of characters that we have learned through this lesson. Rewrite each character in the row next to its radical.

名　旁　另　哥　相　惯　旅　姐　妹　右　运
椅　机　情　连　功　送　员　远　忙　极　动

方	
女	
口	
木	
辶	
忄	
力	

7. Character sleuth: Look for the phonetic

Group the characters below in terms of their rhymes or near-rhymes. Write the characters that rhyme with each other in the column on the right. Write the shared part of each character in the column on the left. For all of these characters, the shared part is the "phonetic," the part of the character that provides a clue to its pronunciation. The first set of rhymes is completed for you. There are fourteen additional sets of characters that rhyme or partially rhyme and share a phonetic component among these characters.

红	又	右	请	马	星	爸	完	旁	饺	放	坏
相	爬	姓	张	口	情	工	友	弟	妈	生	远
码	长	第	较	房	吗	院	吧	想	还	功	把

phonetic	characters that rhyme or almost rhyme and share a phonetic component
工	工，红，功

8.   Scrambled sentences

Rewrite these phrases as sentences, putting the words in the correct order to match the English translations.

a. 长 **chéng** / 爬 / 从来 / 我 / 过 / 没

I have never climbed the Great Wall.

b. 选 / 老师 / 的 / 东西 / 送 / 我 / 帮助 / 妹妹 / 请 / 我 / 给

Please help me select something to give as a gift to my younger sister's teacher.

c. 椅子 / 的 / 书包 / 别 / 上 / 在 / 你 / 把 / 放

Don't put your book bag on the chair.

d. 你 / 左边 / 房间 / 房间 / 厕所 / 的 / 的 / 在 / 在 / 你 / 右边 / 还是

Is the bathroom to the right of your room or to the left of your room?

9.   Dictionary skills

Following the instructions in Lesson 17 of the Textbook, look up these characters in a Chinese dictionary and provide the requested information.

a. 被
   pronunciation:
   meaning:
   one two-character word or phrase in which it occurs:

b. 丢
   pronunciation:
   meaning:
   one two-character word or phrase in which it occurs:

c. 城
   pronunciation:
   meaning:
   one two-character word or phrase in which it occurs:

10.   Find the incorrect characters

Zhang Dawei has written an email to his friends back home about a trip that he took recently, but he has written ten characters incorrectly. Read the passage aloud, circle the mistakes, and correct them on the answer sheet below.

> 放寒假的时后，我跟几个同学做火车到中国男方去旅行。我的一个同学弟一天在火车站就把照想机给 **diū** 了。本来以为出去玩是一件很让人高行的事请，可是他当然很生汽也很难过，我们也不高兴，但是我们学会了出去旅行一定要小心看好自己的东四。你帮助我拿书包，我帮助你看东西。我们旅行了一个星期左友，没有再让人生气的事情。

a. ____   b. ____   c. ____   d. ____   e. ____

f. ____   g. ____   h. ____   i. ____   j. ____

11.   Reading for the main ideas

You have not learned all of the characters in the following paragraph, but you have learned all of the structures and much of the vocabulary. Read the paragraph for the main ideas and answer the questions that follow in English.

> 我想选音乐的专业，但是我父母劝我不要学音乐，他们希望我学医。他们认为喜欢唱歌，喜欢听音乐跟选专业是两件很不相同的事情。学音乐，毕业以后不容易找工作。找到工作，挣的钱也不会多。我问他们为什么一谈到选专业，他们就会想到钱。我跟他们说我觉得钱一点都不要重要。他们说我现在觉得钱不重要，因为我一没钱就给家里打电话要钱。我真跟他们说不清楚。

a. This paragraph reports a conversation between three people. Who are they?

b. What were they discussing?

c. There was a disagreement among them. What was it about?

12.　A conversation between Dawei and Guoqiang

Read this conversation and answer the questions that follow in English. (You have learned all of the characters so if you find any that you don't recognize, look them up in the textbook and learn them.) Then, translate lines F.–K. into English.

A.　国强：你知道吗？你的老师有名。

B.　大为：我当然知道我的老师有名。你有名，我也有名，我们都有名字。

C.　国强：我的意思是你的老师很有名。

D.　大为：有名不是有名字吗？

E.　国强：不是，有名是很多人都知道你、很多人都知道你的名字的意思。你跟我都有名字，但是我们没有名。

F.　大为：那么有名，他一定有很多钱了。

G.　国强：对，他很有钱。

H.　大为：他很有名，很有钱，一定也很有学生了。

I.　国强：你不可以说很有学生，只能说有很多学生。

J.　大为：为什么有很多钱可以说很有钱，而有很多学生不能说很有学生呢？

K.　国强：我也不知道。我是中国人。我只知道你不可以这样说，可是我不知道你为什么不可以这样说。

a. This conversation is about similar phrases with very different meanings. What are the phrases?

b. What do the phrases mean?

13. Some good advice

Rewrite this advice in Chinese characters. Write the word **diū** in Pinyin.

Chūqu lǔxíng de shíhou, zuì hǎo bǎ nǐ de xìngmíng、diànhuà hàomǎ hé zhù de dìfang dōu xiě zài yī zhāng zhǐ shàng, fàng zài nǐ de shūbāo lǐ.

Yàoshi nǐ de shūbāo (diū) le, bié de rén zhǎodào yǐhòu, kànjian nǐ de míngzì hé diànhuà hàomǎ, kěyǐ gěi nǐ dǎ diànhuà.

Focus on structure

1. Practice with 把 (Use and Structure note 26.1)

a. 请把这张 **biǎo tián** 一下。

- 把你的中文名字写下来。
- 把你的英文名字写下来。

b. "出生日期"是什么意思？英文怎么说？请把你的出生日期写一下。

c. 你是男的还是女的？请你写一下。

d. **Tián** 完以后请把这个 **biǎo** 给老师看看。

中文姓名 （请一正楷填写）	□1 男 □2 女	□1 境内居民 □2 港澳居民 □3 台籍人士 □4 外籍人士	出生日期 年　　月　　日		
pīnyīn /英文姓名（请按护照 "大写"填写，姓与名之间以空格分开）					

2. Big numbers (Use and Structure note 26.3)

Here are numbers involving 10,000 and multiples of 10,000, written in Arabic numerals. Rewrite them in Chinese numerals, as in the example. Use characters for everything except **wàn** 10,000.

Example:

27,460　　→　　两 **wàn** 七千四百六

a. 12,385　　→

b. 61,222　　→

c. 150,500   →

d. 478,606   →

e. 5,478,000   →

f. 9,999,999   →

g. 12,345,678   →

3.   International currency conversion (Use and Structure notes 26.2, 26.3)

How much is the US dollar worth in other currencies? Here are the conversion rates as of when this book was written, rounded off to the nearest dollar. The international abbreviations of the currency names are provided.

- Rewrite them in Mandarin, using characters for everything except **wàn** *10,000* and **yuán** *dollar*, as in the example.
- Then, go online and look up the most current conversion rates and add a sentence stating the rate. You can use a website such as the Universal Currency Converter website (http://www.xe.com/ucc/) to find the most current rates.

Example:
1,000 USD = 6,782 CNY (Chinese Yuan) (also abbreviated as RMB 人 **mín bì**)
一千美 **yuán** 等于六千七百八十二 CNY

现在 _____

a. 10,000 USD = 13,960 SGD (Singapore Dollars)

现在 _____

b. 500 USD = 16,100 TWD (New Taiwan Dollars)

现在 _____

c. 99,000 USD = 105,290 CAD (Canadian Dollars)

现在 _____

d. 1,500 USD = 131,143 JPY (Japanese Yen)

现在 _____

e. 189,000 USD = 151,738 EUR (Euro)

现在 _____

4.   More or less this amount (Use and Structure note 26.10)

Provide a short answer to each question in Mandarin, using 左右 or 差不多 in each answer.

a. How many students are in each Chinese class? _____

section 1	section 2	section 3
19	20	21

b. What is the age of these students? _____

student 1	student 2	student 3	student 4	student 5	student 6
18	17¹/₂	17¹/₂	18¹/₂	18	18¹/₂

c. What is the price of computer model number 0335? _____

store A	store B	store C
$790	$810	$805

d. How long did students take to complete the test? _____

student 1	student 2	student 3
45 minutes	50 minutes	40 minutes

5.   Almost that amount (Use and Structure note 26.10)

Provide a short answer to each question in Mandarin based on the information in parentheses, using 差不多 in each answer.

a. How long has Xiao Zhang studied Chinese? (one year and eleven months)

b. How much money does Xiao Ye get paid each month for her summer job? (￥1995)

c. How long did Xiao Wang sleep last night? (nine hours fifty minutes)

d. How much is the annual tuition fee at Xiao Zhang's college in the United States? ($39,500)

6. Get people to do things (Use and Structure note 26.6)

Translate these sentences into Mandarin, using 请, 叫, or 让 in each sentence.

a. Let's invite our teachers to dinner, okay?

b. You should tell your roommate to study Chinese.

c. My mom makes me wear socks when the weather is cold.

d. If your friends don't want to drink beer, you shouldn't make them drink it.

e. I want to ask your older brother to help me study Chinese.

f. Mom told the children to clean up the room. (There are two correct choices.)

g. The doctor told me to take this medicine. (There are two correct choices.)

7. Passive (Use and Structure note 26.4)

Translate these sentences into English.

a. 这件事 **bèi** 他知道了。

b. 他还不到二十岁就喝酒，**bèi** 他的爸爸看见了。

c. 我的手机 **bèi** 我弟弟用坏了。

Translate these sentences into Mandarin, using **bèi** in each sentence, and writing characters where we have learned them.

d. While I was studying in the library, my computer was stolen by someone.

e. Sorry, the dumplings we made today were all eaten up by the teachers.

8.   Hypothetical situations with 要是 (Use and Structure note 26.7)

Answer the questions in complete Mandarin sentences.

a. 要是有人给你一百 **wàn** 块钱你会做什么?

b. 要是你的中文课没有考试,你还会 **fù** 习功课吗?

c. 要是你的同屋身体不舒服,你会做什么?

d. 要是你的同屋把你的可乐喝完了,你会不会生气? 为什么?

e. 要是你把电 **nǎo** 给 **diū** 了,你会怎么样?

9.   Translate into English

Translate these sentences into English.

a. 听说北京现在有 1,700 **wàn** 人左右。

b. 我的同屋把我昨天刚买的可乐给喝了。

c. 我写的功课 **diū** 了。不能给老师,等于我昨天晚上什么都没做。

d. 明天会下 **yǔ**。**Kǒng** 怕我们不能去爬山了。

e. 今天下雪下得这么大,我以为没有课了呢。

f. 我以为今天的考试会很难。没想到容易得不得了。

g. 我昨天晚上把我的经 **jì** 课的课本给 **wàng** 在图书馆了。

h. 你这样说就等于你不 **xīwàng** 我们跟你一起去。

10. Translate into Mandarin

Translate these sentences into Mandarin, using characters where we have learned them.

a. I thought (mistakenly) that I wouldn't be able to buy American food in China.

b. From today on, I will practice writing a few characters every day.

c. My mom said that if I can't come home this weekend, she can come to school to see me.

d. (1) We asked Xiao Xie's mom to teach us how to make dumplings.

   (2) She is having us come to her house this weekend to learn.

e. That child is really afraid of his father, but he isn't afraid of his mother.

f. I'm afraid I might be too busy to go to the cafeteria to eat, so I have a lot of food in my room.

g. If you are going to go to the bathroom in the train station, you should ask your friends to watch your things.

11. Scrambled sentences

Rewrite these phrases into sentences, putting them in the right order to match the English translations.

a. 说/ 你 / 你 / 父母 / 你 / 把 / 想 / **zhuānyè** / 应该 / 跟 / 一下 / 选 / 的 / 的

   You should discuss which major you want to choose with your mother and father.

b. 早就 / **yán** / 了/ 不 / 要是 / 我 / 老师 / 选 / 课 /那个 / 那门

   If that teacher weren't strict I would have taken his course long ago.

c. 功课 / 看/ 你 /把 / 然后 / 去 / 请 / 电 **yǐng** / 做完 / 先 / 再

   First finish your homework and then go see a movie.

d. 了 / 考试 / 汉字 / 要是 / 没有 / 就 / 好 / 明天

   It would be good if there wasn't a Chinese-character test tomorrow.

e. 时候 / 在 / 书 / 的 / 谁 / 你 / 考试 / 看 / 让

   Who told you to look at the book while taking the test?

Focus on communication

1.   Dialogue comprehension

Study the Lesson 26 Narrative and Dialogue. Then, read the following statements and indicate whether they are true (T) or false (F).

a. (   ) 大为的 **biǎo** 妹以前没来过中国。

b. (   ) 大为有时间 **dài biǎo** 妹跟同学去爬长 **chéng**，因为现在是寒假。

c. (   ) 他们去爬长 **chéng** 的那天下雪，所以人很少。

d. (   ) 大为的照相机是他哥哥买的。

e. (   ) 那个相机要一 **wàn** 多块美 **yuán**。

f. (   ) 大为的同学觉得，一定有人把相机 **tōu** 走了。

g. (   ) 除了相机以外，大为还 **diū** 了 **hù** 照。

h. (   ) 大为的相机是在厕所里 **diū** 的。

i. (   ) 大为觉得不用请 **biǎo** 妹看着相机，因为他一会儿就回来。

j. (   ) 工作人员跟大为说，以后一定要 **zhù** 意自己 **dài** 的东西。

k. (   ) 大为 **tián** 了一张 **biǎo**，**xīwàng** 如果相机找到了，工作人员可以告诉他。

2.   What do you say?

What do you say in each of the following situations? Type your answers, using characters where we have learned them, and email them to your Chinese teacher.

a. You lost your cell phone and you ask the staff person to help.

b. You want to know how much $1,000 USD is in RMB.

c. You apologize to your friend because you accidentally left her coat in the subway station, and now you can't find it.

d. When the teacher announces that the exam will begin in five minutes, you wonder what to do because you thought the exam was next week and you did not prepare for it.

e. You explain to your friends that you still live with your parents because you don't want to leave them.

f. You are talking to your father about job hunting: You have applied for five jobs so far. Google is your first choice, but you think it's a long shot.

g. Your friend looks very agitated. Ask him not to be mad and tell you what happened. Also offer to help.

h. Tell your roommate you are very upset because you accidentally lost the gift that your boyfriend just gave you.

i. You volunteer as a receptionist in a clinic. Tell a patient to fill out the form first, and then sit in a nearby chair and wait for a few minutes.

j. As a librarian, instruct a visitor on how to apply for a library card. (Tell him to fill out the form with his name, address, and phone number.)

k. Advise your friend not to wear leather shoes today. You're afraid that if he wears leather shoes, he won't be able to climb the Great Wall.

3. Complete the mini-dialogues

Use the structure in parentheses to complete each mini-dialogue.

a. A: 你怎么没穿你最喜欢的那件大衣？

   B: _____。（**bèi**）

b. A: 你为什么不早一点买火车 **piào**？你不知道春节的火车 **piào** 最难买吗？

   B: _____，没想到 **piào** 已经卖完了。（以为）

c. A: 这个照相机我没看过，是从哪儿来的？

   B: 是我 _____ 从美国 **dài** 回来的。（让）

   A: 多少钱？

   B: 不贵。_____。（左右；等于）

d. Teacher: "己"这个字跟"已经"的"已"差不多。

   Student: 好，我 _____。（**zhù** 意）

e. A: 我已经三个星期没有看见你了，这个周末你有时间吗？

   B: 对不起，_____。（**kǒng** 怕）

f. A: 你离开了这么 **jiǔ**，也不给我打电话，真难过！

   B: 别生气，现在我回来了，_____，我不会离开你了。（从...起）

4.   Complete and translate

Using the context as your guide, choose the correct expression to complete each sentence, and then translate the sentences into English.

a. 我以为你明天才会来，_____。
   1) 我已经把房间 **shōushi** 干净了
   2) 所以我放假了，可以 **dài** 你出去玩
   3) 没想到你今天就到了

   English:

b. 昨天早上我送朋友去火车站，_____ 去 **guàng** 商店，很晚才回家。
   1) 然后
   2) 以前
   3) 再说

   English:

c. 今年 **shǔ** 假我大概不会去中国。八月的天气太 **rè** 了，**bìng** 且，_____。
   1) 我没有去过北京
   2) 我早就想去爬长 **chéng** 了
   3) **fēi** 机 **piào** 贵得不得了

   English:

5.   Who is he?

a. 这个人可以帮助你做什么？

b. 什么地方会有这 **zhǒng** 人？

c. 你去找这 **zhǒng** 人的时候，他会怎么帮你？

6. All about emotions

Answer each of the following questions in complete Mandarin sentences, based on the information in the illustration, as in the example.

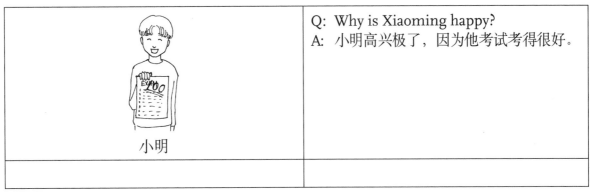

小明	Q: Why is Xiaoming happy? A: 小明高兴极了，因为他考试考得很好。

a. 美雪		Q: Why is Meixue unhappy? (boyfriend left) A:
b. 王刚		Q: Why is Wang Gang so tired? (jogged 3 hours) A:
c. 高同		Q: Why is Gao Tong so anxious? (filling out college application) A:
d. 文音		Q: Why is Wenyin mad to death? (younger sister wore and ruined her skirt) A:

7.   I lost my favorite... Part I

Think about one item that was special to you but got lost (maybe returned later). Answer the following questions about that particular experience in complete Mandarin sentences.

a. 你 **diū** 的东西是什么？

b. 你是什么时候拿到这个东西的？

c. 这个东西是谁送给你的？你知道那是在哪儿买的吗？多少钱？

d. 这个东西为什么很 **zhòng** 要？

e. 这个东西是什么时候 **diū** 的？

f. 这个东西是在哪儿 **diū** 的？你为什么会去那儿？

g. 请你说一下那天 **diū** 东西的经过。

h. 东西 **diū** 了以后，你觉得怎么样？(*For* **Example:** 为什么特别难过，或者特别生气？)

i. 你发现东西 **diū** 了以后，请别人帮忙了吗？

j. 东西最后找到了吗？如果找到了，是怎么找到的？

k. 这件事情以后，你会特别 **zhù** 意什么？

8.   I lost my favorite... Part II

Use your answers from Exercise 7 to write a paragraph about an "I lost..." experience. Your paragraph should be at least 150 characters in length.

_____

_____

_____

_____

_____

_____

_____

_____

Lesson 27 Workbook

 Listening and speaking

Structure drills

(audio online)

1. NP V 起来 AdjV *NP is AdjV to V* (Use and Structure note 27.1)

You will hear a phrase describing an action and a noun phrase. Rephrase the sentence using NP V 起来 AdjV, saying that *the noun phrase is AdjV to V*, as in the example. Translations of the example sentences are provided.

Example:
You will hear: 听那个很有意思的 **gù** 事。 *Listen to that very interesting story.*
You will say: 那个 **gù** 事听起来很有意思。 *That story is interesting to listen to.*
Click "R" to hear the correct response: 那个 **gù** 事听起来很有意思。

(a)   (b)   (c)   (d)   (e)   (f)   (g)   (h)

2. Expressing *both...and* with **jì**...又 (Use and Structure note 27.5)

You will hear a statement describing a noun phrase with two qualities. Rephrase the statement with **jì**...又, as in the example.

Example:
You will hear: 这个学生很 **cōng** 明也很用功。
You will say: 这个学生 **jì cōng** 明又用功。
Click "R" to hear the correct response: 这个学生 **jì cōng** 明又用功。

(a)   (b)   (c)   (d)   (e)   (f)   (g)   (h)   (i)   (j)

3.   V₁ 起来 AdjV₁ V₂ 起来 AdjV₂ (Use and Structure note 27.7)

You will hear a statement describing an action in two different ways. Rephrase the statement with V₁ 起来 AdjV₁ V₂ 起来 AdjV₂, as in the example.

Example:

You will hear: 包饺子，很容易说，很难做。
You will say: 包饺子，说起来容易，做起来难。
Click "R" to hear the correct response: 包饺子，说起来容易，做起来难。

(a)   (b)   (c)   (d)   (e)   (f)   (g)   (h)

4.   把…V-**chéng** *taking something and turning it into something else* (Use and Structure note 27.9)

You will hear two noun phrases followed by a verb. Use them to form a sentence saying that you took the first noun phrase and turned it into the second one, as in the example.

Example:

You will hear: 七点、一点、听
You will say: 我把七点听 **chéng** 一点了。
Click "R" to hear the correct response: 我把七点听 **chéng** 一点了。

(a)   (b)   (c)   (d)   (e)   (f)   (g)   (h)   (i)   (j)

5.   In fact it is not at all like that (Use and Structure notes 27.8, 27.12)

You will hear a statement about what someone believes. Reply that, in fact, the situation is not like that, using **shíjì** 上 and 并 + NEG, as in the example.

Example:

You will hear: 我以为中文很难学。
You will say: **Shíjì** 上，中文并不难。
Click "R" to hear the correct response: **Shíjì** 上，中文并不难学。

(a)   (b)   (c)   (d)   (e)   (f)   (g)   (h)   (i)   (j)

Listening for information

1.   Cooking ingredients

(CD2: 18)   Chef Liu is talking about the ingredients for two dishes. Listen to her and circle the ingredients used in each dish.

a. First dish: ginger, tofu, sugar, soy sauce, green onion, fish, vinegar, pork, garlic

b. Second dish: ginger, tofu, sugar, soy sauce, green onion, fish, vinegar, pork, garlic

2.   A dinner party

Aimei and several of her friends had dinner together in a Chinese restaurant. Each of them (CD2: 19) ordered some dishes. Listen to Aimei's description of the dinner and complete the table with the names of the dishes that each person ordered (in Pinyin).

姓名	中国菜
Àiměi	
Zhāng Xīn	
Liào Tiānmíng	
Páng Yàoguāng	

3.   Stinky tofu

Listen to the story of the dish "stinky tofu," and answer the questions that follow in (CD2: 20–21) complete Mandarin sentences, using characters where we have learned them. The story includes two words that we have not learned, but you should be able to follow the story without knowing precisely what these two words mean.

a.

b.

c.

4.   Chicken with green onions

Listen to the recipe for **cōngyóu jī** *chicken with green onions*, and answer the questions that (CD2: 22–23) follow in complete Mandarin sentences. Use characters where we have learned them. The word **zhēng** means *steam*.

a.

b.

c.

d.

e.

5. Doctor's instructions

(CD2: 24) Chongwen hurt his leg (**tuǐ**) while playing ball. His doctor is telling him what he should do every day to recover. Write down the doctor's instructions about exercising and taking medicine in English. The narrative contains one word that you have not yet learned. It refers to something that Chongwen should do. Write that word in Pinyin in the appropriate place in the table, paying attention to tones.

exercise	medicine
1.	1.
2.	2.
3.	

6. A conversation

(CD2: 25) You are chatting with a Chinese friend about cooking. Answer her questions in Mandarin, based on your own experience. Use characters where we have learned them.

a.

b.

c.

d.

e.

f.

7. In the library

(CD2: 26–27) Listen to the librarian's instructions to Mike about applying for a library card (**jiè** 书 **zhèng**), and then provide a short answer in Mandarin to each question.

a.

b.

c.

d.

e.

8.   Telephone message

Zhiqiang has left you a phone message about tonight's dinner plans. Write an email to him in Chinese responding to each of his questions.

(CD2: 28)

> Your email responding to each of Zhiqiang's questions:

9.   Dialogue I

Listen to the conversation between Tom and his friend Huiru about Beijing. Answer the questions based on the dialogue.

(CD2: 29)

a. What is Tom's summer plan?
   1) travel
   2) do research
   3) work
   4) study

b. What is Tom specifically asking about?
   1) the road situation
   2) finding a suitable apartment
   3) transportation in the city
   4) safety in the community

c. What does Huiru say about riding a bicycle?
   1) Bicycles are often stolen.
   2) Bicycle riding is convenient.
   3) Bicycle riding is not cheap.
   4) Bicycle riding saves time.

10.   Dialogue II

Kathy is asking Jianmin to teach her how to cook Chinese food. Listen to their conversation and answer the following questions. The conversation includes a few words that you have not learned, but you should still be able to follow the main points and answer all of the questions.

(CD2: 30)

a. What does Kathy say about the difference between American and Chinese food?
   1) It is harder to cook American food.
   2) It is easier to eat Chinese food.
   3) It is common to have shredded meat in Chinese dishes.
   4) It is difficult to use chopsticks when eating meat.

b. What should be added when marinating the meat mentioned in the dialogue?
  1) garlic
  2) cooking wine
  3) green onion
  4) hot oil

c. What does Kathy want to learn?
  1) how to cut meat
  2) how to choose the right meat
  3) how to cook meat in various ways
  4) how to marinate meat

 # Reading and writing

Focus on Chinese characters

1. Number of strokes

Indicate the number of strokes used in writing each of the following characters.

a. 懂 _____   f. 备 _____

b. 客 _____   g. 热 _____

c. 鱼 _____   h. 练 _____

d. 准 _____   i. 筷 _____

e. 鸡 _____   j. 久 _____

2. Which character?

Circle the character in each line that corresponds to the meaning on the left.

a. **bìng** (**bìngqiě** *moreover*)   共   并

b. **ròu** *meat*   肉   内

c. **rù** *enter*   入   八

d. **wǔ** (**zhōngwǔ** *noon*)   久   午

e. **zhòng** (**zhòngyào** *important*)   懂   重

f. **zhǒng** *type of*   种   钟

g. **qié** (**qiézi** *eggplant*)   茄   加

h. **liàn** (**liànxí** *practice*)   连   练

i. **fā** (**fā shāo** *have a fever*)   友   发

j. **zhǔn** *accurate*   谁   准

k. **kè** *guest*   客   宫

l. **bèi** (**zhǔnbèi** *prepare*)   各   备

3.   First strokes

Write the first two strokes of each of the following characters.

a. 久 _____   f. 备 _____

b. 筷 _____   g. 共 _____

c. 发 _____   h. 午 _____

d. 肉 _____   i. 茄 _____

e. 种 _____   j. 鱼 _____

4.   Missing strokes

Complete each character by writing in the missing strokes.

a.   扌丿   **rè** *hot*

b.   又′   **jī** *chicken*

c.   丷   **bìng** *(not) at all*

d.   冫   **zhǔn** *accurate*

e.   忄艹   **dǒng** *understand*

f.   纟   **liàn** (**liànxí** *practice*)

g.   丿   **rù** *enter*

h.   宀   **kè** *guest*

i.   火   **chǎo** *stir-fry*

j.   夕   **bèi** (**zhǔnbèi** *prepare*)

5. Total strokes

Rewrite this list of characters, arranging the characters in terms of their total number of strokes. Begin your list with the character with the fewest strokes.

懂	练	发	久	客	备	热	茄	入	午	种	共	重	准	鱼	鸡	并	炒	肉	筷

6. Radicals

Here is a list of characters that we have learned through this lesson. Rewrite each character in the row next to its radical.

懂	第	热	茄	寒	练	情	等	穿	英	算
净	茶	冷	然	客	级	惯	花	次	绍	筷

忄	
灬	
艹	
冫	
宀	
纟	
竹	

7. Character sleuth: Look for the phonetic

Group the characters below in terms of their rhymes or near-rhymes. Write the characters that rhyme with each other in the column on the right. Write the shared part of each character in the column on the left. For all of these characters, the shared part is the "phonetic," the part of the character that provides a clue to its pronunciation. The first set of rhymes is completed for you. There are fourteen additional sets of characters that rhyme or partially rhyme and share a phonetic component among these characters.

吗	块	懂	中	练	极	识	筷
想	种	连	炒	请	较	妈	放
认	码	级	人	话	饺	快	重
少	活	方	钟	相	情	只	房

phonetic	characters that rhyme or almost rhyme and share a phonetic component
重	重，懂

8.   Scrambled sentences

Rewrite these phrases as sentences, putting the words in the correct order to match the English translations.

a. 容易 / 我 / 不 / 筷子 / 发现 / 用 / 并

I realized that it is not at all easy to use chopsticks.

b. 以前 / 得 / 课 / 你 / /功课 / 上 / 准备

Before going to class, you have to prepare the lesson.

c. 想法 / 我们 / 的 / 说 / 你 / 你 / 跟 / 请 / 说 / 一 / 把

Please tell me your opinion.

d. 不 / 我 / 我 / 认识 / 你 / 哥哥 / 以为 / 你 / 的

I assumed you didn't know my older brother.

9. Dictionary skills

Following the instructions in Lesson 17 of the Textbook, look up these characters in a Chinese dictionary and provide the requested information:

a. 简

pronunciation:

meaning:

one two-character word or phrase in which it occurs:

b. 费

pronunciation:

meaning:

one two-character word or phrase in which it occurs:

c. 借

pronunciation:

meaning:

one two-character word or phrase in which it occurs:

10. Find the incorrect characters

Ye Youwen has dashed off this email to one of her friends as she waits for guests to arrive. She is in such a hurry that she has written ten characters incorrectly. (One is written incorrectly two times.) Read the passage aloud, circle the mistakes, and correct them on the answer sheet below.

> 客人很块就要道了。一共来五个，都是我的同学。我爸爸妈妈请他们来我家吃五
> 饭。来以前他们说不要客气，不用谁备很多吃的东西。吃什么不种要。种要的是在
> 一气谈谈话，认只一下我的父母。因为我父母不会说英文，所以他们来我家吃反可
> 以跟我父母连习说中文，并且可以练习用快子吃饭。

a. ____   b. ____   c. ____   d. ____   e. ____

f. ____   g. ____   h. ____   i. ____   j. ____

11. Reading for the main ideas

The following paragraph contains a few characters that we have not yet learned, but you should be able to "read around them" and understand the main points of the passage. Read the paragraph for the main ideas and answer the questions that follow in English.

> 自助餐
>
> 中文有的时候很麻烦。比方说，有一个说法是从英文借来的，但是你不可以把借来的英文都说出来，都说清楚。说清楚就不对了。"自助餐"就是这样。自是自己。助是帮助。餐在这里就是饭的意思。自助餐实际上就是自己帮助自己的饭。但是你不可以这样说。中国人不懂什么是自己帮助自己的饭。你只能说自助餐。

a. 自助餐是什么？

b. 你认为什么时候吃自助餐很方便？

c. 写这个 **gù** 事的人为什么说"中文有的时候很麻烦"？

12.   Translation into English

Translate the following conversation into English.

国强：大为，你最喜欢的中国菜是什么？

大为：我喜欢吃肉，所以我最喜欢的是做两次的肉。

国强：做两次的肉？我怎么没听说过？

大为：你怎么没听说过。上个周末我们一起去吃饭我就要的这个菜。你吃了很多。

国强：那是回 **guō** 肉，不是做两次的肉。

大为：为什么叫回 **guō** 肉？

国强：回 **guō** 肉就是把肉先做一次，再让肉回到 **guō** 里一次，一共做两次。

大为：请你再说一次。肉，一共做几次？

国强：做两次。

大为：所以是做两次的肉。

Focus on structure

1.   Both this and that (Use and Structure note 27.5)

Translate these sentences into Mandarin using the structure **jì AdjV₁ 又 AdjV₂**.

a. Stir-fried eggs with tomatoes is both cheap and simple.

b. Eggplant with yuxiang sauce is both fragrant and delicious.

c. Those dishes are both beautiful and expensive.

d. The ingredients for cooking fish are both simple and inexpensive.

2.   Describing things in terms of two qualities (Use and Structure note 27.7)

Translate these sentences into Mandarin using the structure **V₁ 起来 AdjV₁ V₂ 起来 AdjV₂**.

a. Dumplings are easy to make and delicious to eat.

b. Chinese characters are beautiful to look at but hard to write.

c. This kind of clothing is comfortable to wear and easy to wash.

d. This kind of song is beautiful to listen to but difficult to sing.

3.   More practice with V-chéng (Use and Structure note 27.9)

These sentences all include resultative verbs in which the ending is **chéng**. Translate them into English.

a. 他常常把"问老师"说成"**wěn** (*kiss*) 老师"。

b. 炒菜以前，你得先把肉 **qiē chéng** 块儿。

c. **Zāogāo**，我不小心把"人"写 **chéng**"入"了。

d. 我把她看 **chéng** 她妹妹了。

e. 二十块钱常常写 **chéng** ¥20。

4.   Borrow and loan (Use and Structure note 27.13)

Translate these sentences into English.

a. 请把你的 **bǐ** 借给我。

b. 你最好别跟别人 **jiè** 东西。

c. 要是你想买车你可以从 **yín** 行 **jiè** 钱。

d. 他跟我 **jiè** 了好几本书。

e. 你 **yuàn** 意不 **yuàn** 意把你的电 **nǎo jiè** 给别人？

5.   Scrambled sentences

Rewrite these phrases into sentences, putting them in the right order to match the English translations.

a. **wèi** 道 / 贵 / 很好 / 饭馆 / 并 / 菜 / 那家 / 而且 / 的 / 不

The dishes in that restaurant taste good, moreover they aren't at all expensive.

b. **tiáoliào** / 菜 / 放了 / **xiāng** / 吧 / 这个 / 不少 / **wén** 起来 / 一定 / 真

This dish is very fragrant to smell. They certainly put in a lot of seasonings.

c. 以外 / 有 / 筷子 / **wǎn** / 我 / **pán** 子 / 除了 / 和 / 也

Besides chopsticks, I also have bowls and plates.

d. 的 / 不 / 了 / 我 / 我 / 发现 / **gòu** / 刚 / 钱

I just realized I don't have enough money.

e. **yán** / 这 / 关心 / 个 / **jì** / 又 / 很 / 学生 / 老师 / 很

This teacher is both very strict and also cares about her students.

6.   Translation into English

Translate these sentences into English.

a. 我去图书馆 **jiè** 书。图书馆没有这本书。老师把他的 **jiè** 给我了。

b. **Shíjì** 上，说中文并不难。难的是写汉字。

c. 现在的经 **jì** 不太好。大学 **bìyè** 生找工作，说起来容易做起来难。

d. 今天的中文功课是想一个你小的时候听的 **gù** 事，明天用中文给老师和同学 **jiǎng**。

e. 快过春节了。**Shāng** 店的东西都在打折。比方说，有的打九折，有的打八五折，还有的打七折。

f. 这个人在吃的方 **miàn** 一点都不 **jiǎngjiu**，可是在穿的方 **miàn** 非常 **jiǎngjiu**。

g. 这个周末是大为的生日。我们请他来我们的宿舍喝酒。我们 **shǒu** 先 **shōushi** 房间，然后把脏衣服洗干净，最后去买 **pí** 酒和吃的东西。

h. 下个星期六我们一起去长 **chéng** 玩，你 **dài** 吃的，我 **dài** 喝的，早上六点学校门口见。一 **yán** 为定。

7.   Translation into Mandarin

Translate these sentences into Mandarin, using characters where we have learned them.

a. I don't like to go on the web and chat with other people. I think it is too much of a waste of time.

b. This weekend we are going to go climb the Great Wall. Do you want to (are you willing to) come with us?

c. Before returning to my home country, I definitely want to learn how to cook a few authentic Chinese dishes.

d. I study Chinese together with Xiao Wang. We study Chinese together with Professor Zhang.

e. He lived in China for several years, so the Chinese that he speaks is very authentic.

f. I think your way of doing things is not correct. Let's try another method, okay?

g. Actually, there is no problem with this method. (Use 并.) The problem is that you don't understand it.

h. I don't have enough time. I definitely won't be able to finish the homework tonight.

Focus on communication

1. Dialogue comprehension

Study the Lesson 27 Narrative and Dialogue. Then, read the following statements and indicate whether they are true (T) or false (F).

a. (　) 中国菜 **jiǎngjiu** 看起来漂亮、**wén** 起来 **xiāng**，吃起来有 **wèi** 道。

b. (　) 美丽最会做的中国菜就是鸡 **dàn** 炒西红 **shì** 和鱼 **xiāng** 茄子。

c. (　) 鱼 **xiāng** 茄子有 **cōng**，**jiāng**，**suàn**，**táng** 等等的 **tiáoliào**，可是没有鱼。

d. (　) 美丽想请国强的妈妈教她做鱼 **xiāng** 茄子。

e. (　) 谢太太认为，中国菜不一定都很难做。有的家常菜又好吃又容易做。

f. (　) 鸡 **dàn** 炒西红 **shì** 要放 **táng**、**yán** 和 **cōng**。

g. (　) 做鸡 **dàn** 炒西红 **shì** 的时候，鸡 **dàn** 别 **wàng** 了多炒几分钟。

h. (　) 做鸡 **dàn** 炒西红 **shì** 的时候，把西红 **shì** **qiēchéng** 块儿，不要放进 **guō** 里炒，放在炒好的鸡 **dàn** 上就可以了。

i. (　) 美丽跟谢妈妈 **jiè** 了一个 **guō**，回家练习做中国菜。

2. What do you say?

What do you say in each of the following situations? Type your answers, using characters where we have learned them, and email them to your Chinese teacher.

a. You want to start a story with "Once upon a time…".

b. You are making eggplant with yuxiang sauce. Ask your sister to wash the eggplants and cut them into small pieces.

c. You want to ask your Chinese friend to teach you a simple yet delicious Chinese dish.

d. You promise your little brother that if he goes to bed early you will tell him a story.

e. Apologize to your grandma that you can't go visit her this weekend because there's not enough time. You thought next Monday was still a holiday (a day off), but later you realized that it's not.

f. Imagine saying "I do" (I'm willing to!) when you marry someone in China.

g. Your friend insists on taking you out to the movies. Make a deal with your friend that movie tickets are his treat, but dinner is on you.

h. Say a few nice words to compliment a dish that your mom cooked that is on the dinner table. (For example, what it smells like, what it looks like, etc.)

i. You have just taken a bite of a wonderful dish. It's so tasty that you want the hostess to tell you what seasonings are (put) in it.

j. Name one dish that you like the best and provide at least two reasons for your choice.

k. You try to convince your parents to learn how to use the internet. Name a few advantages. (Use the phrase "for example.")

l. You need to borrow a wok and some ginger from your neighbor because you want to practice making scallion-ginger chicken. Explain to your neighbor that you found the recipe (way of making it) online.

m. Instruct your kitchen helper to cut the meat into strips (条) that are not too long and not too short.

3. Complete the mini-dialogues

Use the structure in parentheses to complete each mini-dialogue.

a. A: 给 **hái** 子选名字什么最重要？

   B: 给 **hái** 子选名字 _____。（**jiǎngjiu**）

b. A: 你给我 **jiǎng jiǎng**，一双好的鞋子应该怎么样？

   B: _____。（V 起来）

c. A: **Dōng** 天去爬长 **chéng** 怎么样？

   B: 很多人认为 _____。（**shíjì** 上）

d. A: 你明天几点钟回来？

   B: 大概 _____ 吧。 (use two numbers in a row)

e. Wife: 你怎么会穿黄色的 **chènshān**？黄 **chènshān** 跟这条 **kù** 子一点也不 **pèi**。

   Husband: 真的吗？那我去 _____。（V-**chéng**）

f. A: 没想到北京这么冷，这次旅 **yóu** 我只 **dài** 了 **chènshān** 来，这几天怎么 **bàn** 呢？

   B: _____ 没关系，我可以 **jiè** 给你一件大衣。（**gòu**）

g. A: 你教我做一个地道的美国菜，怎么样？

   B: 没问 **tí**。就做 _____ 好了。_____（**jì**…又）

4.   Complete and translate

Using the context as your guide, choose the correct expression to complete each sentence, and then translate the sentence into English.

a. 大家都以为中国菜里的 **yóu** 特别多，**shíjì** 上 _____。
   1) 地道的中国菜并不是这样。
   2) 大家都喜欢吃，因为 **jì** 方便又便宜
   3) 炒菜的时候我不喜欢放那么多 **yóu**。

   English:

b. 买衣服最重要是大小 **héshì**，也就是说，_____
   1) 打折的时候去买衣服正好。
   2) 买衣服的时候一定要试穿。
   3) 有没有大一号的？

   English:

c. 炒鸡 **dàn** 一点儿也不难。你看，_____。
   1) 下次我做给你吃
   2) 两三分钟就炒好了
   3) 一定要用筷子打 **yún**

   English:

5.   Goldilocks and the Three Bears

Here is the story *Goldilocks and the Three Bears* in Chinese. Look at the illustration and fill in the blanks to complete the story. Research online if you are not familiar with the story.

a. 很久很久以前，_____ 叫 Goldilocks。有一天，她 _____ 一个房子里。

b. 她看到 **zhuō** 上有 _____ **zhōu** (*porridge*)。第一 **wǎn** 太 _____，

_____，_____，所以 Goldilocks 就

把 _____。

c. 然后，Goldilocks 看到三把椅子。第一把太 _____，

_____，_____，

所以 Goldilocks 就坐下来，可是，她不小心把 _____。

d. 后来，Goldilocks 走进房间里，看到 _____。她太累了，

就在 _____。

e. **Xióng** (*bear*) 爸爸、**xióng** 妈妈和小 **xióng** 回到家，_____ （i. **shǒu** 先，ii. 然后，

iii. 后来），小 **xióng** 看到他的 **zhōu** 不见了，说：是谁 _____？

_____ （i. **shǒu** 先，ii. 然后，iii. 后来）小 **xióng** 看到他的椅子坏了，就更生气

了，他说：我的椅子 **bèi** _____？

f. _____ （i. **shǒu** 先，ii. 然后，iii. 后来）他们走进房间里，看到 Goldilocks

_____。小 **xióng** 生气得不得了。_____

_____

_____。 (*So scared that she jumped out of the bed and ran out.*)

6. Cinderella (**Huī Gūniang** *Dust Girl*)

Part I. Describe each scene, using the words provided in parentheses. Here are the words and phrases we have not yet learned that you will need to tell the story: 后母 *stepmother*, 王子 *prince*, **xiān** 女 *fairy godmother*, A 跟 B **jiéhūn** *A gets married to B*, **zhī** (*classifier for one shoe*).

a.	(打 **sǎo**)
	_____
	_____
	_____

b.

(难过、帮助、送给)

_____

_____

_____

c.

(cān 加、wǔ 会)

_____

_____

_____

d.

(离开、跑、diū)

_____

_____

_____

e.

(试穿、V 不下)

_____

_____

_____

f.

_____

_____

_____

Part II. The complete story Working with a partner, compare each other's sentences from Part I and work together to write the story of Cinderella in Mandarin, starting with "Once upon a time…" Your story should be at least 150 characters in length.

_____

_____

_____

_____

_____

_____

_____

_____

7. A recipe for 西红 **shì dàn huā tāng** (*soup*) *tomato egg drop soup*

Part I. The following is a recipe for 西红 **shì dàn huā tāng** *tomato egg drop soup*. The recipe is divided into three sections, and each section includes illustrations of the process.

For each section:

- Complete the sentences.
- Put the sentences in the correct order so that they form a cohesive set of instructions for making tomato egg drop soup.
- Translate the recipe into English.

The additional vocabulary items that you need for this recipe are: **tāng** *soup*, **huā** *flower*, **gǔn** *boil*, and **jiǎo** *stir*. Translations are also provided in the recipe.

a.	A. 先准备好 _____ 、 _____ 和一个鸡 **dàn**。
	B. 再加两 **wǎn** 水。
	C. 然后，放一点 **yóu** 在 **guō** 里，**yóu** 热了以后，把_____ 一起放 _____ **fān** 炒一下。
	D. **Shǒu** 先，把西红 **shì qiē** _____，把 **cōng qiē** _____。
Order:	
English translation:	

b.	A. 最后放一点 **yán**，试试 **wèi** 道。 B. 把 **dòufu qiē** _____，等水 **gǔn** (*boil*) 了以后， 放 _____。 C. 水 **gǔn** (*boil*) 了，再把 **dàn** _____。一边放，一边 用筷子 **jiǎo** (*stir*) 一下。 D. **Dòufu** 放进去以后，把鸡 **dàn** 打开，放 _____， 用筷子 _____。
Order:	
English translation:	
c.	A. 因为 **dàn** 打在 **tāng** 里看起来跟 **huā** (*flower*) 差不多， B. 一两分钟以后，西红 **shì dàn huā tāng** _____。 C. 所以叫 **dàn huā tāng**。
Order:	
English translation:	

Part II.   Imagine you are teaching a novice in the kitchen how to make tomato egg drop soup. Using the descriptions above, follow the style of the Lesson 27 Narrative in the Textbook and write a paragraph. Make it clear and encouraging for this person that you are teaching. You can throw in some tips along the way.

_____

_____

_____

_____

_____

8. A recipe

Think about your favorite simple dish (a pasta dish, pizza, sandwiches, dessert, etc.). Follow the steps in Exercise 7 and write the recipe below. Use the supplementary vocabulary in this Lesson or consult a dictionary for words you don't know. Work with your classmates to type all of your recipes in Chinese (using Pinyin for characters we have not learned) and prepare a cookbook of simple Western dishes in Chinese.

_____

_____

_____

_____

_____

_____

_____

_____

_____

_____

_____

9. How-to: Describing a process in Chinese

Write step-by-step instructions explaining how to do one of the processes on the following list, or select your own topic to write about.

Step I: Pick a topic.

Sample processes:

- How to compare and shop for the cheapest airfare online.
- How to prepare for a job interview.
- How to prepare for a big annual sale of your favorite produce or store. (For example, what you can do ahead of time to get ready for the sale.)
- How to lose weight in a healthy way (both dieting and exercise tips).
- How to be a good host/hostess at a party.
- How to choose the right major for you.
- How to comfort a friend who just had an accident/lost something/broke up with someone/got fired, etc.
- Your topic: _____

Step II.   Brainstorm your idea in English.

1. _____

2. _____

3. _____

4. _____

Things to avoid: _____

Things to pay special attention to: _____

_____

Other tips: _____

Step III.   Use the above ideas to write step-by-step instructions in Chinese. In your instructions, use the expressions **shǒu** 先、然后、再、一边...一边...、**zhù** 意、别...、把..., and 最后.

_____

_____

_____

_____

_____

_____

_____

_____

_____

_____

_____

Lesson 28 Workbook

 Listening and speaking

Structure drills

1. Chèn X 的时候 *taking advantage of a time when X*, Part I
   (Use and Structure note 28.3)

You will hear a statement saying what someone is doing, followed by a location phrase. Say that the person is taking advantage of the time when he is at that location to do the action, as in the example.

Example:

You will hear: 小叶学做中国菜，在北京
You will say: 小叶 **chèn** 在北京的时候学做中国菜。
Click "R" to hear the correct response: 小叶 **chèn** 在北京的时候学做中国菜。

(a)   (b)   (c)   (d)   (e)   (f)   (g)   (h)

2. Chèn X 时候 *taking advantage of a time when X*, Part II
   (Use and Structure note 28.3)

You will hear a statement saying what someone is doing, followed by a statement saying that someone else is doing a different action. Say that the second person is taking advantage of the time the first person does some action to do a different action, as in the example.

Example:

You will hear: 他写 **xìn**，我去打电话。
You will say: **Chèn** 他写 **xìn** 的时候，我去打电话。
Click "R" to hear the correct response: **Chèn** 他写 **xìn** 的时候，我去打电话。

(a)   (b)   (c)   (d)   (e)   (f)   (g)   (h)

3.　Not as good as (Use and Structure note 28.5)

You will hear a statement saying that some situation is better than another in some way. Summarize the information using 不如 to say that one situation is not as good as the other, as in the example.

> **Example:**
> *You will hear:* 学中文比学日文有用。
> *You will say:* 我觉得学日文不如学中文。
> *Click "R" to hear the correct response:* 我觉得学日文不如学中文。

(a)　　(b)　　(c)　　(d)　　(e)　　(f)　　(g)　　(h)

4.　It can't get any better than this (Use and Structure note 28.6)

You will hear a statement describing the quality of person or thing. Say that the person or thing has as much of that quality as is possible, as in the example.

> **Example:**
> *You will hear:* 非常便宜的书
> *You will say:* 这本书再便宜不过了。
> *Click "R" to hear the correct response:* 这本书再便宜不过了。

(a)　　(b)　　(c)　　(d)　　(e)　　(f)　　(g)　　(h)　　(i)　　(j)

5.　Done for this reason (Use and Structure note 28.9)

You will hear a statement saying that someone has done some action for some reason. Use the structure 为了 NP 而 VP to say that the action was done for that reason, as in the example.

> **Example:**
> *You will hear:* 因为我想去中国，所以我在学中文。
> *You will say:* 我为了去中国而学中文。
> *Click "R" to hear the correct response:* 我为了去中国而学中文。

(a)　　(b)　　(c)　　(d)　　(e)　　(f)　　(g)　　(h)

Listening for information

1.　Beijing one-day tour

Miss Huang at Shanghao Travel Agency is describing the itinerary and fee for a one-day tour in Beijing. Listen to her description and provide the information in English for the following form.

(CD2: 34)

Beijing One-Day Tour		
Tour time schedule	Start time: _____ End Time: _____	
Scenic spots visited		places
	morning	_____
	afternoon	_____
Meals included:	_____	

Fee per person:
   individual
   groups of five or more
	_____
	
	_____	

2. Math questions

(CD2: 35) You will hear three math word problems. Answer each question in English.

a.

b.

c.

3. Studying Chinese

(CD2: 36) This is the first meeting of Teacher Ye's Chinese class. Several students explain why they are studying Chinese. Listen to each student's statement and fill in the reason in English for each student.

student	reason
#1	
#2	
#3	
#4	

4. Change of plans

Mr. Zhao, a travel agent, has left a message for you. Listen to the message and write an instant message to him in Mandarin, answering his questions. **(CD2: 37)**

> Instant message to Mr. Zhao:

5. Ma Rong's trip

Ma Rong is talking about his summer trip. Based on his narration, indicate whether the following statements are true (T) or false (F). **(CD2: 38)**

a. (   ) Ma Rong traveled in three countries.

b. (   ) Ma Rong saved a lot of money because of the help from the travel agency.

c. (   ) Ma Rong is fluent in French, so it is easy for him to travel in France.

d. (   ) The trip lasted three weeks.

e. (   ) They found Italy to be the most fun country, so they stayed there the longest time.

6. On the airplane

You will hear an announcement from a flight attendant on a flight to Guangzhou. Answer the questions that follow in Mandarin, based on the announcement. **(CD2: 39–40)**

a.

b.

c.

d.

e.

f.

7. Check in at a hotel

(CD2: 41–42) Yang Tianren is checking in at a hotel. Listen to the dialogue between him and the hotel receptionist. Then, answer the questions that follow in Mandarin based on their conversation.

a.

b.

c.

d.

e.

8. A conversation

(CD2: 43) You are studying in China. Your Chinese roommate wants to know about traveling in the USA. Answer her questions in Mandarin based on your own experience. Use characters where we have learned them.

a.

b.

c.

d.

e.

f.

9. Listen and write

(CD2: 44–45) You will hear an announcement from Mr. Wang, a tourist guide. Listen to what he is telling his group and answer the questions that follow in Mandarin, based on his announcement.

a.

b.

c.

d.

e.

f.

10. Dialogue

Miss Chen is calling the front desk from her hotel room. Listen to the dialogue between her **(CD2: 46)** and the hotel clerk. Choose appropriate answers, based on the dialogue.

a. What is the problem with Miss Chen's room?
  1) There is no internet connection.
  2) The TV is broken.
  3) The bathroom is dirty.
  4) The room is too small.

b. What was the hotel clerk's first response to Miss Chen's request?
  1) He will send someone to check the room.
  2) He will find another single room for her.
  3) He will find a bigger room for her.
  4) He will give her free internet connection.

c. What will Miss Chen do after the conversation with the clerk?
  1) go to another hotel
  2) pay less for the room
  3) get one night free for the room
  4) move to a bigger room

Reading and writing

Focus on Chinese characters

1. Number of strokes

Indicate the number of strokes used in writing each of the following characters.

a. 唱 _____   f. 复 _____

b. 街 _____   g. 飞 _____

c. 影 _____   h. 址 _____

d. 单 _____   i. 歌 _____

e. 游 _____   j. 故 _____

2. Which character?

Circle the character in each line that corresponds to the meaning on the left.

a. **gē** *song*   歌   哥

b. **gù** (**gùshi** *story*)   古   故

c. **jì** (**jīngjì** *economics*)   济   际

d. **jià** (**jiàqian** *price*)   价   介

e. **jiē** *street*   行   街

f. **lā** (**kǎlā OK** *karaoke*)   立   拉

g. **piào** *ticket*   漂   票

h. **dān** (**jiǎndān** *simple*)   单   草

i. **jì** (**jìhuà** *plan*)   汁   计

j. **yóu** (**lǚyóu** *travel*)   游   放

k. **yè** (**shāngyè** *business*)   并   业

l. **shì** (**diànshì** *television*)   视   规

3. First strokes

Write the first two strokes of each of the following characters.

a. 带 _____   f. 址 _____

b. 飞 _____   g. 单 _____

c. 卡 _____   h. 歌 _____

d. 影 _____   i. 餐 _____

e. 划 _____   j. 故 _____

4. Missing strokes

Complete each character by writing in the missing strokes.

a.   癶   **cān** (**zǎocān** *breakfast*)

b.   亻   **jià** (**jiàqian** *price*)

c.   氵   **yóu** (**lǚyóu** *travel*)

d.   覀   **piào** *ticket*

e.   礻   **shì** (**diànshì** *television*)

f.   丨   **yè** (**shāngyè** *business*)

g.   彳   **fù** (**fùxí** *review*)

h.   阝   **jì** (**guójì** *international*)

i.   宀   **shí** (**shíjìshàng** *actually, in reality*)

j.   彳   **jiē** *street*

5.   Total strokes

Rewrite this list of characters, arranging the characters in terms of their total number of strokes. Begin your list with the character with the fewest strokes.

拉	票	际	影	实	带	视	价	址	游	划	街	济	故	单	计	复	卡	餐	唱

6.   Radicals

Here is a list of characters that we have learned through this lesson. Rewrite each character in the row next to its radical.

午   客   济   地   认   千   流   寒   别   游   识
划   活   坐   实   到   歌   单   容   欢   坏   计

氵	
欠	
十	
讠	
宀	
土	
刂	

7. Character sleuth: Look for the phonetic

Group the characters below in terms of their rhymes or near-rhymes. Write the characters that rhyme with each other in the column on the right. Write the "phonetic," the shared part of each character, in the column on the left. There are at least eleven sets of characters that rhyme or partially rhyme and share a phonetic component among these characters.

可　　只　　筷　　先　　少　　漂　　功　　快
钟　　炒　　价　　请　　歌　　懂　　种　　哥
介　　选　　重　　红　　块　　票　　识　　情

phonetic	characters that rhyme or almost rhyme and share a phonetic component

8. Scrambled sentences

Rewrite these phrases as sentences, putting the words in the correct order to match the English translations.

a. 中国 / 中文 / 为 / 来 / 他 / 学 / 而 / 到 / 是 / 了 / 的

It was in order to study Chinese that he came to China.

b. 好做 / 好吃 / 不 / 可是 / 我 / 中国 / 认为 / 饭

I figure Chinese food is delicious but not easy to cook.

c. 手机 / 好用 / 上网 / 太 / 个 / 可以 / 但是 / 这 / 不

This cell phone can access the internet but it is not easy to use.

d. 你 / 买 / 为 / 酒 / 的 / 些 / 是 / 这

This alcohol was bought for you.

9. Dictionary skills

Following the instructions in Lesson 17 of the Textbook, look up these characters in a Chinese dictionary and provide the requested information.

a. 信

    pronunciation:

    meaning:

    one two-character word or phrase in which it occurs:

b. 交

    pronunciation:

    meaning:

    one two-character word or phrase in which it occurs:

c. 剩

    pronunciation:

    meaning:

    one two-character word or phrase in which it occurs:

10. Find the incorrect characters

Zhang Dawei has written an email home explaining how people buy tickets in China, but he has written ten characters incorrectly. Read the passage aloud, circle the mistakes, and correct them on the answer sheet below. Then, translate the passage into English.

> 在美国卖飞机漂，如果你买来回票，飞几票的家钱会更宜一些。可是实济上在中国不是这样，所以有的人到一个地房去旅行，去的时后坐飞机，会来的时候坐火车。火车票北飞机票好买。

a. ____   b. ____   c. ____   d. ____   e. ____

f. ____   g. ____   h. ____   i. ____   j. ____

English:

11. Reading for the main ideas

The following paragraph contains a few characters that we have not yet learned, but you should be able to "read around them" and understand the main points of the passage. Read the paragraph for the main ideas and answer the questions that follow in English.

> 很多青年人喜欢跟朋友一起去酒吧。在那里他们可以聊天、看球赛或认识新的朋友。可是旅馆为什么要有酒吧呢？住旅馆的人，家一定不在附近。如果你的家不在附近，可能在旅馆的附近你也没有朋友。那么，你跟谁一起喝酒呢？如果你想在酒吧认识一些新的朋友，可是因为你的家不在附近，所以你马上又要离开这个地方。你要离开这个地方，为什么还要在这儿认识新朋友呢？我不知道什么样的人会去旅馆的酒吧喝酒。

a. What is the main topic of this paragraph?

b. Which two groups of people does the author compare in this paragraph?

c. What is the paradox (the contradiction) that the author presents in this paragraph?

12.   Add the punctuation

Add punctuation to the following paragraph, and then translate it into English. You should add a total of six commas, three periods, and one question mark to the passage.

书店是卖书的商店但是酒店不是卖酒的商店有的旅馆的名字叫酒店有的饭馆的名字也叫酒店旅馆一定可以睡觉而且常常有饭馆和酒吧而饭馆一定不能睡觉有的卖酒有的不卖你可以告诉我酒店真正的意思是什么吗

English:

Focus on structure

1.   Good to do (Use and Structure note 28.1)

Answer each of the following questions in complete Mandarin sentences, using the structure 好 + ActV and the verb provided in parentheses. Then, translate your responses into English.

a. 你的同屋唱歌唱得怎么样？（听）

   A:

English:

b. 你觉得这个手机怎么样？（用）

   A:

English:

c. "学生 **zhī** 友" 卡拉 **OK** 在哪儿？你知道吗？（找）

A:

English:

d. 小王的女朋友怎么样？（看）

A:

English:

e. 学校旁边的餐厅的菜怎么样？（吃）

A:

English:

2.   Take advantage (Use and Structure note 28.3)

Here is a list of places that Xiao Zhang's cousin hopes to visit while she is in Asia, along with something she hopes to do in each place. Write a sentence in Mandarin for each situation, saying that she wants to *take advantage of the time that she is in that place* to do each thing.

a. travel in Shanghai: see the Bund

b. see her older brother in Beijing: eat famous Beijing Roast Duck

c. in Japan: eat Japanese food

d. in Sichuan: eat spicy food

e. in Beijing: climb the Great Wall

f. visit friends in Taiwan: drink tea

3.   Do the math! Fractions and percentages (Use and Structure note 28.4)

Rewrite a.–d. as numerical fractions, as in the example.

Example:

三分 **zhī** 二   →   2/3

a. 七分 **zhī** 五   →

b. 十分 **zhī** 一   →

c. 十五分 **zhī** 八   →

d. 六分 **zhī** 五   →

Rewrite e.–h. in Mandarin, as in the example.

Example:

2/3 → 三分 **zhī** 二

e. 9/10 →

f. 8/9 →

g. 1/4 →

h. 1/20 →

Rewrite i.–l. as numerical percentages %.

i. 百分 **zhī** 二 →

j. 百分 **zhī** 一 →

k. 百分 **zhī** 二十五 →

l. 百分 **zhī** 四十 →

4. Not as good (Use and Structure note 28.5)

Answer each question with 不如, saying that the first choice is not as good as the second, and then translate your answers into English.

a. 你觉得蓝色的 **kù** 子和 **hēi** 色的 **kù** 子一样吗？
   A:

   English:

b. 在中国学中文和在美国学中文一样吗？
   A:

   English:

c. 中国电影和美国电影一样吗？
   A:

   English:

d. 你觉得 **duànliàn** 身体，**pǎo bù** 和打球一样吗？
   A:

   English:

e. 坐汽车去学校和自己开车去学校一样吗？
   A:

   English:

5.   Focus on the purpose or beneficiary (Use and Structure note 28.9)

Translate the following sentences into English.

a. 你应该为了你的 **jiāng** 来而用功学习。

b. 他为了 **duànliàn** 身体而 **cān** 加 **jiàn** 身房，可是 **cān** 加了以后，只去过两、三次。

c. 为了你的身体好，做饭的时候少放一点 **yán** 吧。

d. 为了去中国旅游，我现在在图书馆工作 **zhèng** 钱。

e. 为了上一个好大学，很多中学生周末去上课，准备考试。

6.   Scrambled sentences

Rewrite these phrases into sentences, putting them in the right order to match the English translations.

a. 朋友 / 我 / 中国 / 个 / 要 / 一 / **chèn** / 机会 / 认识 / 些 / 这 / 多

   I want to take advantage of this opportunity to make a few more Chinese friends.

b. 功课 / 做完 / 要 / 你 / 吗 / 明天 / 的 / **jiāo** / 了

   Have you finished doing the homework that we have to hand in tomorrow?

c. 吃 / 没 / 想 / **kǎoyā** / 有 / 早餐 / 我 / 人

   I think no one eats roast duck for breakfast.

d. 时间 / 又 / 钱 / 地铁 / **shěng** / **shěng** / 坐 / **jì**

   Taking the subway saves both time and money.

e. 坐 / **miǎnfèi** / 北京 / 公共 / 在 / 老人 / 汽车

   In Beijing old people ride the bus for free.

7.   Translation into English

Translate these sentences into English.

a. 这种手机最近很流行，百分 **zhī** 八十的学生都有。

b. 今年的工作很好找。百分 **zhī** 六十五的 **bì** 业生在 **bì** 业以前就找到了工作。

c. 有这样一个难得的好朋友带你在中国旅行是一个非常难得的机会。

d. 很多人喜欢运动只是喜欢看比 **sài**。

我认为看比 **sài** 不如 **cān** 加比 **sài**。

Cān 加比 **sài** 可以 **duànliàn** 身体。

e. 友文 **chèn** 在中国学习的时候学会了几个地道的中国菜。

f. 我们学的中文是 **biāo** 准的中文。你的说法不 **biāo** 准。

8.   Translate into Mandarin

Translate these sentences into Mandarin, using characters where we have learned them.

a. Xiao Xie wants to use the time during spring break to prepare (for) a very big exam.

b. Teacher, I didn't understand what you said. Please go over it again.

c. Because you don't have credit, (so) the bank didn't give you a credit card.

d. Economic conditions in the USA this year are very good.

e. When I am traveling, I am not interested in famous sites and historic places.

f. If the room rate in that hotel does not include breakfast, and the internet is not free, please do not make a reservation in (reserve) that hotel.

g. Nowadays a lot of college students recognize that studying Japanese is not as good as studying Chinese.

h. Some tourist sites sound really good but actually aren't that good.

Focus on communication

1.   Dialogue comprehension

Study the Lesson 28 Narrative and Dialogue. Then, read the following statements and indicate whether they are true (T) or false (F).

a.   (   ) 大为和他 **biǎo** 妹这几天都在北京。

b.   (   ) 大为和他 **biǎo** 妹新的、旧的旅游 **jǐng** 点都去了。

c.   (   ) 大为去 **Xiù** 水街 **guàng** 得很高兴。

d.   (   ) 大为的 **biǎo** 妹常常来中国看他。

e.   (   ) 大为打算开车带着 **biǎo** 妹去上海看看。

f.   (   ) 大为给旅行社打电话的那天是星期六。

g.   (   ) 他打算去上海玩五天。

h.   (   ) 大为想 **dìng jiāotōng** 方便而且比较便宜的酒店。

i.   (   ) 打八五折的机票就是 **jiǎn** 价八块五。

j.   (   ) 从北京到上海坐飞机要坐一天。

k.   (   ) 星期五没有打折的机票，所以坐火车比飞机好。

l.   (   ) 坐火车回北京 **jì** 便宜又可以 **shěng** 旅馆钱。

m.   (   ) 大为想知道有没有比坐火车 **gèng** 好的方法。

n.   (   ) 大为和 **biǎo** 妹会在上海睡三个晚上。

o.   (   ) 旅行社 **dìng** 的酒店离什么都很近，还可以 **miǎn fèi** 上网。可是早餐得出去吃。

p.   (   ) 大为要 **fù** 现金，因为旅行社不让他用 **xìn** 用卡。

2.   What do you say?

What do you say in each of the following situations? Type your answers, using characters where we have learned them, and email them to your Chinese teacher.

a.   You call the travel agent and ask him to book a round-trip plane ticket to Shanghai.

b.   You call the travel agent to inquire about the cheapest round-trip plane ticket to China.

c.   As a travel agent, ask your client if she can leave on Thursday instead of Friday because flight tickets are much more expensive on weekends.

d.   As a travel agent, convince your client to book a double room, rather than reserving two single rooms, because it saves a lot of money.

e.   Apologize to your client that you don't take credit cards. It's cash only.

f.   As a clerk at the lost and found counter, ask the customer to briefly describe his lost cell phone.

g.   Tell your travel agent the ideal hotel you would like to book (including room type, location and price).

h.   Ask for the address of the travel agency so that you can pick up the tickets tomorrow afternoon yourself.

i.   Explain to your out-of-town guests that they have to go to _____ (a place of your choice) because their visit is a rare (hard to obtain) event.

j.   Tell the salesperson that if she can give you 50% off, nothing would be better than that.

k.   You complain that from yesterday until now, you've only completed one-third of your homework. There are still two-thirds unfinished.

l.   Persuade your friend to go to the party with you by telling him that he should grab this opportunity to meet more girls.

m.   Ask your Chinese friend what's the most trendy and famous restaurant in Beijing.

n.   Warn your friend not to drag you to karaoke because you sing worse than anyone.

o.   Discuss with your friend the pros and cons of purchasing a soft-sleeper train ticket.

p.   Ask the person on the other end of the phone to repeat what he just said because you didn't hear it clearly a moment ago.

3.　Complete the mini-dialogues

Use the structure in parentheses to complete each mini-dialogue.

a. A: 这个周末很多商店打折，有的店打三折、有的打五折。

　　B: 真的吗？那 ＿＿＿＿＿＿＿＿＿＿＿＿＿＿＿＿＿＿＿。（**chèn**…机会）

b. A: 你那么会做菜，做几个好菜请我吃吧！

　　B: ＿＿＿＿＿＿＿＿＿＿＿＿＿＿＿＿＿＿＿＿＿。（A 不如 B）

c. A: 这个旅馆怎么样：离车站十分钟，单人间，可是加床不要钱。

　　B: 听起来很好，如果 ＿＿＿＿＿＿＿＿＿＿＿＿＿＿＿。（再好不过了）

d. A: 这么大的 pizza 你一个人吃得完吗？

　　B: 当然吃不完。＿＿＿＿＿＿＿＿＿＿＿＿＿＿＿。（X分 **zhī** Y）

e. A: 你不是不喜欢运动吗？怎么开始上 **jiàn** 身房了呢？

　　B: ＿＿＿＿＿＿＿＿＿＿＿＿＿＿＿＿＿＿＿＿＿。（为了…而）

f. A: 我女朋友的父母请我去她家吃饭，你觉得我应该带什么好呢？

　　B: ＿＿＿＿＿＿＿＿＿＿＿＿＿＿＿＿＿＿＿＿＿（最好）

g. A: 每次我带朋友回来我爸爸就不高兴。他说我们的 **shēng** 音太大了。

　　B: 很 **jiǎn** 单。你就＿＿＿＿＿＿＿＿＿＿＿＿＿＿（**chèn**…的时候）

4.　Multiple choice

Using the context as your guide, choose the correct expression to complete each sentence, and then translate the sentences into English.

a. 星期一的机票比周末的便宜得多，如果 ＿＿＿＿＿＿ 就再好不过了。
　　1) 坐火车比坐飞机便宜
　　2) 你能星期一走
　　3) 星期六下午有机票

　　English:

b. 你难得 ＿＿＿＿＿＿，一定要 **chèn** 这个机会去 **fù** 近的旅游 **jǐng** 点。
　　1) 来一次加 **zhǒu**
　　2) 给我打电话
　　3) 喜欢旅游

　　English:

c. 这个房间一个晚上三百二十块，房间里有两张单人床，另外，＿＿＿＿＿＿＿。

    1) 打电话和上网都 **miǎn fèi**

    2) 请帮我 **dìng** 两间旅馆

    3) 一共 **dāi** 几天？

English:

5.   For rent

Below are two rental advertisements. Fill in the blanks with the words given, according to the context. Each word may be used more than once.

fù 近	张	又	另外
jiāotōng	离	**hán**	左右

> Advertisement #1:
>
> 单人房出 **zū**。一个月四百五十块。＿＿＿＿＿＿学校很近，走路五分钟。就在地铁站旁边，
>
> ＿＿＿＿＿＿方便。＿＿＿＿＿＿有商店、书店和电影院。房间里 **miān** 有 **zhuō** 子、椅子和
>
> 一＿＿＿＿＿＿单人床，**kuān** 带 **miǎn fèi**，不＿＿＿＿＿＿水电 (*water and electricity: utility*)，
>
> 跟同屋一起用一间厕所。

> Advertisement #2:
>
> 房间出 **zū**。一个月五百六十块。房间＿＿＿＿＿＿大又干净。里 **miān** 有双人床，电视、
>
> 书 **jià** 和 **guì** 子。＿＿＿＿＿＿，还有自己的厕所。＿＿＿＿＿＿水电，**kuān** 带 **miǎn fèi**。
>
> 到学校开车十五分钟＿＿＿＿＿＿，＿＿＿＿＿＿最近的地铁站差不多十分钟。

6.   Reading comprehension

Read the above two rental advertisements again, and then answer the following questions in Mandarin.

a. 什么人会喜欢第一个房间？为什么？

b. 什么人会喜欢第二个房间？为什么？

c. 如果是你，你会选哪一个房间，为什么？

7.   Form a cohesive paragraph

Rewrite these sentences, putting them in the correct order to form a cohesive paragraph about making reservations by phone in China.

a. 他们帮你找到旅馆以后，你可以问一问房间里有没有 **kuān** 带上网。

b. 这样你的旅馆就 **dìng** 好了。

c. 你先告诉他们你打算住几天，和你想住什么样的房间。

d. 最后你还可以问一下住旅馆的钱 **hán** 不 **hán** 早饭。

e. 在中国打电话 **dìng** 旅馆很方便也很容易。

f. 你觉得都可以了以后，你再把你的 **xìn** 用卡的号 **mǎ** 告诉他们。

g. 如果有，**kuān** 带是不是 **miǎn fèi**。

h. 另外你可以跟他们说你想住在城市的什么地方。

8.   Travel package jargon

Below are two very common expressions you will see in travel advertisements. Read the expressions, and then answer the questions below each one.

a. 机加酒两人同行一人半价
   1) 你觉得什么是 "机加酒"？

   2) "两人同行一人半价" 是什么意思？

b. **Xìn** 用卡机 **chǎng miǎn fèi jiē** 送。
   1) 什么是 "**jiē** 送"？

   2) **Shēn** 请这张 **xìn** 用卡有什么好的地方？

9. Write a travel advertisement

Write a short paragraph to promote this travel package. Your advertisement should be at least 100 characters in length.

(Vocabulary note: **Xiānggǎng** *Hong Kong*)

---

3 days/2 nights

HONG KONG Holiday Package

From March 01–31, [this year]

Book 2 weeks in advance to get US$10 discount!

US$280 per person

Package includes:

Round-trip air ticket via Hong Kong Express

Round-trip airport–hotel pickup

2 nights hotel accommodation at *Mountain View* or *Riverside Hotel*

Daily breakfast, free internet

Half-day city tour

AA STAR TRAVEL (681-2375/ Reserv_AAstar@yahoo.com)

_____

_____

_____

_____

_____

10. Reading

Read the following paragraph, and then answer the questions.

坐火车、飞机和汽车哪个最方便？

春节到了，每个人都想回家跟家人过年。到 **dǐ** 坐火车、飞机和汽车哪个最 **héshì**？别以为坐飞机一定是最贵的。我为大家看了一下今年的情 **kuàng**：比方说你在西 **ān** 工作，要回上海过年。从西 **ān** 到上海的飞机票，除 **xī** 夜那天下午打三折，只要三百八十元，时间不到两个钟头。而西 **ān** 到上海的火车票，**yìngwò** 两百九十，**ruǎnwò** 四百元，要花二十个钟头。汽车票价是三百五十元，要坐十七个钟头左右。所以，大家在买票以前，上网或者是给旅行社打电话，选一个 **jì shěng** 钱又方便的方法回家过年。

---

a. 你觉得，谁会 **yuàn** 意坐火车回上海？

b. 如果是你，你会选哪个？飞机、火车还是汽车？为什么？

11. Planning your spring break

You and your friends are going on a four-day trip to _____ (a destination of your choice) during spring break. Work in pairs to do a little research online about the expense (flight/train/rental car/lodging). Follow the style of Exercise 10 and write a paragraph to compare these choices.

Part I. Planning   In the following table, note your travel plans in English.

Destination: _____

Choice of transportation: (at least two options)

	option one	option two	(option three)
cost			
time			
pros			
cons			

Choice of lodging: (at least two options)

	option one	option two	(option three)
cost			
location			
pros			
cons			

Part II.   Write a paragraph in Mandarin comparing these choices and explaining your final choices of transportation and lodging. Your paragraph should be at least 120 characters in length.

_____

_____

_____

_____

_____

_____

_____

_____

Lesson 29 Workbook

 Listening and speaking

Structure drills

1. To each his own (Use and Structure note 29.1)

You will hear a statement saying that two people will do similar actions. Rephrase the information, saying that *each will do her own thing,* as in the example.

> **Example:**
> *You will hear:* 你回你的宿舍，我回我的宿舍。
> *You will say:* 我们 **gè** 回 **gè** 的宿舍。
> *Click "R" to hear the correct response:* 我们 **gè** 回 **gè** 的宿舍。

(a)   (b)   (c)   (d)   (e)   (f)   (g)   (h)

2. Every which way (Use and Structure note 29.2)

You will hear a statement saying that someone has done some action but has not reached the result that they wanted. Rephrase the information, saying that the person has done the action *every which way* and has not reached the desired result, as in the example.

> **Example:**
> *You will hear:* 我没找到我的手机。
> *You will say:* 我找来找去，还是没找到我的手机。
> *Click "R" to hear the correct response:* 我找来找去，还是没找到我的手机。

(a)   (b)   (c)   (d)   (e)   (f)   (g)   (h)

3.   Not unless (Use and Structure note 29.4)

You will hear a statement saying that if you don't do something, something else will not happen. Restate the information, saying that *unless* you do something, something else will not happen, as in the example.

Example:
You will hear: 如果你不帮助我，我不能写完读书报告。
You will say: 除非你帮助我，要不然我写不完读书报告。
Click "R" to hear the correct response: 除非你帮助我，要不然我写不完读书报告。

(a)   (b)   (c)   (d)   (e)   (f)   (g)   (h)   (i)   (j)

4.   More and more, Part I (Use and Structure note 29.7)

You will hear a statement saying that an action is happening *more and more* in a certain way. Restate the information, saying that *the more* something happens, *the more* of some quality it has, as in the example.

Example:
You will hear: 雨下得越来越大。
You will say: 雨越下越大。
Click "R" to hear the correct response: 雨越下越大。

(a)   (b)   (c)   (d)   (e)   (f)   (g)   (h)

5.   More and more, Part II (Use and Structure note 29.7)

You will hear a statement about doing something with some object. Restate the information, saying that *as for that object, the more* you do it *the more* some quality results, as in the example.

Example:
You will hear: 我 **ài** 吃 **là** 的菜。
You will say: **Là** 的菜，我越吃越 **ài** 吃。
Click "R" to hear the correct response: **Là** 的菜，我越吃越 **ài** 吃。

(a)   (b)   (c)   (d)   (e)   (f)

6.   More and more, Part III (Use and Structure note 29.7)

You will hear a statement about two situations. Restate the information, saying that *the more* the first action happens, *the more* true the second situation is, as in the example.

Example:
You will hear: 老师 **jiǎng yǔ** 法，我不懂。
You will say: 老师越 **jiǎng yǔ** 法，我越不懂。
Click "R" to hear the correct response: 老师越 **jiǎng yǔ** 法，我越不懂。

(a)   (b)   (c)   (d)   (e)   (f)   (g)   (h)

7.   Whatever you do (Use and Structure note 29.8)

You will hear a question asking what you are going to do. Reply that you will do whatever the other person does, as in the example.

Example:
You will hear: 你选什么课？
You will say: 你选什么课，我就选什么课。
Click "R" to hear the correct response: 你选什么课，我就选什么课。

(a)   (b)   (c)   (d)   (e)   (f)   (g)   (h)   (i)   (j)

8.   I'll do whatever I want (Use and Structure note 29.8)

You will hear a question asking what you are going to do. Reply that you will do whatever you want, as in the example.

Example:
You will hear: 你选什么课？
You will say: 我想选什么课就选什么课。
Click "R" to hear the correct response: 我想选什么课就选什么课。

(a)   (b)   (c)   (d)   (e)   (f)   (g)   (h)   (i)   (j)

Listening for information

1.   What do they need?

You will hear five statements about five people's physical states. Based on the statements, choose the item that each person needs most.

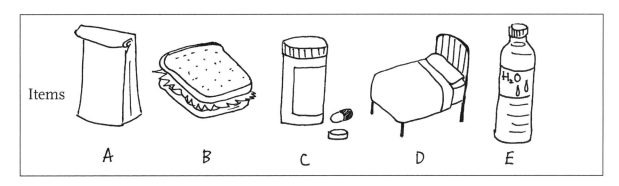

Items

A   B   C   D   E

a.   b.   c.   d.   e.

2.   More and more

(CD2: 52) You will hear four statements about Xiao Wang's daily life. Write down (in English) the reason and result that each statement describes.

statement	reason	result
1		
2		
3		
4		

3.   Ordering dinner

(CD2: 53) You will hear three customers ordering food and drink in a restaurant. Write their orders in English on the following form.

customer	dish	drink
1		
2		
3		

4.   Food delivery

(CD2: 54–55) Peiru is placing a telephone order at a nearby restaurant. Listen to her talking with the service person. Then, listen to the questions that follow, and answer them in Mandarin.

a.

b.

c.

d.

e.

f.

5.   McDonald's in China

You will hear a radio commercial for McDonald's Restaurants (**màidāngláo**) in China. **(CD2: 56)**
Listen to the commercial and write down the main points in English.

> Main points in the commercial:

6.   Birthday celebration

You and Zhang Xin are planning a birthday celebration for your good friend Cai Wen. **(CD2: 57)**
Zhang Xin left a voice message for you. Listen to the message and write an email in
Mandarin responding to her questions.

> Your response:

7.   A conversation

Your friend from China is asking you about dining in the USA. Listen to each question and **(CD2: 58)**
answer it in Mandarin.

a.

b.

c.

d.

e.

f.

8.   Study-abroad experience

(CD2: 59) Jackie is talking about her experience studying in China. Listen to her talk, and then indicate whether each of the following statements is true (T) or false (F). We have not learned the word she uses for 'study abroad' but you should be able to identify it within the context of her talk.

a. (   ) Jackie thinks it is best to live in a university dormitory.

b. (   ) Jackie recommended the Chinese Program in Yunnan to everyone.

c. (   ) Jackie learned a lot about the daily life of Chinese people during her study abroad.

d. (   ) Jackie's Chinese improved by talking with her Chinese roommate.

 9.   Travel plans

(CD2: 60) He Xiang is telling her friends about her trip. Answer the following questions, based on her description.

a. How did they arrange the trip?
   1) with a travel agency
   2) by themselves
   3) via the college student center
   4) through a traveler's hotline

b. Which fact about Hainan is true?
   1) Hainan is larger than Taiwan.
   2) The weather there is always warm.
   3) The mountain area on the island is cool.
   4) Not many tourists are on the island.

c. Which of the following facts about their trip is true, based on He Xiang's description?
   1) They spent more than four hours on the plane to Hainan.
   2) They stayed in Hainan for a week.
   3) They ate special local food every day.
   4) They enjoyed all kinds of fruit.

 10.   Dialogue

(CD2: 61) Mr. and Mrs. Wang are talking about their Friday dinner plans. Answer the following questions, based on their conversation.

a. What fact correctly describes Mr. Wang's reservation?
   1) He reserved a table for twelve people.
   2) He ordered a meal of ten dishes.
   3) He reserved a private room.
   4) He made the reservation at a Cantonese restaurant.

b. What did Mr. and Mrs. Wang say about Mr. and Mrs. Zhang?
   1) They may not come for dinner.
   2) They will come later due to another event.
   3) They do not eat meat or fish.
   4) They like that restaurant very much.

c. What food or drink will they likely order?
   1) roast duck
   2) a pork dish
   3) beer
   4) soft drinks

Reading and writing

Focus on Chinese characters

1. Number of strokes

Indicate the number of strokes used in writing each of the following characters.

a. 报 ＿＿   f. 健 ＿＿

b. 肚 ＿＿   g. 迎 ＿＿

c. 忘 ＿＿   h. 费 ＿＿

d. 预 ＿＿   i. 像 ＿＿

e. 换 ＿＿   j. 紧 ＿＿

2. Which character?

Circle the character in each line that corresponds to the meaning on the left.

a. **jué** (**juédìng** *decide*)   决   快

b. **qīng** *green-blue*   情   青

c. **tīng** (**cāntīng** *cafeteria*)   订   厅

d. **gòu** *enough*   句   够

e. **bǎo** *full*   饱   抱

f. **fù** (**fùjìn** *vicinity*)   附   腐

g. **fèi** *expense, fee*   费   附

h. **yù** (**yùdìng** *make a reservation*)   顺   预

i. **wèi** *flavor, aroma*   末   味

j. **yíng** (**huānyíng** *welcome*)   迎   卯

k. **xiàng** *resemble*   像   象

l. **jiàn** (**jiàn shēn** *exercise, work out*)   建   健

3.   First strokes

Write the first two strokes of each of the following characters.

a. 香 _____   f. 预 _____

b. 风 _____   g. 紧 _____

c. 瓶 _____   h. 附 _____

d. 线 _____   i. 费 _____

e. 换 _____   j. 糖 _____

4.   Missing strokes

Complete each character by writing in the missing strokes.

a.   千   **xiāng** *fragrant*

b.   纟   **xiàn** *thread, line*

c.   彳   **yíng** (**huānyíng** *welcome*)

d.   口   **wèi** *flavor, aroma*

e.   亡   **wàng** *forget*

f.   厂   **tīng** (**cāntīng** *cafeteria*)

g.   并   **píng** *bottle*

h.   冫   **jué** (**juédìng** *decide*)

i.   扌   **bào** *report*

j.   勹   **gòu** *enough*

5. Total strokes

Rewrite this list of characters, arranging the characters in terms of their total number of strokes. Begin your list with the character with the fewest strokes.

肚	醋	瓶	费	川	预	忘	香	决	附	像	订	紧	换	风	报	饱	青	够	线

6. Radicals

Here is a list of characters that we have learned through this lesson. Rewrite each character in the row next to its radical.

厕　酒　换　紧　忘　像　净　预　决　绍　练
冷　思　打　准　级　醋　厅　颜　想　健　价

心	
西	
冫	
纟(糸)	
厂	
扌	
亻	
页	

7. Character sleuth: Look for the phonetic

Group the characters below in terms of their rhymes or near-rhymes. Write the characters that rhyme with each other in the column on the right. Write the "phonetic," the shared part of each character, in the column on the left. There are at least twelve sets of characters that rhyme or partially rhyme and share a phonetic component among these characters.

房　饱　并　订　想　土　请　钟　旁
厅　少　重　汽　肚　种　炒　瓶　长
张　情　相　院　包　远　懂　气　放

phonetic	characters that rhyme or almost rhyme and share a phonetic component

8.   Scrambled sentences

Rewrite these phrases as sentences, putting the words in the correct order to match the English translations.

a. 茄子 / 觉得 / 鱼 / 糖醋 / 鱼香 / 不如 / 我

I think that sweet and sour fish is not as good as eggplant in yuxiang sauce.

b. 准备 / 菜 / 的 / 做 / 住 / 学 / 中国 / 中国 / 她 / 几年 / 为了 / 地道 / 去

In order to learn how to cook authentic Chinese food, she is preparing to go to China to live for a year.

c. 为 / 菜 / 的 / 这 / 特别 / 你 / 个 / 是 / 做

This dish was made especially for you.

d. 特别 / 川菜 / 很 / 味道 / 的

The flavor of Sichuan cuisine is unique.

9.   Dictionary skills

Following the instructions in Lesson 17 of the Textbook, look up these characters in a Chinese dictionary and provide the requested information:

a. 读
   pronunciation:
   meaning:
   one two-character word or phrase in which it occurs:

b. 饿

pronunciation:

meaning:

one two-character word or phrase in which it occurs:

c. 各

pronunciation:

meaning:

one two-character word or phrase in which it occurs:

10. Find the incorrect characters

Xiao Zhang has written an email to one of his friends from Chinese class back in the USA, but he has written ten characters incorrectly. Circle his mistakes and write the correct characters in the answer sheet below. Then, translate the paragraph into English.

学交附近新开了一家四川风味的餐听。我作天给他们的丁餐热线打电话订了一个糖醋鱼、一个鱼相茄子和一瓶可口可乐，让他们把菜关到我的宿舍。菜很块就送到了。味到很好，我吃得很包。饱得我都快走不动了。看来我得多去几次建身房了。

a. _____   b. _____   c. _____   d. _____   e. _____

f. _____   g. _____   h. _____   i. _____   j. _____

English:

11.   Reading for the main ideas

The following paragraph contains a few characters that we have not yet learned, but you should be able to "read around them" and understand the main points of the passage. Read the paragraph for the main ideas and answer the questions that follow in English.

饮食和文化

有的人认为从吃的东西的样子上，就能看出来中国文化和美国文化很不相同。中国人都喜欢吃饺子。从外边看，看不出来饺子里边有什么，可能是鸡肉的，也可能是牛肉的。可能是茄子的，也可能是西红柿的。这些东西都包在饺子里边了。只有吃的时候才能知道。而美国的"三明治"和"汉堡包"呢，是肉的还是鱼的，有没有西红柿，从外边可以看得清清楚楚。有的人说中国的文化和美国的文化也是这样。中国人做一件事情，你从外边看不出来为什么，而美国人做一件事情你就可以看出来。你觉得这种说法对吗？

---

a. What is the author comparing in this paragraph?

b. 三明治 and 汉堡包 are foods commonly eaten in the USA. Based on the pronunciation of the characters that you know in each food name, and *without* looking up the words online or in a dictionary or asking your teacher, identify each of these foods.

c. What is the author's theory about the difference between the things that he is comparing? Do you agree? Why or why not?

Focus on structure

1.   Unless you do this (Use and Structure note 29.4)

Meili and Youwen are talking about a trip that Meili is planning to Sichuan. Youwen is giving Meili advice. Translate a.–c. into English, and d.–e. into Mandarin.

a. 除非你早一点订票，要不然你可能买不到 **ruǎnwò** 票。

b. 除非你订商业区的饭店，要不然 **jiāotōng** 不会方便。

c. 四川很多地方不用 **xìn** 用卡。除非你带现金，要不然你买不了东西。

d. I have heard that hotels have broadband internet connections but the rooms don't have computers. Unless you bring your own computer you won't be able to use the internet.

e. Unless you are used to hearing Sichuan people speak, you may not understand what they say.

2. **The more you do it (Use and Structure note 29.7)**

Guoqiang is asking Dawei about a number of things. Translate Dawei's responses into Mandarin.

a. Q: 你觉得川菜怎么样？

A: _____

(I think it's really spicy. But it's strange. The more I eat it, the more I like it.)

b. Q: 经济课怎么样？

A: _____

(The more I study, the harder it gets.)

c. Q: 你喜欢喝茶还是喝可乐？

A: _____

(I prefer tea. The more cola I drink, the thirstier I get.)

d. Q: 我们今天吃饺子，好不好？

A: _____

(I don't want to eat dumplings again. The more I eat them, the fatter I get.)

3. **As you please, Part I (Use and Structure note 29.8)**

Translate a.–d. to English, and translate e.–h. into Mandarin, using the pattern QW 就 QW.

a. 哪个旅行 **shè** 便宜我们就跟哪个旅行社订。

b. 你把相机 **jiè** 给谁了我就去跟谁要回来。

c. 哪件事重要我们就先做哪件事。

d. 你说什么地方好玩我们就去什么地方。

e. I'll go wherever you go.

f. We'll select whatever method saves money.

g. We'll stay (live) at whatever hotel you make reservations for.

h. We'll go whenever it is convenient.

4.   As you please, Part II (Use and Structure note 29.8)

Youwen and Meili are both in a good mood as they finish a day of shopping and are discussing plans for the rest of the day. Write the responses to each of these suggestions in complete Mandarin sentences, using the pattern QW 就 QW, and using the question word in parentheses after each suggestion.

a. 这双鞋很不 **cuò**。你看，我买不买？（什么）

b. 我们去咖啡馆喝一点咖啡吧。（哪儿）

c. 我们晚上吃中国饭，行吗？（什么）

d. 我们请那个新的学生跟我们一起吃饭吧。（谁）

e. 吃饭以后，我们去看那个日本电影，好不好？（哪）

5.   Scrambled sentences

Rewrite these phrases into sentences, putting them in the right order to match the English translations.

a. 穿 / 应该 / **pí** 鞋 / 好的 / 要 / 一双 / 舒服 /越 / 越

With an expensive pair of shoes, it should be that the more you wear them the more comfortable they are.

b. 四川菜 / 有 / 的 / 吃饭 / 哪儿 / 上 / 好吃 / 就 / 哪儿 / 我们

Wherever there is delicious Sichuan food, let's go there to eat. (Let's go eat wherever there is delicious Sichuan food.)

c. 看 / 特别 / 开开 / 新车 / 舒服 / 你 / 开起来

Drive it and see. New cars are very comfortable to drive.

d. 会 / 不 / 下雨 / 明天 / 一定

It won't necessarily rain tomorrow. (It may not rain tomorrow.)

e. 做 / **ài** 吃去 / 妈妈 / 菜 / 吃 / 吃来 / 还是 / 最 / 的 / 我

I've eaten everywhere, and I think that the food that mom cooks is the best.

f. 那么 / 不 / 一 **bān** / 少 / 中国 / 让 / 穿得 / 父母 / **hái** 子

Chinese parents generally don't let their children wear so little.

6. Translate into English

Translate these sentences into English.

a. 青菜、水果会让你越吃越年 **qīng**。

b. 这个照相机我越看越喜欢，如果便宜一点就再好不过了。

c. 你试试看这个手机用起来容易不容易。

d. 虽然商店都在打折，但是我看来看去也没有看到一件喜欢的衣服。

e. 我每天 **dú** 书 **dú** 累了，就出去走一走，放 **sōng** 一下。

f. 自己做饭不一定比去外边买麻烦。

g. 做作业可以大家在一起做，但是考试只能 **gè** 写 **gè** 的。

h. 我为了帮他找书包，已经在车站里外跑来跑去跑了半个钟头了。

7. Translate into Mandarin

Translate these sentences into Mandarin, using characters where we have learned them.

a. His story made us feel like the more we listened the sadder we were.

b. Try it and see. I think that this pen may be broken.

c. Ask and see whether she wants to go traveling with us.

d. The most expensive restaurants are not necessarily the most delicious.

e. Listen. Is that Xiao Wang's voice?

f. Let's have a little talk. Why did you decide to change majors?

g. There aren't any good restaurants in the vicinity. We've eaten all around and every time we go to that Cantonese restaurant.

h. This is the time when the roads are most crowded. Unless you take a subway, you won't be able to get to the airport in an hour.

Focus on communication

1.   Dialogue comprehension

Study the Lesson 29 Narrative and Dialogue. Then, read the following statements and indicate whether they are true (T) or false (F).

a. (   ) 春假 **jiéshù** 以后，大家又忙着学习。

b. (   ) 学校附近的中国餐馆多极了，可是国强连想都没想就决定要吃四川菜。

c. (   ) 他们没有订位子就去餐厅了，所以服务员要他们等三十分钟。

d. (   ) 大为又 **kě** 又 **è** 不想等，所以他们决定换一家餐厅。

e. (   ) 他们先点了 **pí** 酒和可乐。

f. (   ) 餐厅里没有 **bīng** 茶。

g. (   ) 大为 **ài** 吃四川菜，可是他觉得四川菜太 **là** 了。

h. (   ) 上次大为来这家饭馆吃四川菜，后来吃坏肚子了。

i. (   ) 他们一共点了六个菜，都是 **là** 的。

j. (   ) 服务员上 **cuò** 菜，所以送了他们一个烧茄子。

k. (   ) 美丽最 **ài** 吃茄子，她一高兴就多给了一些小费。

l. (   ) 他们把菜都吃完了，还打包了一个鱼香茄子带走。

m. (   ) 你可以预先打电话给这家餐馆订餐。

2.   What do you say?

What do you say in each of the following situations? Type your answers, using characters where we have learned them, and email them to your Chinese teacher.

a.   Ask your mom to teach you a couple of her specialty dishes.

b.   Ask the waiter to bring you a glass of water without ice. Explain to your friend that in general you do not drink ice water.

c.   Invite everyone to come to your house for a karaoke party this Saturday because you want everyone to relax after the exam.

d.   You just made a dish. Ask your friend to have a taste of your authentic _____ (dish of your choice).

e.   You have just arrived at the restaurant. Tell the waiter your last name, and say that you have a reservation for 6:30 for a party of seven.

f. As a waiter, apologize to your customer that the restaurant is very crowded right now, and tell him that the possible wait time is an hour and a half. Ask the customer for his last name and ask him how many people are in his party.

g. You refuse to go shopping with your friend now (V 不了) because you are thirsty and hungry and tired.

h. Tell the waiter you don't drink hot tea. Ask what other drinks they have.

i. Tell your mom you'll eat whatever she has because you are starving.

j. Ask the waiter to switch the chicken cubes in *gongbao chicken* to tofu because you don't eat meat.

k. As a waiter, ask the customers if they want to take the leftover dishes home.

l. As a waiter, thank your customers for coming and invite them to come back again next time.

m. You are wondering (thought it was really strange) where you placed the beer and juice that you just bought.

3.   Complete the mini-dialogues

Use the structure in parentheses to complete each mini-dialogue.

a. A: 你这么喜欢看电影，那你说说看，哪国的电影最好看？

   B: 这很难说，_____。（**gè** 有 **gè** 的）

b. A: 你怎么 _____？（V 来 V 去）

   B: 因为我穿这件 **chènshān** 看起来最 **shòu**!

c. A: 真 **zāogāo**，我怎么忘了带钱了？

   B: _____，要不然我们就回不了家了。
   （**Xìngkuī**）

d. Patient (calling): 请问，我可以跟叶 **Yī** 生 **yuē** 今天下午看 **bìng** 吗？

   Receptionist: 对不起，今天下午人特别多，_____。
   （除非 ... 要不然 ...）

e. A: 怎么样，这家饭馆的川味 **niú** 肉 **miàn** 做得地道吧？

   B: 真不 **cuò**，_____。（越 V 越）

f. A: 这双鞋看起来这么小，我怎么可能穿得了？

   B: _____ （VV看）

g. A: 今天这么热，你想去哪儿？

   B: _____ （QW 就 QW）

4.   Complete and translate

Using the context as your guide, choose the correct expression to complete each sentence, and then translate the sentences into English.

a. 在商店 **diū** 了钱包 (*wallet*) 很难找回来。除非 _____，要不然大概没有 **xīwàng**。
   1) 你找到了
   2) 你把地址和电话给服务员
   3) 你刚走出来就发现，马上回去找

   English:

b. 这个旅行社 **guǎng** 告的 **jǐng** 点我都没有兴趣，看来看去 _____。
   1) 我觉得我还是跟朋友自己出去旅行吧
   2) 贵极了
   3) 我什么地方都想去

   English:

c. 对不起，那本书已经卖完了，我们刚跟商店订了书。这样吧，_____
   1) 这两本书 **miǎn** 费送给你。
   2) 给我你的电话号码，书送来了我就给你打电话。
   3) 你为什么一定要买那本书？

   English:

5.   Ordering in a restaurant

Part I.   Read the following passage about Xiao Zhang's birthday celebration dinner, using the context to help you choose the correct word or phrase to complete each sentence.

　　这个周末是我的生日。小谢上星期开始就 _____（a. 用 b. **chèn** c. 拿）我不 **zhù** 意的时候，_____（a. **yuē** b. 带 c. 订）了小高，小叶和小王、在最近新开的四川饭馆 _____（a. 点 b. 带 c. 订）了位子。昨天下课，他来学校 **jiē** 我，路上什么也没有说，我觉得 _____（a. 累 b. 麻烦 c. **qíguài**）极了。等我 _____（a. 认为 b. 以为 c. 发现）大家都在饭馆门口等我，我高兴得不得了，没想到他们这么早就帮我 _____（a. 过 b. 吃 c. **yuē**）生日。小高说，_____（a. 只要 b. **yuàn** 意 c. 为了）给我一个 *surprise*，小谢计划了很久呢。

　　这家饭馆的拿手菜 _____（a. 可能 b. 当然 c. **kǒng** 怕）是四川菜。我最 **ài** 吃 **là** 的，所以我 _____（a. 马上 b. 事先 c. 决定）点了 **là** 子鸡 **dīng** 和 **gōngbǎo niú** 肉。小高喜欢吃青菜，她点了 **bái** 菜和鱼香茄子。小谢说我们点什么他 _____（a. 都 b. 也 c. 就）吃什么，不过他一定要点青 **dǎo pí** 酒。还帮我们都点了可乐和 **bīng** 茶。小王说他不能吃 **là** 的，_____（a. 另外 b. **xìngkuī** c. 再说）这家餐厅也有不 **là** 的菜。他怕吃 **là** _____（a. 可是 b. 而且 c. 所以）最喜欢吃 **dòufu**，就要了一个烧 **dòufu**，还点了一个糖醋鱼。小叶觉得这些菜已经 _____（a. 不够 b. 很地道 c. 够了），所以她只点了麻 **là** 饺子，因为她说 _____（a. 从来 b. 到 **dǐ** c. 的 **què**）没吃过 **là** 饺子，想 **cháng cháng** 看。小谢点了 **mǐ** 饭，不过服务员说他们的炒饭特别有名，所以我们又把

mǐ 饭 _____（a. 换成 b. 炒成 c. 加）炒饭，还特别请他们别放 **là** 的，这样小王就可以吃了。

等服务员 _____（a. 点菜 b. 上菜 c. 打包）的时候，我们一边喝 **yǐnliào** 一边 **liáo** 天。这家饭馆上菜上得很块，一下子 _____（a. 除非 b. 除了 c. 并且）烧 **dòufu** 以外，别的菜都来了。_____（a. 然后 b. 后来 c. 以后）服务员发现他忘了帮我们点烧 **dòufu**，马上说这个菜送给我们，另外，再送了一个 西红 **shì** 炒鸡 **dàn**。

这些菜 _____（a. **jì** b. 虽然 c. 而且）好吃又地道，我们都吃得饱得不得了。开学以后大家忙着学习，_____（a. 难过 b. 难得 c. 最好）有机会在一起吃饭，我觉得这是最好的生日 **lǐ wù**！

Part II.　Answer the following questions about the passage in Part I in Mandarin.

a. 为什么他们昨天吃饭？昨天到 **dǐ** 是不是小张的生日？

b. 这个生日晚会是谁计划的？谁来 **cān** 加了？

c. 他们点的菜，哪些是 **là** 的？哪些不 **là**？

d. 为什么他们点了炒饭？炒饭 **là** 不 **là**？

e. 请你 **tián** 一下这个 **biǎo**:

	小张	小谢	小高	小叶	小王
喜欢吃什么/不能吃什么					
点了什么菜					

f. 西红 **shì** 炒鸡 **dàn** 为什么不算钱？

g. 小张的生日 **lǐ wù** 是什么？

6.　What did they say?

You are a participant at the dinner party described in Exercise 5. Write (or type) in Mandarin what each person said in the following situations.

a. Xiao Zhang was eager to find out where Xiao Xie was taking him in the car. So he kept asking Xiao Xie where exactly ("after all") they were going.

b. Xiao Xie explained why he picked this particular restaurant for Xiao Zhang.

c. Xiao Xie insisted that they order beer because Xiao Zhang was turning twenty-one!

d. Xiao Gao knows Xiao Wang does not eat spicy food. She suggested some non-spicy dishes to Xiao Wang.

e. Xiao Ye was very excited when she discovered "spicy dumplings" and decided to give them a try.

f. The waiter recommended that they order fried rice instead of white rice.

g. Xiao Wang asked the waiter about the missing simmered tofu. The waiter apologized for it and made amends immediately.

h. Xiao Xie asked the waiter to bring the bill. The waiter asked if they wanted to take the leftovers with them.

i. Xiao Zhang expressed his gratitude to everyone after dinner.

j. The waiter saw them off at the door.

7.   Restaurant jargon

This exercise includes very common expressions used in Chinese restaurants. You have not learned all of them, but you should be able to figure out the meanings from the context. Read each sentence and answer the questions that follow about its meaning.

a. 这边吃还是外带？
  1) 你觉得"外带"的意思是什么？

  2) 你觉得这句话是什么时候说的？
     A. 在饭馆门口的时候
     B. 要点菜的时候
     C. 吃饱的时候

  3) 你觉得"外带"和"外送"有什么不一样？

b. 对不起，我们不接 **shòu** 订位，也不 **shōu xìn** 用卡。
  1) 你觉得什么是"接 **shòu**"？

  2) 请问去这个饭馆一定得带什么？

c. 你觉得"加 **miàn** 不加价"是什么意思？

d. 如果要把 **bái miàn** 换成黄 **miàn**，请先告知。
  1) 你觉得"请先告知"是什么意思？

  2) 这家饭馆的 **miàn** 一 **bān** 都是 **bái miàn** 还是黄 **miàn**？

e. 一家红茶店的门口 **tiē** 着一张 **guǎng** 告："买大送小"。你觉得，"大"和"小"是什么？

f. 你觉得"今日特餐"是什么意思？

8. Give me some advice

Xiao Mei always has trouble making decisions. Luckily she has good friends who are always there for her. Read the situations below involving Xiao Mei and her friends. Use the two structures that express condition: 如果…就 and 除非…要不然, to complete everyone's reply. For each situation, come up with your own suggestion at the end as well, using either of the structures.

Situation 1:

小美：我现在有两个工作机会。一个在学校餐厅，一个在离学校半个钟头的书店。餐厅的工作没有意思，但是时间很不 **cuò**。书店的工作我比较喜欢，可是离学校太远了。怎么 **bàn**？

青青：别去书店。除非＿＿＿＿＿＿＿＿＿＿＿＿＿＿，要不然我觉得去书店太麻烦了。

天明：我觉得书店的工作比较好。一个星期工作几天？如果＿＿＿＿＿＿＿＿＿＿＿＿，我可以送你去。

心宜：你还是去书店吧。书店可以学到很多事。除非这个工作跟你以后的工作没有关系，要不然 ＿＿＿＿＿＿＿＿＿＿＿＿＿＿＿＿。

Your suggestion: ＿＿

Situation 2:

小美：快帮我决定，买这条红色的 **qún** 子好，还是买那件 **bái** 色的 **chènshān** 好？

青青：这个红色穿在你身上有点 **qíguài**。除非这条 **qún** 子正在打折，＿＿＿＿＿＿＿＿＿＿＿＿＿＿＿＿＿＿＿＿＿＿＿＿＿＿＿＿。

天明：当然买 **bái** 色的 **chènshān**！＿＿＿＿＿＿＿＿＿＿＿＿＿＿＿，**pèi** 什么都好看。红 **qún** 子也不 **cuò**，如果 ＿＿＿＿＿＿＿＿＿＿＿＿＿＿，就两件都买吧。

心宜：你先想一想你有几件 **bái chènshān**。＿＿＿＿＿＿＿＿＿＿＿＿＿＿＿＿＿＿＿＿，要不然我觉得你应该买红 **qún** 子，有时候也得换个不一样衣服的吧！

Your suggestion: ＿＿

Lesson 30 Workbook

Listening and speaking

1. S 把NP₁ V 作 NP₂ *S sees/calls NP₁ NP₂* (Use and Structure note 30.5)

You will hear three noun phrases, followed by either 看作 or 叫作. Use the information to say the subject considers/calls NP₁ NP₂, as in the example.

> **Example:**
> *You will hear:* 中国人，汉语的标准语，**pǔ** 通话，叫作
> *You will say:* 中国人把汉语的标准语叫作 **pǔ** 通话。
> *Click "R" to hear the correct response:* 中国人把汉语的标准语叫作 **pǔ** 通话。

(a)　　(b)　　(c)　　(d)　　(e)　　(f)

2. Marking the verb in a noun description: 所 V 的, Part I
(Use and Structure note 30.6)

You will hear a statement involving a noun phrase in which the description involves a verb. Restate the information, adding 所 before the verb, as in the example. Notice that in many of these sentences, the main noun (the noun that follows the description + 的) is omitted.

> **Example:**
> *You will hear:* 这就是他问的问题。
> *You will say:* 这就是他所问的问题。
> *Click "R" to hear the correct response:* 这就是他所问的问题。

(a)　　(b)　　(c)　　(d)　　(e)　　(f)　　(g)

3. Marking the verb in a noun description: 所 V 的, Part II
(Use and Structure note 30.6)

You will hear a sentence involving a subject, verb, and object. Restate the information as a description of the object, placing 所 before the verb, as in the example. Translations are provided for the example to help you understand the structure.

Example:
You will hear: 他学方言。 *He studies dialects.*
You will say: 他所学的方言 *the dialects that he studies*
Click "R" to hear the correct response: 他所学的方言 *the dialects that he studies*

(a)   (b)   (c)   (d)   (e)   (f)   (g)   (h)   (i)   (j)

4. **Wúlùn** + QW *no matter (who, what, when, where, how, what quality)*
(Use and Structure note 30.8)

You will hear a sentence followed by a question phrase. Restate the sentence using **wúlùn** and the question phrase to say *no matter (who, what, when, where, how, what quality)*, as in the example.

Example:
You will hear: 学生都得 **cān** 加考试。（谁）
You will say: **Wúlùn** 谁都得 **cān** 加考试。
Click "R" to hear the correct response: **Wúlùn** 谁都得 **cān** 加考试。

(a)   (b)   (c)   (d)   (e)   (f)   (g)   (h)   (i)

5. **Jíshǐ** S$_1$ 也 VP/S$_2$ *even if/even though S$_1$, VP/S$_2$*
(Use and Structure note 30.10).

You will hear two actions. Restate these using *jíshǐ*… 也 to say that *even if/even though* the first action occurs, the second will not occur.

Example:
You will hear: 我知道，我不告诉你
You will say: **Jíshǐ** 我知道，我也不告诉你。
Click "R" to hear the correct response: **Jíshǐ** 我知道，我也不告诉你。

(a)   (b)   (c)   (d)   (e)   (f)   (g)   (h)   (i)   (j)

6. A 跟 B 没有直接的关系 *There isn't a direct connection between A and B*

You will hear two phrases. Say that there isn't any direct relationship between the two phrases, as in the example.

Example:

You will hear: 书写，发音

You will say: 书写跟发音没有直接的关系。

Click "R" to hear the correct response: 书写跟发音没有直接的关系。

(a)   (b)   (c)   (d)   (e)   (f)   (g)

7. Influencing others: 影 **xiǎng**

You will hear a statement saying that doing something influences other people or other things. Restate the sentence, saying that doing something *has an influence on* others, as in the example.

Example:

You will hear: 你大 **shēng** 说话影 **xiǎng** 别人学习。

You will say: 你大 **shēng** 说话对别人学习有影 **xiǎng**。

Click "R" to hear the correct response: 你大 **shēng** 说话对别人学习有影 **xiǎng**。

(a)   (b)   (c)   (d)   (e)   (f)   (g)

Listening for information

1. The Tower of Babel

(CD2: 65) You will hear five students talking about the dialects they speak. Based on their statements, fill out the form.

student	hometown	dialect spoken	alternative name for the dialect
#1			
#2			
#3			
#4			
#5			

2. Learning Chinese

Mali is describing her experience learning different aspects of Chinese. Listen to her (CD2: 66) description and write down her comments in English.

aspects	experience
characters	
pronunciation	
tones	
grammar	

3. Two cuisines

Mark is asking his roommate Wang An, an exchange student from China, about Hunan (CD2: 67–68) and Sichuan cuisines. Answer the questions that follow in Chinese characters, based on Wang An's reply. His reply includes one word that you have not learned, but you should be able to "listen around" that word and understand his remarks.

a.

b.

c.

d.

4. Self-reflection

(CD2: 69–71) Wen Ding, Baojia, and Xiao'ai are taking turns talking about their strengths and weaknesses. Listen to their remarks, and write down their self-evaluations in English, using the form below.

person	strengths	weaknesses
1. Wen Ding		
2. Baojia		
3. Xiao'ai		

5. Language study commercial

(CD2: 72) You will hear a radio commercial for a language-study program. Listen to the commercial and write (in English) the three main points stated in the commercial.

Three main points of the commercial:

1.

2.

3.

6. A conversation

(CD2: 73) Your Chinese friend is asking you some questions about your experience learning Chinese. Listen to each question and answer it in Mandarin.

a.

b.

c.

d.

e.

f.

7. Class presentation

You will hear a phone message from Shuting about the class presentation. Listen to her **(CD2: 74)** message and write an email responding to her questions. The message includes two words that you have not learned, but you should be able to "listen around" the words and guess their meanings.

> Your email responding to Shuting's phone message:

8. Dialogue I

Nike is telling Zufang about the Chinese linguistics course that he is taking this semester. **(CD2: 75)** Answer the questions, based on their conversation.

a. What is the focus of the Chinese linguistics course taken by the male student?
   1) history
   2) characters
   3) grammar
   4) dialects

b. What led him to take this Chinese linguistics course?
   1) He is a linguistics major.
   2) He is studying Chinese.
   3) He is not clear about Chinese grammar.
   4) The professor is excellent.

c. What other course is he taking?
   1) Introduction to Linguistics
   2) Phonology
   3) American Dialects
   4) English Grammar

9. Dialogue II

Yaru and Weisi are discussing where to live while in college. **(CD2: 76)**

a. Why does the male student want to move out of his home?
   1) His home is far from the university.
   2) He wants to be away from his parents.
   3) He would like to try campus life.
   4) He and his good friend want to share a place.

b. What does the female student say about living in a dorm?
1) It is close to the classrooms.
2) You need to get used to living with other people.
3) You will meet many interesting people.
4) It is much more expensive.

c. What is it like living off-campus, according to the woman?
1) It is inexpensive.
2) It is convenient.
3) It is lonely.
4) It is far from the school.

 # Reading and writing

Focus on Chinese characters

1.   Number of strokes

Indicate the number of strokes used in writing each of the following characters.

a. 错 _____   f. 怪 _____

b. 题 _____   g. 之 _____

c. 湾 _____   h. 德 _____

d. 底 _____   i. 标 _____

e. 笔 _____   j. 既 _____

2.   Which character?

Circle the character in each line that corresponds to the meaning on the left.

a. **jiè** *borrow, loan*   借   错

b. **hái** *child*   该   孩

c. **chéng** *become, turn into*   城   成

d. **dǐ** (**dàodǐ** *in fact, after all*)   低   底

e. **gè** *each*   各   备

f. **jiǎn** (**jiǎndān** *simple*)   简   筒

g. **bǐ** *pen*   笺   笔

h. **tōng** (**pǔtōng** *ordinary*)   通   桶

i. **shěng** *save*   省   告

j. **jiǎng** *speak*   井   讲

k. **jiē** *pick up a guest*   搂   接

l. **tí** (**wèntí** *question, problem*)   提   题

3.   First strokes

Write the first two strokes of each of the following characters.

a. 各 ____   f. 通 ____

b. 既 ____   g. 湾 ____

c. 之 ____   h. 台 ____

d. 简 ____   i. 孩 ____

e. 成 ____   j. 错 ____

4.   Missing strokes

Complete each character by writing in the missing strokes.

a.   亠   **yán** (**yǔyán** *language*)

b.   彳   **dé** (**Déguó** *Germany*)

c.   忄   **guài** (**nánguài** *no wonder*)

d.   小   **shěng** *save*

e.   夕   **gè** *each, every*

f.   亻   **jiè** *borrow, loan*

g.   ⼂   **bǐ** *pen*

h.   讠   **yǔ** (**yǔyán** *language*)

i.   卩   **jì** *both*

j.   广   **dǐ** (**dàodǐ** *in the end, after all*)

5. Total strokes

Rewrite this list of characters, arranging the characters in terms of their total number of strokes. Begin your list with the character with the fewest strokes.

题	省	简	湾	既	怪	底	成	言	德	各	之	借	错	通	孩	台	讲	接	语	笔

6. Radicals

Here is a list of characters that we have learned through this lesson. Rewrite each character in the row next to its radical.

通	题	游	拉	错	种	流	报	借	怪	订
语	计	迎	情	湾	像	讲	健	预	标	接

忄	
亻	
扌	
页	
讠	
氵	
木	
辶	
钅	

7. Character sleuth: Look for the phonetic

Group the characters below in terms of their rhymes or near-rhymes. Write the characters that rhyme with each other in the column on the right. Write the "phonetic," the shared part of each character, in the column on the left. There are eleven sets of characters that rhyme or partially rhyme and share a phonetic component among these characters.

五	远	爬	间	完	错	瓶	把	厅	简	客	忘
百	妹	玩	各	少	钟	懂	小	重	京	味	忙
中	炒	爸	订	并	醋	园	语	影	种	怕	吧

phonetic	characters that rhyme or almost rhyme and share a phonetic component

8.   Scrambled sentences

Rewrite these phrases as sentences, putting the words in the correct order to match the English translations.

a. 的 / 特点 / 方言 / 各 / 各 / 中国 / 有

As for Chinese dialects, each has its own characteristics.

b. 子 / 的 / 孩 / 错 / 那 / 菜 / 真 / 个 / 做 / 不

The food that the child cooked is really not bad.

c. 会 / 会 / 德 / 讲/ 底 / 语 / 你 / 不 / 到

Can you really speak German?

d. 笔 / 把 / 我 / 你 / 借 / 请 / 的 / 给

Please loan me your pen.

9. Dictionary skills

Following the instructions in Lesson 17 of the Textbook, look up these characters in a Chinese dictionary and provide the requested information.

a. 处

  pronunciation:

  meaning:

  one two-character word or phrase in which it occurs:

b. 猜

  pronunciation:

  meaning:

  one two-character word or phrase in which it occurs:

c. 使

  pronunciation:

  meaning:

  one two-character word or phrase in which it occurs:

10. Find the incorrect characters

Xiao Zhang has written this essay for his Chinese class, but he has written eight characters incorrectly. Circle his mistakes and write the correct characters in the answer sheet below. Then, translate the paragraph into English.

> 我觉得汉语非常难学。弟一，汉语里有 **shēngdiào**，但是英语里没有 **shēngdiào**。如国你的语言里没有 **shēngdiào**，让你去学一个有 **shēngdiào** 的语言，你相能容易吗？第二，学汉语，就得学汉字。岁然很多语言不月汉字，但是有的语言，北方说日语，就用汉字。日木人学汉语就会觉得容易得多，因为他们没有汉字的门题。第三，英语和法语，或者别的一些西方的语言里边有的字在以前是一样的，现在的写法和说法也茶不多。但是英语和中文没有这样的关系。所以我觉得中文比法文难学。

a. _____   b. _____   c. _____   d. _____

e. _____   f. _____   g. _____   h. _____

English:

11.   Reading for the main ideas I

The following paragraph contains a few characters that we have not yet learned, but you should be able to "read around them" and understand the main points of the passage. Read the paragraph for the main ideas, and then respond to the requests and questions that follow in English.

其实，方言不一定都是哪个地方的语言。在同一个地方，不同的人说话也不一样，这也是方言。比方说，读过很多年书的人，跟没有上过学的人说话就不一样。他们之间的这种语言上的差别也是方言之间的差别。

a. State the main topic of this paragraph in one word.

b. How would the author define this word?

c. Give an example from English that supports the author's definition of this word.

12.   Reading for the main ideas II

Read the following paragraph for the main ideas, and then respond to the requests and questions that follow in English.

方言就是一个地方的语言。在很早很早以前，交通不方便，不同地方的人来往很少，人们只说自己那个地方的语言，这样就有了很多方言。在英国的英语里和美国的英语里都有方言。**Lúndūn** 人说的话就跟英国其他地方的话不一样。在美国南方话和北方话也有很大的差别。就是在北方，**Niǔyuē** 人和 **Bōshìdùn** 的人说话也不一样。这些方言的差别都比较小，而中国的方言差别比较大。

a. According to the author, what is one reason why a language has different dialects?

b. The author says that there can be dialects within dialects. Give some examples of this, based on the information in the paragraph.

c. What does the author say about the difference between the dialects of English and the dialects of Chinese?

Focus on structure

1.   Definitions (Use and Structure note 30.1)

Here is a list of items and their descriptions. Write a sentence for each, saying that an item with this description is called [name of item], as in the example. Then translate your sentences into English.

Example:

在中国大 **lù**，标准语言，**Pǔ** 通话   →   在中国大 **lù**，标准语言叫作 **Pǔ** 通话。

a. 一个地方说的语言，方言   →

English:

b. 两个东西不同的地方，差别   →

English:

c. 饭馆最有名的菜，拿手菜   →

English:

d. **lìshǐ** 上有名的地方，名 **shèng gǔjì**   →

English:

e. 中国人吃饭用的东西，筷子   →

English:

2.   Strengths and weaknesses (Use and Structure note 30.7)

Answer each of the following questions in complete Mandarin sentences, using characters where we have learned them.

a. 你自己的长 **chu** 是什么？

b. 你觉得坐飞机的 **duǎnchu** 是什么？

c. 手机的用 **chu** 是什么？

d. 你觉得中文的难 **chu** 是什么？

e. 喝酒的坏 **chu** 是什么？

3.   No matter what (Use and Structure note 30.8)

Complete these sentences by adding a clause that begins with **wúlùn** to match the English translations.

a. _____ , **jiāo** 通都很方便。

   No matter where you want to go, the transportation is very convenient.

b. 谢妈妈很会做菜，_____ 。

   Mama Xie is a very good cook. Whatever you want to eat, she can cook it.

c. 中文作业你非做不可。_____ 。

   You have to do the Chinese homework. No matter whether you are busy or not, you still have to do it.

d. 这个菜是我女朋友做的。_____ 。

   This dish was made by my girlfriend. Whether it tastes good or not, I have to eat it.

e. 我父母今天从美国来看我。_____ 。

   My parents are coming from the USA to see me. No matter what time they arrive, I have to go to the airport to pick them up.

4.   Even if, even though (Use and Structure note 30.10)

Complete these sentences by adding a clause that begins with **jíshǐ** to match the English translations.

a. 这里的 **jiāo** 通很方便。_____ 。

   The transportation here is very convenient. Even if you don't have a car, you can go anywhere.

b. 谢妈妈很会做菜，_____ 。

   Mama Xie is a very good cook. Even if she has never cooked a dish before, she can cook it.

c. 中文作业你非做不可。_____ 。

   You have to do the Chinese homework. Even if you are very busy, you still have to do it.

d. 这个菜是我女朋友做的。_____ 。

   This dish was made by my girlfriend. Even though it doesn't look very delicious, I still have to eat it.

e. **Pǔ** 通话的四 **shēng** 不难学。_____ 。

   The four tones of Putonghua are not too difficult to learn. Even if the language that you speak does not have tones, you will still be able to learn them.

5.   She did it this way (Use and Structure note 30.11)

Translate each sentence into Mandarin, using <u>AdjV AdjV 地 +VP</u> to express the way that Xiao Gao performed each action.

a. Xiao Gao listened carefully to what the teacher said.

b. Xiao Gao slowly completed all of her homework.

c. Xiao Gao quickly straightened up her room.

d. Xiao Gao reviewed the characters well. (She worked hard on this task)

6.   Scrambled sentences

Rewrite these phrases into sentences, putting them in the right order to match the English translations.

a. 就 / 话 / 的 / 是 / **pǔ** 通人 / 说 / **pǔ** 通话

   Putonghua is the language that ordinary people speak.

b. 事 / 是 / 的 / 的 / 就 / 今天 / 今天 / 做完 / 长 **chu** / 我

   My strength is that I finish today's work today.

c. 什么 / 打 / 问 / 你 / 问题 / 可以 / 电话 / **wúlùn** / 来 / 我 / 有 / 都

   Whatever questions you have, you can phone me and ask.

d. 来 / **chèn** / 是 / 人 / 打折 / 到 **chu** / 东西 / 商店 / 的 / 里 / 都 / 买

   The store is full of people taking advantage of the sale to buy things.

e. 的/ 喜欢 / 是 / 是 / 而 / 所 / 经济 / 音乐 / 我 / 不

   What I like isn't economics but music.

7.   Translate into English

Translate these sentences into English.

a. 他去过很多地方，会说好几种不同的方言。

b. 我 **cāi** 你完全没有听懂老师在课上所说的话。

c. 我连有四个 **shēngdiào** 的 **pǔ** 通话都说不好，怎么能学有九个 **shēngdiào** 的 **Guǎng** 东话呢？

d. 他们之间的事情，我所知道的不多。

e. 对我来说，汉字最难学。我可以只学说话，不学书写吗？

f. **Pǔ** 通话和北京话在语法、发音和 **cíhuì** 上的差别都不大。

g. 在中国大 **lù** 的中国人只用简体字，在台湾的中国人只用 **fán** 体字，而在美国学汉语的学生有的既要学简体字，又要学 **fán** 体字。

h. 这门课 **jī** 本上没有考试，但是有很多功课和 **dú** 书报告。

i. 你把这个功课分成三天做，就不会觉得那么多了。

j. 你既不运动又吃得多，难怪会 **pàng**。

8.   Translate into Mandarin

Translate these sentences into Mandarin, using characters where we have learned them.

a. No wonder he didn't come to class today. It turns out he was sick.

b. Whether I study Chinese or not next semester depends upon whether or not I have time.

c. My roommate makes loud phone calls (loudly makes phone calls) every night and interferes with (influences) my studying.

d. Simplified characters, from the perspective of foreign students, are not at all easy.

e. I've already asked you many times. Is this teacher in fact difficult or not?

f. Everyone has her own strengths and weaknesses.

g. Today is the last test of this semester. Even though I am sick, I have to go take (participate in) the test.

h. I've always considered you a good friend.

i. Actually, how much you sleep and what your grade is on tests have a direct relationship.

Focus on communication

1. Dialogue comprehension

Study the Lesson 30 Narrative and Dialogue. Then, read the following statements and indicate whether they are true (T) or false (F).

a. ( ) **Pǔ** 通话和国语是现 **dài** 汉语的标准语。

b. ( ) 汉语的方言 **jī** 本上有七种。只说汉语的人，什么方言都听不懂。

c. ( ) 方言和方言之间的差别，有的大，有的小。

d. ( ) 虽然说不同方言的人可能 **hù** 相听不懂，但是写出来的文字，一定看得懂。

e. ( ) 外国学生学汉语难 **chu** 是，书写和发音没有直接的关系。

f. ( ) 大为昨天去吃饭的餐厅里，服务员跟他们说 **Pǔ** 通话，可是服务员之间说的是方言。

g. ( ) 方言和方言之间，除了发音是最 **zhǔ** 要的不同以外，**cíhuì** 和语法一 **bān** 差别不大。

h. ( ) 小张的老师说学汉语的学生如果不离开北京，就不 **xū** 要学方言。

i. ( ) 在中国，全国的小孩子上学以后都要学 **Pǔ** 通话。

j. ( ) 台湾跟大 **lù** 一样，也用简体字。

k. ( ) 学简体字还是 **fán** 体字，**jī** 本上你应该自己决定，没有好或者不好。

2. What do you say?

What do you say in each of the following situations? Type your answers, using characters where we have learned them, and email them to your Chinese teacher.

a. Answer your friend's question about studying in China or in Taiwan. Explain to her that each has its own advantages and it's hard to tell which one is better.

b. As a travel agent, explain to your client that after the discount and the $80 off, if you pay with cash, this train ticket is basically 50% off.

c. Tell your friend the main differences between American English and British English.

d. As a fruit vendor, advertise your promotion: every day after 9:30, no matter what fruit they purchase, it's 50 cents apiece.

e. After you have taken one bite, tell your friend that the "la zi ji ding" is in fact <u>not</u> as spicy as he thought and urge him to give it a try.

f. As a teacher, tell your students that they should ask you directly if they have questions instead of asking other classmates.

g. When your friend thanks you for your help, tell him there's no need to say thank you between you and him because of course friends should help each other!

h. Ask your friend to guess how many languages you speak.

i. Tell your friends about at least one of your strengths and weaknesses.

j. Complain about how crowded this place is—there are people everywhere.

k. Tell your friends whether you are learning traditional or simplified characters. Briefly explain the advantages and disadvantages of the type of characters you are learning, and explain the main reason why you are learning that form of characters.

l. Tell your classmates the person who influenced you the most.

m. After your boyfriend explained that the girl you saw with him the other day was his cousin, you are relieved and say "that explains it." You also joke that no wonder he's not afraid of you getting mad at all.

n. Ask your friend to divide the cake (**dàngāo**) into six pieces.

3.   Complete the mini-dialogues

Use the structure in parentheses to complete each mini-dialogue.

a. A: 大家都说美国人不讲 **jiu** 做菜，你觉得呢？

　B: ＿＿＿＿＿＿＿＿＿＿＿＿＿＿＿＿＿＿＿＿＿＿＿＿＿＿＿。（**Qí** 实…）

b. A: 我昨天刚从中国回来。去了一个月，玩得高兴极了。

　B: 我怎么不知道你去中国了？＿＿＿＿＿＿＿＿＿＿＿＿＿＿＿＿。（难怪…）

c. A: 你觉得这么晚了我们还找得到东西吃吗？

　B: 当然！＿＿＿＿＿＿＿＿＿＿＿＿＿＿＿＿＿＿＿＿＿＿。（到 **chù** 都是）

d. A: 我已经每天去上课了，为什么我的成 **jì** 还是没有进 **bù**？

　B: 如果 ＿＿＿＿＿＿＿＿＿＿＿＿＿＿＿＿＿＿＿＿，**jíshǐ** ＿＿＿＿＿＿＿＿＿＿
＿＿＿＿＿＿＿＿＿＿＿＿＿＿＿＿，成 **jì** 还是不会进 **bù** 。（**jíshǐ**…）

e. A: 你的老师怎么这么关心你们？真难得。

　B: 王老师 ＿＿＿＿＿＿＿＿＿＿＿＿＿＿＿＿＿＿＿，所以他非常关心我们。（看作…）

4.   Complete and translate

Using the context as your guide, choose the correct expression to complete each sentence, and then translate the sentences into English.

a. 我现在才知道，中国人一 **bān** 不喝 **bīng** 的。难怪 _____
  1) 餐厅里不卖 **bīng yǐnliào**。
  2) **suān** 辣 **tāng** 这么有名。
  3) 吃得太 **là** 的时候喝什么呢？

  English:

b. 很多人不知道，四川菜 _____ 不都是 **là** 的。
  1) 到底
  2) **qí** 实
  3) **jíshǐ**

  English:

c. 老师：因为"筷子"听起来跟"快子"一样，所以，送别人筷子意思就是 **xīwàng** 别人"快一点有孩子"。

  学生： _____。
  1) **Yuàn** 者上 **gōu**
  2) **Yuán** 来如 **cǐ**
  3) 一言为定

  English:

d. 最近的天气越来越冷，晚上出去 **jíshǐ** _____ 还是冷得不得了。
  1) 穿了大衣、**dài** 了 **ěrzhào**，手 **tào**，
  2) 不穿大衣
  3) 事先订位

  English:

e. A: 我要去上海工作一年，到底我 **xū** 要不 **xū** 要学上海话？

  B: 完全不 **xū** 要，_____ 你自己有兴趣。
  1) 难怪
  2) **xìngkuī**
  3) 除非

  English:

5. Cantonese and Mandarin

Part I. Using the context as your guide, complete this paragraph by filling in the blanks with the appropriate words below.

发现	当然	比方说	听起来
另外	**jī** 本上	有名	而

说到汉语的方言，最 _____ 的大概就是 **Guǎng** 东话了。如果你去中国 **chéng** *(China-town)*，你会 _____，很多人只说 **Guǎng** 东话，不说 **Pǔ** 通话。**Guǎng** 东话和 **Pǔ** 通话所用的 **cíhuì** 差不多，可是因为发音不同，_____ 完全不一样。**Guǎng** 东话有八个 **shēngdiào**，_____ **Pǔ** 通话只有四个。在语法上，**Guǎng** 东话和 **Pǔ** 通话 _____ 差不多，可是有些字放的地方跟 **Pǔ** 通话不太一样。_____，**Pǔ** 通话里的"多吃点儿"，在 **Guǎng** 东话里说"吃多点儿"。_____，**Gǔ** 汉语 *(Classical Chinese)* 对 **Guǎng** 东话的影 **xiǎng** 很大。**Pǔ** 通话里的"多少"，**Guǎng** 东话说"几多"。"几多"就是从 **Gǔ** 汉语里头来的。虽然有这些不同，但是两个语言所用的书写文字是一样的。所以，说 **Guǎng** 东话看得懂中文书，说 **Pǔ** 通话的人去 **Xiānggǎng** *(Hong Kong)* 玩，_____ 也看得懂街上写的字了。

Part II. True or false   Read the paragraph again, and decide whether each of the following statements is true (T) or false (F).

a. (　) 在美国的中国 **chéng** 里常常会听到 **Guǎng** 东话。

b. (　) **Guǎng** 东话的 **shēngdiào** 比 **Pǔ** 通话多。

c. (　) **Guǎng** 东话和 **Pǔ** 通话之间的差别，在语法上比在发音上大得多。

d. (　) **Guǎng** 东话有很多 **Gǔ** 汉语所用的 **cíhuì**。

e. (　) 这两个语言说出来不一样，写出来也完全不一样。

Part III. Think and write   你 **cāi cāi** 看，说 **Guǎng** 东话的人如果要学中文，会有什么难 **chu**，哪方 **miàn** 特别容易？（如果你有说 **Guǎng** 东话的朋友，就去问问他们。） Your response should be at least 120 characters in length.

_____

_____

_____

_____

_____

6. American English vs. British English I

Using the context as your guide, as well as your knowledge of American English and British English, choose the most appropriate word in each group to complete this paragraph.

_____（a. 在 b. 对 c. 从）很多学英语的人来说，美式英语和英式英语都是英语。_____（a. 实际上 b. 说到 c. 另外）这两个语言_____（a. **hù** 相 b. 等于 c. 之间）还是有一些不同。最 **zhǔ** 要的差别就是_____（a. 发音 b. 文字 c. 语法）。所以有人说，美国人到英国去旅行，也_____（a. 不一定 b. 一定 c. **kǒng** 怕）完全听得懂他们说的话。听不懂有的时候也是因为一些_____（a. 语法 b. **cíhuì** c. 语音）上的差别。比方说，"elevator" 在英式英语里_____（a. 叫做 b. 分成 c. 看作）"lift"。也就是说，_____（a. **xìngkuī** b. 的 **què** c. **jíshǐ**）你看到 "lift"，如果你不知道这个字的意思，你还是不知道那就是 "电 **tī**"。另外，美式英语和英式英语在文字的写法上也有一点不一样。美式英语的 "color"，英式英语_____（a. 写成 b. 写好 c. 写到）"colour"，多了一个 "u"，_____（a. 但是 b. 而 c. 也就是说）"theater" 和 "center" 在英国成了 "theatre" 和 "centre"。

7. American English vs. British English II

Answer the following questions in Mandarin, based on your opinions and experience. You can consult outside sources to help you find the information you need to answer some of these questions. Your Chinese teacher may have you work on these questions in small groups and report your findings to the class.

a. 除了 "elevator/lift" 以外，请你说说美式英语和英式英语里头几个不一样的 **cíhuì**。

b. 除了 "color/colour" 和 "theater/theatre" 以外，你还能想到哪些 **cíhuì** 在美式英语和英式英语里头的写法不一样？请写出两个。

c. 你比较喜欢美式英语还是英式英语，为什么？

d. 你说的是哪一个，美式英语还是英式英语？你听得懂另外一个吗？

e. 除了美国和英国以外，还有哪些国家的人也说英语？

f. 有的时候因为说的英语不同，两个人之间也会 **hù** 相听不懂。请你讲一个发生在你自己身上的事情。

8.   Form a cohesive paragraph

Rewrite these sentences, putting them in the correct order to form a cohesive paragraph about a difference between Putonghua and Beijing dialect.

a. 在 **Pǔ** 通话里没有那么多的 "**er**"。

b. 有很多人以为北京话就是 **Pǔ** 通话，实际上北京话跟 **Pǔ** 通话不一样。

c. 我觉得 "听懂" 比 "好听" 重要得多，所以请你跟我说 **Pǔ** 通话，别说北京话。

d. 北京人说话有很多 "**er**" 的 **shēng** 音。

e. 对我们外国学生来说，如果你说得很快，而且有很多 "**er**" 的 **shēng** 音，就很难听懂。

f. 有的人觉得 "**er**" 的 **shēng** 音很好听。

9.   An objective view

The paragraph below, from Part C of the Lesson 30 Dialogue, illustrates a way to present your opinion about some topic and to support your opinion with facts.

Part I.   Examine this paragraph. Identify <u>the topic, the narrator's opinion, information that supports the narrator's opinion</u>, and <u>the conclusion</u>. What is the purpose of the last sentence in the paragraph?

说到简体字和 **fán** 体字，各有各的好 **chu**。很难说哪个比较好。比方说，写简体字笔 **huà** 少、省时间、可是很多人认为 **fán** 体字比较漂亮也容易认。 想学哪个，完全看你自己的 **xū** 要。现在中国大 **lù** 用简体字，而台湾用 **fán** 体字。中国的汉字有几千年的 **lìshǐ**，对附近的国家影 **xiǎng** 也很大。

Part II.   Using the same structure as in the paragraph in Part I, write about two of the following topics. Your goal is not to persuade your listener one way or the other, but to offer a neutral presentation, stating the facts of both sides. When you offer examples to support both sides, you can use the following expressions to introduce and connect your statements: 而且、再说、另外…. Your essays should each be at least 100 characters in length.

Suggested topics

a. 学中文 vs. 学西 **bānyá** 文 *(Spanish)*

b. 自己做午饭 vs. 在学校餐厅吃午饭

c. 上大学的时候住 **sùshè** vs. 住家里

d. 放假的时候从学校坐飞机回家 vs. 开车回家

e. 带朋友去 **guàng** 名 **shèng gǔjì** vs. 带朋友去 **guàng** 街买打折的东西

f. 买 **ruǎnwò** 的火车票 vs. 买 **yìngwò** 的火车票

g. 旅行的时候带一个好的照相机 vs. 带一个可以照相的手机

h. 朋友生日的时候送 **lǐwù** vs. 送红包或者 **lǐqùan** *(gift certificate)*

i. Your choice of topic: _____

First topic: _____

说到 _____, 各有各的 _____。很难说哪

个比较好。比方说, _____

_____, 可是 _____

_____。想选哪个, 完全 _____

_____。

_____

_____。

Second topic: _____

说到 _____, 各有各的_____。很难说哪

个比较好。比方说, _____

_____, 可是 _____

_____。想选哪个, 完全 _____

_____。

_____

_____。

Lesson 31 Workbook

 Listening and speaking

Structure drills

1. Because of this (Use and Structure note 31.1)

You will hear a noun phrase followed by a verb phrase stating that an action cannot be done. Restate the information with **yóu** 于 *due to, because of*, saying that due to the noun phrase, the action cannot be done, as in the example.

Example:
You will hear: 喝酒，不能开车
You will say: **Yóu** 于喝酒的关系，我不能开车。
Click "R" to hear the correct response: **Yóu** 于喝酒的关系，我不能开车。

(a)　(b)　(c)　(d)　(e)　(f)　(g)　(h)　(i)　(j)

2. Be interested in, Part I (Use and Structure note 31.3)

You will hear a pronoun, name, or noun phrase referring to a person or people, followed by a noun phrase or action. Restate the information by saying that the person is interested in the noun phrase or action, as in the example.

Example:
You will hear: 大为，中国文化
You will say: 大为对中国文化感兴趣。
Click "R" to hear the correct response: 大为对中国文化感兴趣。

(a)　(b)　(c)　(d)　(e)　(f)　(g)　(h)　(i)　(j)

3.   Be interested in, Part II (Use and Structure note 31.3)

You will hear a noun or noun phrase referring to people, followed by a noun phrase, verb phrase, or clause. Restate the information, saying that the subject is <u>not</u> interested in the noun phrase, verb phrase, or clause, as in the example.

> **Example:**
> *You will hear:* 我，你的考试成 **jì**
> *You will say:* 我对你的考试成 **jì** 不感兴趣。
> *Click "R" to hear the correct response:* 我对你的考试成 **jì** 不感兴趣。

(a)   (b)   (c)   (d)   (e)   (f)   (g)   (h)

4.   Something that concerns this (Use and Structure note 31.4)

You will hear a statement about an object that someone likes, or the object of some action. Restate the information using the structure 跟 NP₁ 有关的 NP₂, as in the example. An English translation of the example is provided to help you to understand the structure.

> **Example:**
> *You will hear:* 我喜欢看经济的书。 *I like to read economics books*
> *You will say:* 我喜欢看跟经济有关的书。 *I like to read books concerning economics.*
> You will hear the correct response: 我喜欢看跟经济有关的书。 *I like to read books concerning economics.*

(a)   (b)   (c)   (d)   (e)   (f)   (g)   (h)

5.   For one thing…and for another thing (Use and Structure note 31.5)

You will hear a situation followed by two things to consider about it. Restate the information with 一方面…另一方面…, as in the example.

> **Example:**
> *You will hear:* 选什么 **zhuān** 业，要想到自己的兴趣和毕业以后找工作。
> *You will say:* 选什么 **zhuān** 业，一方面要想到自己的兴趣，另一方面要想到毕业以后找工作。
> *Click "R" to hear the correct response:* 选什么 **zhuān** 业，一方面要想到自己的兴趣，另一方面要想到毕业以后找工作。

(a)   (b)   (c)   (d)   (e)   (f)   (g)   (h)   (i)   (j)

6.   Not only…but also… (Use and Structure note 31.6)

You will hear a situation followed by two things that must be done concerning the situation. Restate the information, using 既 VP₁ 也 VP₂ to present the things that must be done, as in the example.

Example:
You will hear: 选什么 **zhuān** 业，要想到自己的兴趣和毕业以后找工作。
You will say: 选什么 **zhuān** 业，既要想到自己的兴趣，也要想到毕业以后找工作。
Click "R" to hear the correct response: 选什么 **zhuān** 业，既要想到自己的兴趣，也要想到毕业以后找工作。

(a)   (b)   (c)   (d)   (e)   (f)   (g)   (h)   (i)   (j)

Listening for information

1.   Job search

You will hear five students talking about the kind of jobs they are applying for. Based on (CD2: 79) their statements, fill out the form, including the type of job and the location where they want to work.

student	type of job	location
#1		
#2		
#3		
#4		
#5		

2.   Job application

Malilan has applied for a job in Suzhou. She called the company to follow up on her applica- (CD2: 80) tion. Listen to her phone conversation with the assistant manager of the company, and check the items in the list that have been received, completed, or decided upon.

items	completed
application letter	
recommendation letters	
résumé	
grade report	
Chinese oral test	
interview date	

3. Message from a friend

(CD2: 81) You will hear a phone message from Bili. Listen to his message and write an email in response to his questions.

> Your email response to Bili's message:

4. Writing an application letter

(CD2: 82) Teacher Zhang is telling the students how to write a good job application letter. Listen to her instructions, and write the four points of her instructions in English.

a.

b.

c.

d.

5. Work experience in China

(CD2: 83) Teacher Pang invites Jenny, who is working in China, to give a talk to the students in her Chinese class. Listen to her talk and write down the work and living experiences in China that she mentions.

working	living

6. A conversation

You are having a job interview with Miss Pan at CK International, a business firm. Listen **(CD2: 84)** to her questions and answer them in Mandarin.

a.

b.

c.

d.

e.

f.

7. Interview experience

You will hear Jiaming describing her interview with a company last Tuesday, followed by **(CD2: 85–86)** five questions in Mandarin. Answer the questions in Mandarin, based on the information that Jiaming provides.

a.

b.

c.

d.

e.

8. Dialogue I

You will hear two friends chatting about their jobs in China. Choose the correct answer for **(CD2: 87)** each question, based on their conversation.

a. What kind of company does the woman work for?
1) a newspaper
2) a TV station
3) a business firm
4) a research center

b. What's the woman's job responsibility in China?
1) She reports economic news on TV.
2) She analyzes economic policy.
3) She writes articles on economics.
4) She collects critical economic news.

c. What is the man's job responsibility in China?
   1) He is an expert at bringing US companies to China to invest.
   2) He is a contact person between the USA and a Chinese company.
   3) He is a consultant helping to establish trading companies in China.
   4) He is an adviser on how to promote US products.

d. What will the man do after next month?
   1) He will switch to a better-paid job.
   2) He will work for a US company.
   3) He will advance his Chinese writing skills.
   4) He will study international relations.

 9.   Dialogue II

(CD2: 88) Shanmu is asking his teacher to write a letter of recommendation. Choose a correct answer for each question, based on their conversation.

a. What does Teacher He particularly need to explain in the recommendation letter?
   1) Shanmu's academic achievement
   2) Shanmu's communication skills
   3) Shanmu's Chinese proficiency
   4) Shanmu's work experience

b. Why has Juanjuan not been to the USA yet?
   1) Juanjuan and Shanmu just met.
   2) Juanjuan cannot obtain a visa.
   3) It is expensive to travel to the USA.
   4) She does not have time.

c. What will Juanjuan do in the USA?
   1) travel
   2) work
   3) study
   4) visit friends

d. What will Shanmu do right after arriving in the USA?
   1) start working
   2) visit the company
   3) find a place to live
   4) rest for several days

Reading and writing

1.   Number of strokes

Indicate the number of strokes used in writing each of the following characters.

a. 毕 _____   f. 短 _____

b. 望 _____   g. 面 _____

c. 安 _____   h. 希 _____

d. 纸 _____   i. 处 _____

e. 愿 _____   j. 被 _____

2.   Which character?

Circle the character in each line that corresponds to the meaning on the left.

a. **xū** (**xūyào** *need*)   需   雷

b. **xìn** *letter*   信   這

c. **shēn** (**shēnqǐng** *apply*)   申   車

d. **lì** (**lìshǐ** *history*)   厉   历

e. **gǎn** (**gǎn xìngqu** *interested in*)   咸   感

f. **bèi** *by*   被   披

g. **duǎn** *short*   知   短

h. **xī** (**xīwàng** *hope*)   杀   希

i. **bì** (**bìyè** *graduate*)   毕   毕

j. **chù** (**chángchu** *strength*)   处   外

k. **yuàn** (**yuànyì** *willing*)   愿   感

l. **miàn** *side, face*   而   面

3.   First strokes

Write the first two strokes of each of the following characters.

a. 感 _____   f. 纸 _____

b. 毕 _____   g. 申 _____

c. 需 _____   h. 望 _____

d. 广 _____   i. 处 _____

e. 安 _____   j. 希 _____

4.   Missing strokes

Complete each character by writing in the missing strokes.

a.   礻   **bèi** *by*

b.   ⺊   **bì** (**bìyè** *graduate*)

c.   夕   **chù** (**chángchu** *strength*)

d.   ⻐   **duǎn** *short*

e.   ⼇   **jiāo** (**jiāotōng** *communication*)

f.   一   **lì** (**jiǎnlì** *résumé*, **lìshǐ** *history*)

g.   冂   **shēn** (**shēnqǐng** *apply*)

h.   亻   **xìn** *letter*

i.   厉   **yuàn** (**yuànyì** *willing*)

j.   ⼄   **zhǐ** *paper*

5.   Total strokes

Rewrite this list of characters, arranging the characters in terms of their total number of strokes. Begin your list with the character with the fewest strokes.

望	需	纸	感	面	短	被	历	广	毕	安	愿	交	申	信	希	处

6.   Radicals

Here is a list of characters that we have learned through this lesson. Rewrite each character in the row next to its radical. Use this as an opportunity to review these characters. If you do not know the pronunciation or meaning of a character on the list, look it up and practice it.

广　雪　借　宿　肚　望　脏　安　线　应　宜
带　客　意　需　实　价　思　纸　希　像　练
知　寒　便　服　健　愿　底　绍　短　信　床

月	
亻	
雨	
心	
巾	
纟	
矢	
广	
宀	

7.   Character sleuth: Look for the phonetic

Group the characters below in terms of their rhymes or near-rhymes. Write the characters that rhyme with each other in the column on the right. Write the "phonetic," the shared part of each character, in the column on the left. There are at least eleven sets of characters that rhyme or partially rhyme and share a phonetic component.

毕　末　女　活　交　忙　错　玩　该　订
爸　饺　五　听　右　孩　票　客　较　味
远　漂　忘　妹　爬　把　厅　口　如　重
园　各　校　语　望　话　醋　懂　完　比

phonetic	characters that rhyme or almost rhyme and share a phonetic component

8. Scrambled sentences

Rewrite these phrases as sentences, putting the words in the correct order to match the English translations.

a. 事 / 不 / 件 / 请 / 千万 / 把 / 这 / 他 / 你 / 告诉 / 要

Please absolutely do not tell him about this matter.

b. 一定 / 兴趣 / 兴趣 / 不 / 对 / 你 / 感 / 感 / 你 / 的 / 人

People you are interested in are not always interested in you.

c. 流行 / 这 / 鞋 / 既 / 式样 / 便宜 / 也 / 双

This pair of shoes is not only cheap, the style is also in fashion.

d. 为 / **shàn** 于 / 工作 / 人 / 介绍 / 她

She is good at finding (introducing) jobs for people.

9. Dictionary skills

Following the instructions in Lesson 17 of the Textbook, look up these characters in a Chinese dictionary and provide the requested information.

a. 留
   pronunciation:
   meaning:
   one two-character word or phrase in which it occurs:

b. 封
   pronunciation:
   meaning:
   one two-character word or phrase in which it occurs:

c. 祝

pronunciation:

meaning:

one two-character word or phrase in which it occurs:

10. Find the incorrect characters

Xiao Zhang has written this letter to Xiao Ye, but he has written ten characters incorrectly. Circle his mistakes and write the correct characters in the answer sheet below. Then, translate the paragraph into English.

我马上就比业了。很多同学早九希忘能毕业了，可是我很怕。从小的时候到现再，我一真都在上学。上学的时后，我爸爸妈妈给我钱。学生的生活，对我来说，再习惯不过了。毕业就要白己找工作，不能让爸爸妈妈给我钱，可是我从来没有找过工作，也从来没有工作过。一想道在报纸上找有关工作的广告，写间历、申青信和请老师帮我写 **tuījiàn** 信等等，我就很紧张。我要是一直可以上学就好了。

a. _____   b. _____   c. _____   d. _____   e. _____

f. _____   g. _____   h. _____   i. _____   j. _____

English:

11.   Reading for the main ideas I

The following paragraph contains a few characters that we have not yet learned, but you should be able to "read around them" and understand the main points of the passage. Read the paragraph for the main ideas and respond to the requests and questions that follow in English.

大为的英文名字是 David。老师给他的中文名字是"大为"。开始的时候，他很不喜欢。他觉得他的中文名字跟英文名字差不多。老师告诉他为什么给他这个名字以后，他不但很喜欢他的名字，而且还常常跟别人讲他名字的意思。中国人给小孩子名字的时候很注意名字的意思。"大为"并不是英文"David"的声音，"大为"是"大有作为"。"大有作为"的意思是不管做什么都可以做得很好，很有成绩。老师希望他将来能大有作为。现在大为就要毕业了。他希望能在中国工作一段时间。他在申请工作，希望能在中国大有作为。

a. State the main topic of this paragraph in <u>one</u> word.

b. State the two main pieces of information that the author provides about this word.

c. What is the connection that the author wants the reader to make about these two pieces of information?

12.   Reading for the main ideas II

Read the following paragraph for the main ideas, and then respond to the requests and questions that follow in English.

工作和兴趣既有关系，也没有关系。当然，如果你找到一个你有兴趣的工作，你愿意做的工作，你一定可以做好。但是在经济不好的时候，工作不多，能找到工作就很不错了。因为你需要钱，所以不管你对这个工作有兴趣还是没兴趣，你都得做。开始的时候，你可能没有兴趣，很可能慢慢儿地就有兴趣了。

a. State the topic of this paragraph in two or three words.

b. The author says that this topic poses a paradox. What is the paradox?

c. What do economic conditions have to do with this topic?

Focus on structure

1.   Due to this (Use and Structure note 31.1)

Here is a set of reasons and results. Express each relationship in a complete Mandarin sentence, using the structure **yóu** 于 (NP) 的关系 or **yóu** 于 S₁, S₂.

a. the weather   →   the party will be indoors (开会 *hold a party*)

b. bad grades (academic record)   →   he decided not to apply to college this year

c. her insufficient experience   →   the company wasn't willing to hire her

d. history   →   way of writing in Taiwan and mainland China is different

2.   Expressing interest (Use and Structure note 31.3)

Here are a few things that Dawei has become interested in while he has been studying in China. Use the structure 对 (NP) 感兴趣 to say that he is interested in each of these things.

a. Chinese history   →

b. international trade   →

c. Sino–American (中美) relations →

d. Chinese dialects   →

3.   Something that concerns this (Use and Structure note 31.4)

Here is what Dawei has been doing to follow up on his interests. Translate these sentences to Mandarin, using the structure 跟 NP₁ 有关的 NP₂.

a. Because he is interested in Chinese history, he reads a lot of books having to do with Chinese history.

b. Because he is interested in international trade, he is applying to companies that involve trade.

c. Because he is interested in Sino–American relations, he has taken a lot of courses that have to do with China.

d. Because he is interested in Chinese dialects, he has also taken a few courses that concern Chinese language.

4.   For one thing…, and for another thing (Use and Structure note 31.5)

Translate these sentences to English.

a. 找工作，一方面要自己 **nǔlì**，另一方面要有朋友帮助。

b. 我这次考得不好，一方面是因为我准备得不够，另一方面考试的 **què** 很难。

c. 我下星期去上海，一方面是去旅游，另一方面是去看一个老同学。

d. 我想 **chèn** 今年夏天到上海去工作。一方面看看朋友，另一方面多了 **jiě** 一下上海现在的情 **kuàng**。

5.   Not only… but also (Use and Structure note 31.6)

Dawei is preparing for a job interview tomorrow by making a list of things that he is good at. Express each of these in Mandarin, using the structure 既 VP₁ 也 VP₂.

a. can speak English and can also speak Chinese

b. conscientious and hardworking and willing to help others

c. have study abroad experience and have work experience

d. like to work with others and like to work on my own

6.   What are they good at? (Use and Structure note 31.8)

Translate the following sentences into English.

a. 王先生 **shàn** 于用最简单的 **tiáoliào** 做出色、香、味都有的菜。

b. 你这么 **shàn** 于学习语言，**jiāng** 来一定要找跟外语有关的工作。

c. 他不 **shàn** 于跟不认识的人说话，所以刚认识他的人，都以为他不愿意跟别人交往。

d. 真正 **cōng** 明的学生很 **shàn** 于安 **pái** 时间，该学习的时候学习，该玩儿的时候玩儿。

e. What are you good at? Write one sentence in Mandarin, stating what you are good at.

7.   By all means don't do that! (Use and Structure note 31.9)

Complete these sentences in Mandarin by adding an action that you absolutely shouldn't do, and then translate them into English.

a. 你在外国旅游的时候，千万 _____ 。
   English:

b. 面谈的时候，千万 _____ 。
   English:

c. 朋友请你吃饭的时候，千万 _____ 。
   English:

d. 考试的时候，千万 _____ 。
   English:

e. 介绍你自己的时候，千万 _____ 。
   English:

8.   Scrambled sentences

Rewrite these phrases as sentences, putting the words in the correct order to match the English translations.

a. 既 / 也 / 经 **yàn** / 经 **yàn** / 大学生 / 大 **bù** 分的 / 工作 / 生活 / 没有 / 没有

   Most college students don't have work experience and don't have life experience.

b. 经 **yàn** / 信心 / 所 / 的 / 不 / 工作 / 而 / 自己的 / 是 / 是 / 你 / 需要 / 对

   What you need is not work experience but confidence in yourself.

c. 都 / 大为 / 跟 / 对 / 感兴趣 / 所有 / **mào** 易 / 的 / 工作 / 跟 / 有关

   Dawei is interested in all jobs that have something to do with trade.

d. 忙 / 都 / **yóu** 于 / **lián** 系 / 少 / 很 / 我们 / 很 / 最近

   Because everyone is very busy, we haven't been in touch very often in recent times.

9.   Translate into English

Translate these sentences into English.

a. **Yóu** 于现在的经济情 **kuàng**，刚刚毕业的大学生很难找到工作。

b. 在跟别人交往的时候，要看别人的长处，不要只 **zhǔ** 意短处。

c. 大为对所有跟 **mào** 易有关的工作都感兴趣。

d. 要学好中文，一方面要认真学习、做功课，另一方面要多练习说，不要怕说错。

e. 我的同屋很 **qí** 怪，既不愿意帮助别人，也不愿意别人帮助他。

f. 在上大学的时候，一方面要多跟别人交往，多认识人，另一方面要 **nǔlì dú** 书，不要把时间都花在跟别人交往上。

g. 只有在中国住一 **duàn** 时间，才能真正了 **jiě** 中国的文化。

10.   Translate into Mandarin

Translate these sentences into Mandarin, using the phrase or structure indicated in parentheses.

a. Because of being too nervous and not having confidence in myself, my first job interview was very bad (very not good). (**yóu** 于)

b. Several US universities (colleges) make students know (recognize) both simplified characters and traditional characters. (既…也)

c. My roommate is very good at studying languages. He can speak the languages of many different types of countries. (**shàn** 于)

d. On the web you can often see the expression (way of speaking) "contact us" (**lián** 系 我们). Actually, this is not correct. They ought to say "跟我们 **lián** 系". (实际上)

e. Companies that hire students who are studying abroad help them take their student visas and exchange them for (convert them to) work visas. (换成)

f. You can't use a credit card at that restaurant. When/If you go there to eat lunch, by all means don't forget to take a little cash. (千万)

g. I take my lunch to school every day now. It both saves money and is convenient. (既…也)

Focus on communication

1. Dialogue comprehension

Study the Lesson 31 Narrative and Dialogue. Then, read the following statements and indicate whether they are true (T) or false (F).

a. (   ) 毕业生还没有放假就开始找工作了。

b. (   ) 申请以前，公 **sī** 一定会安 **pái** 你去面谈。

c. (   ) **Liú** 学生如果没有工作 **qiānzhèng** 就不能在中国工作。

d. (   ) 大为已经有十几个面谈了，但是他只喜欢三个。

e. (   ) 大为申请的工作都跟 **mào** 易有关。

f. (   ) 大为想请友文吃饭，因为他已经找到工作了。

g. (   ) 大为找老师说话，因为他想请老师给他写 **tuījiàn** 信。

h. (   ) 面谈的时候一定要对自己有信心。既不能紧张，也别忘了说 **qīngchu** 你的长处。

i. (   ) 面谈的时候，工作经 **yàn** 不是最重要的。让他们了 **jiě** 你的长处更重要。

j. (   ) 大为的长处是语言。还有，中西文化他都了 **jiě**。

k. (   ) **Mào** 易公 **sī** 喜欢工作认真、愿意帮助别人的人。

l. (   ) 跟老师说话以前，大为对自己不太有信心。

2. What do you say?

What do you say in each of the following situations? Type your answers, using characters where we have learned them, and email them to your Chinese teacher.

a. Tomorrow is a holiday. You need to post a sign in Chinese on the door of the school cafeteria that says: "Due to the holiday, the cafeteria is closed today."

b. You work in the Human Resources office. Call a potential candidate to notify her that you'd like to arrange an interview and ask if she's available next Thursday at 10:00 a.m.

c. Politely ask your Chinese teacher to write you a recommendation letter. Explain to her that you want to apply for jobs related to Chinese language.

d. You are at a job fair. Present your application and résumé and tell potential employers that you are interested in their company. Tell them your major and ask them to contact you if they have openings (jobs) related to your major.

e. Ask your friend to prepare you for a job interview tomorrow.

f. Your younger sister is getting ready for her piano recital. Tell her to never ever get nervous and tell her that you have confidence in her.

g. Your friend is heading to a road test to get his driver's license. Wish him good luck and tell him you'll be waiting for his good news.

h. You are currently on a student visa. Ask your potential employer if they would sponsor (help you change into) a work visa if they hire you.

i. As an interviewer, ask the candidate to tell you his/her strengths and weaknesses.

j. Explain to the candidates that the company is looking for someone who is hardworking and has good people skills.

3. Complete the mini-dialogues

Use the structure in parentheses to complete each mini-dialogue.

a. A: 你最近怎么不去那家餐馆吃饭了？

   B: ＿＿＿＿＿＿＿＿＿＿＿＿＿＿＿＿＿＿＿＿＿。（一方面…另一方面…）

b. A: 选 **zhuān** 业最要紧的是什么？

   B: ＿＿＿＿＿＿＿＿＿＿＿＿＿＿＿＿＿＿。（对…感兴趣）

c. A: 明天是小张的生日，我想给他买个 **lǐwù**，你觉得他会喜欢什么？

   B: 买什么都可以，可是 ＿＿＿＿＿＿＿＿＿＿＿＿＿＿＿＿。（千万）

d. A: 他们说的是什么语言？我怎么一点也听不懂？

   B: ＿＿＿＿＿＿＿＿＿＿＿＿＿＿＿＿，难怪你听不懂。（既…也…）

e. A: 你想找哪方面的工作？

   B: ＿＿＿＿＿＿＿＿＿＿＿＿＿＿＿＿＿＿＿＿。（跟…有关）

4. Complete and translate

Using the context as your guide, choose the correct expression to complete each sentence, and then translate the sentence into English.

a. **Yóu** 于 ＿＿＿＿＿＿，愿意买房子的人越来越少。
   1) 房子越做越漂亮
   2) 经济一直很 **zāogāo**
   3) 人越来越多

   English:

b. 只有 ＿＿＿＿＿ 才能省一点钱。

　　1) 如果你不开车

　　2) 你没有车

　　3) 少开车，多坐公共汽车或者地铁

English:

c. A: 找工作越来越难，是不是？

　　B: 是的。对我来说，一方面我没有工作经 **yàn**，另一方面，＿＿＿＿＿＿＿＿，所以，很多公 **sī** 对我不感兴趣。

　　1) 我的中文不够好

　　2) 虽然我对自己有信心

　　3) 如果我能有几 **fēng** 比较强的 **tuījiàn** 信

English:

d. A: ＿＿＿＿＿＿＿。

　　B: 千万别紧张，放 **sōng** 一点儿。

　　1) 我昨天把十几 **fēng** 申请信发出去了

　　2) 时间过得真快，我们下个星期就要毕业了

　　3) 明天晚上我要跟我男朋友的父母吃饭，这是我第一次见到他们

English:

e. A: 下个星期我有个面谈。

　　B: **Zhù** 你好运！＿＿＿＿＿。

　　1) 千万 **jì** 住，穿漂亮一点

　　2) 他们一定很了 **jiě** 你

　　3) 我等你的好 **xiāoxi**

English:

5. Form a cohesive paragraph

Rewrite these sentences, putting them in the correct order to form a cohesive paragraph about preparing for a job interview.

a. 谢谢他们给你这个机会。

b. 回 **dá** (*reply to*) 问题的时候，要想好了以后再说。

c. 找工作的时候，面谈非常重要。

d. 你可以去网上了 **jiě**，也可以问你的老师和朋友。

e. 面谈以后，最好给跟你面谈的人写一 **fēng** 信。

f. 去面谈以前要认真地准备。

g. 在面谈的时候让他们多知道你的长处，让他们觉得你就是他们需要的人。

h. 另外，你要了 **jiě** 他们需要什么样的人。

i. 不要没有完全想好就开始说。

j. 你对 **gù** 人的公司了 **jiě** 得越多越好。

_____

_____

_____

_____

_____

6. Job interview

This is a job interview at a Chinese trading company. Read the questions in Part I and find the matching answers in Part II.

Part I. Questions

a. (   ) 你的长处是什么？短处呢？

b. (   ) 你为什么来申请这个工作？

c. (   ) 有很多申请的人工作经 **yàn** 比你多，说说看我们为什么要 **gù** 用你？

d. (   ) 如果我们决定 **gù** 用你，你有什么问题要问我？

e. (   ) 如果你被 **gù** 用了，你打算做这个工作做多久？

Part II. Answers

Here are answers to the interview questions in Part I. Translate each answer into English. Then match it with the corresponding question, writing the answer letter before the corresponding question in Part I.

A) 我的 **zhuān** 业是经济，而且我大学选了不少跟国际 **mào** 易有关的课。另外，我一直对中美关系很感兴趣。两年以前我就发现了你们公 **sī**。对你们所做的我一直很感兴趣。

English: _____

_____

_____

_____

B) 做了几年，有经 **yàn** 以后，我想回学校学习，希望以后能再回公 **sī** 做更多的事情。

English: _____

_____

C) 虽然我刚毕业，但是我工作起来既 **nǔlì**，又认真。我大学的老师都说我学什么都学得又快又好。另外，从大学开始，每年 **shǔ** 假，我都在我父亲的公 **sī** 帮忙，这也算是有关的工作经 **yàn** 吧。

English: _____

_____

_____

_____

D) 我学中文已经学了七年了，对中西文化都很了 **jiě**，这是我比别人好的地方。而且我 **shàn** 于跟别人交往，又喜欢帮助别人。我最大的问题是我什么都想做好，所以，有的时候会让自己太紧张。

English: _____

_____

_____

_____

E) 我想知道这个工作需要不需要常常到别的国家。我很愿意学习新的东西，所以，如果有旅行的机会，就太好了。

English: _____

_____

_____

_____

7. What's your answer?

Imagine yourself in the same job interview as in Exercise 6. Write down your answer for each question. You can assign the job title yourself so that you can be more specific about your answer; for example, a research assistant in the Department of East Asian Studies, etc.

Job title: _____

a. 你的长处是什么？短处呢？

_____

_____

_____

_____

b. 你为什么来申请这个工作？

_____

_____

_____

_____

c. 有很多申请的人工作经 **yàn** 比你多，说说看我们为什么要 **gù** 用你？

_____

_____

_____

_____

d. 如果我们决定 **gù** 用你，你有什么问题要问我？

_____

_____

_____

_____

e. 如果你被 **gù** 用了，你打算做这个工作做多久？

_____

_____

_____

_____

Lesson 32 Workbook

 Listening and speaking

Structure drills

1. When it comes to this (Use and Structure note 22.1)

You will hear a statement. Rephrase the statement, turning the direct object into the topic with the phrase 在 NP 上, as in the example.

> **Example:**
> *You will hear:* 老师很照顾我们的生活。
> *You will say:* 在生活上，老师很照顾我们。
> *Click "R" to hear the correct response:* 在生活上，老师很照顾我们。

(a)   (b)   (c)   (d)   (e)   (f)

2. It makes me feel this way (Use and Structure note 21.8)

You will hear a sentence saying that someone feels a certain way because of some situation. Restate the information using 让, saying that the situation makes the person feel a certain way, as in the example.

> **Example:**
> *You will hear:* 我很不高兴因为他没来。
> *You will say:* 他没来让我很不高兴。
> *Click "R" to hear the correct response:* 他没来让我很不高兴。

(a)   (b)   (c)   (d)   (e)   (f)

3.   Giving thanks to someone (Use and Structure note 32.3)

You will hear a verb phrase indicating thanks to someone. Use that verb phrase in a sentence, saying that you give thanks to that person, as in the example.

Example:

You will hear: 感谢老师

You will say: 我 **xiàng** 老师表 **shì** 感谢。

Click "R" to hear the correct response: 我 **xiàng** 老师表 **shì** 感谢。

(a)   (b)   (c)   (d)   (e)   (f)   (g)   (h)

4.   It is time (Use and Structure note 16.3)

You will hear a statement saying what someone must do. Restate the sentence, saying that it is time for someone to do that action, as in the example.

Example:

You will hear: 我们应该说再见了。

You will say: 是我们说再见的时候了。

Click "R" to hear the correct response: 是我们说再见的时候了。

(a)   (b)   (c)   (d)   (e)   (f)   (g)

Listening for information

1.   Formal speech

(CD2: 91–92) You will hear two short formal speeches, A and B. Provide information about the speaker, audience, and purpose of each speech in English in the following form.

speech A	
speaker	
audience	
purpose	
speech B	
speaker	
audience	
purpose	

2. Jieke's birthday

It is Jieke's birthday today. Listen to what he says and answer the questions that follow in Mandarin. (CD2: 93–94)

a.

b.

c.

d.

e.

f.

3. An outing

You will hear a phone message from Kaili, who is studying abroad in Taiwan. She suggests (CD2: 95) taking the **Jiéyùn** (*Rapid Transit*) for an outing. Listen to her message and fill in the main points of her message in English.

meeting place and time	
destination	
lunch	
activity after lunch	
how to contact her	

4. Thank-you speech

Listen to Dawei's thank-you speech, and complete the following list in English, providing (CD2: 96) his reasons for thanking each of the people on the list.

person	reason
Teacher Wang	
classmates	
roommate	

5. A conversation

(CD2: 97) A classmate of yours is asking you about the usage and meaning of the new words and expressions in Lesson 32. Answer her questions in Mandarin.

a.

b.

c.

d.

e.

f.

6. Wang Lian's courses

(CD2: 98) Wang Lian is commenting on the courses that she has taken this semester. Summarize her comments for each course in English.

course	comments
culture	
economics	
history	
literature	

7. Dialogue

(CD2: 99) Listen to this conversation between two friends about the coming weekend. Choose the correct answer for each question, based on the conversation.

a. Why did the man call?
  1) to invite the woman to the lake
  2) to tell the woman about the fish that he bought
  3) to remind the woman of the Sunday event
  4) to ask the woman for a favor

b. What is the man worrying about?
  1) Friday's homework
  2) the lake being too far away
  3) the test next Monday
  4) his upcoming trip

c. What will they do on Sunday?
  1) call each other
  2) review Chinese
  3) visit an aquarium
  4) meet for a chat

d. What will the man do on Saturday?
  1) come back from the lake
  2) call the woman
  3) check the internet for information about the lake
  4) send an email to the woman

 # Reading and writing

Focus on Chinese characters

1.   Number of strokes

Indicate the number of strokes used in writing each of the following characters.

a. 留 _____   f. 爱 _____

b. 顾 _____   g. 首 _____

c. 结 _____   h. 严 _____

d. 封 _____   i. 解 _____

e. 其 _____   j. 表 _____

2.   Which character?

Circle the character in each line that corresponds to the meaning on the left.

a. **huán** *return*   还   坏

b. **tǎo** (**tǎojià huánjià** *bargain back and forth*)   对   讨

c. **shǒu** (**shǒuxiān** *first*)   首   宜

d. **shù** (**jiéshù** *conclude*)   束   本

e. **jié** (**jiéshù** *conclude*)   结   给

f. **shǐ** (**lìshǐ** *history*)   史   吏

g. **yán** *strict*   严   广

h. **gù** (**zhàogù** *care for, take care of*)   厕   顾

i. **fēng** (**yī fēng xìn** *a letter*)   刲   封

j. **biǎo** *form*   表   衣

3. First strokes

Write the first two strokes of each of the following characters.

a. 留 _____   f. 讨 _____

b. 解 _____   g. 顾 _____

c. 其 _____   h. 束 _____

d. 爱 _____   i. 封 _____

e. 礼 _____   j. 参 _____

4. Missing strokes

Complete each character by writing in the missing strokes.

a.   *ク*   **jiě** (**liǎojiě** *understand*)

b.   *纟*   **jié** (**jiéshù** *conclude*)

c.   *二*   **biǎo** *form*

d.   *厂*   **gù** (**zhàogù** *care for, take care of*)

e.   *冖*   **shù** (**jiéshù** *conclude*)

f.   *爫*   **ài** *love*

g.   *丌*   **yán** *strict*

h.   *冂*   **shǐ** (**lìshǐ** *history*)

i.   *𠃊*   **liú** *remain*

j.   *丷*   **shǒu** (**shǒuxiān** *first*)

5.   Total strokes

Rewrite this list of characters, arranging the characters in terms of their total number of strokes. Begin your list with the character with the fewest strokes.

爱	表	封	顾	还	结	解	留	其	史	首	束	讨	严	参	礼

6.   Radicals

Here is a list of characters that we have learned through this lesson. Rewrite each character in the row next to its radical. Use this as an opportunity to review these characters. If you do not know the pronunciation or meaning of a character on the list, look it up and practice it.

连	封	男	顾	意	椅	远	感	想	纸	机
束	本	运	各	讲	结	题	语	对	留	线
给	台	史	预	还	计	练	颜	极	绍	标

口	
辶	
木	
心	
页	
纟	
寸	
田	
讠	

7.   Character sleuth: Look for the phonetic

Group the characters below in terms of their rhymes or near-rhymes. Write the characters that rhyme with each other in the column on the right. Write the "phonetic," the shared part of each character, in the column on the left. There are at least eleven sets of characters that rhyme or partially rhyme and share a phonetic component among these characters.

比	王	中	订	请	较	间	其	五
孩	情	语	期	校	钟	厅	饺	钟
青	听	各	交	毕	客	望	该	简

phonetic	characters that rhyme or almost rhyme and share a phonetic component

8.   Scrambled sentences

Rewrite these words and phrases as sentences, putting the words in the correct order to match the English translations.

a. 的 / 是 / 来 / 道 / 你们 / 远 / 而 / 客人

   You are the guests who have come from afar.

b. 短处 / 长处 / 住 / jí 体 / 也 / 在 / 有 / 有 / 里 / 宿舍

   Living in a group dormitory has advantages and disadvantages.

c. 毕业 / 起点 / zhōng 点 / 只 / 大学 / 不 / 是 / 是

   College graduation is not the end point, it is only a starting point.

d. 感谢 / dài 表 / 朋友们 / zhōng 心 / 请 / 我 / 你 / xiàng / 的 / 表 shì / 的

   Please represent me in giving my heartfelt thanks to your friends.

9.   Dictionary skills

Following the instructions in Lesson 17 of the Textbook, look up these characters in a Chinese dictionary and provide the requested information.

a. 途
   pronunciation:
   meaning:
   one two-character word or phrase in which it occurs:

b. 向
   pronunciation:
   meaning:
   one two-character word or phrase in which it occurs:

c. 邮
   pronunciation:
   meaning:
   one two-character word or phrase in which it occurs:

10.   Find the incorrect characters

Xiao Zhang has written this email to one of his friends back home, but he has written ten characters incorrectly. Circle his mistakes and write the correct characters in the answer sheet below. Then, translate the paragraph into English.

我在北京已经助了两年了。刚来的时后，我对北京所有的东西都不西惯。我听不懂北京人说的话，不习惯吃中国反，更不喜欢北京的天汽。先在我不但可以听懂北京话，而且非常喜欢北京话。我们学的 **Pǔ** 同话里边没有很多"儿"的 **shēng** 音，但是北京话里有很多。慢慢儿地，在我说的汉语里边也有很多"儿"的 **shēng** 音了。另外，我现在非长喜欢吃中国饭。中国的地方很大。每个地方的饭都不一样。个种风味都有自己的味到，让你吃了还想吃。最后是北京的天气。我现在也慢慢地习惯了。由于天气的 **biàn** 化，人们穿不同的衣服、吃不同的东西、做不同的运动。这不是让我们的生活更有意思吗？

a. _____   b. _____   c. _____   d. _____   e. _____

f. _____   g. _____   h. _____   i. _____   j. _____

English:

11.   Reading for the main ideas I

The following paragraph contains a few characters that we have not yet learned, but you should be able to "read around them" and understand the main points of the passage. Read the paragraph for the main ideas, and then respond to the requests and questions that follow in English.

> 其实要了解一个国家的文化，最好的办法就是去学习那个国家的语言。首先，人们每天不管做什么都要用语言。人们的想法、说法、和做法都是通过语言来表示的。其次，语言在变化。新的东西、新的想法会有新的词汇来表示。最后，语言有很久很久的历史。人们的传统和习惯都可从语言中找到。通过学习语言来学习文化再好不过了。

a. State the main topic of this paragraph in English in one word.

b. The author says that you can use the topic for some purpose. What is the purpose?

c. Give an example of some specific thing that you can understand by means of this topic.

12.   Reading for the main ideas II

This speech includes a few characters that you have not yet learned, but you should be able to "read around them" and understand its overall meaning. Read the speech, and then respond to the questions that follow in English.

> 同学们，你们好，
>
> 你们两年的在中国留学的生活就要结束了。回过头来看看，你们在各方面的进步都是非常大的。从一句中文不会说，到今天成了半个地道的北京人，你们不但学了中文，更重要的是了解了中国的文化和历史，看到了中国今天的变化。学习语言不是一年两年的事情，是一辈子的事情。你们的中文还会进步，中国在各方面也会进步。希望你们常回来看看。
>
> 再见

a. Who is the audience for this speech?

b. What does the speech let us know about the speaker? Where is the speaker from?

c. What does the speaker believe to be the primary thing that the audience has learned?

Focus on structure

1. **Prepositional phrase + verb phrase (Use and Structure notes 28.9, 31.3, 32.3, and elsewhere)**

In Mandarin, most prepositional phrases precede the verb phrase. Once you have mastered that rule, you still have to decide which preposition to use. Here are four prepositions that we have learned in this course. Complete each sentence by adding the appropriate preposition, and then translate your sentences into English.

给 *for, to*	**xiàng** *toward* (direction, like 往)	对 *to, toward*	为 *on behalf of*

a. 学生应该 ＿＿＿ 老师表 **shì** 感谢。
English:

b. 我们 ＿＿＿ 中国的了解刚刚开始。
English:

c. 我昨天晚上 ＿＿＿ 朋友打电话了。
English:

d. 父母 ＿＿＿ 自己的孩子很 **jiāo'ào**。
English:

e. 孩子出国的时候父母当然很 ＿＿＿ 他们 **dān** 心。
English:

f. 我常常请她 ＿＿ 我们讲 **gù** 事。
English:

g. 他说他 ＿＿ 图书馆走。
English:

h. 老师 ＿＿ 我们介绍中国的情 **kuàng**。
English:

i. 他们 ＿＿ 经济有兴趣。
English:

j. 你不要 ＿＿ 考试那么紧张。
English:

k. 我很感谢老师 ＿＿ 我们严 **gé** 要 **qiú**。
English:

l. 他 ＿＿ 我们走过来了。
English:

2. Translate into English

Translate these sentences from Mandarin into English. Be sure to identify the key structures and any noun description clauses as you prepare your translations.

a. 我父母让我 **dài** 表他们来接你们。

b. 我认为，学习一种语言首先要学好发音，其次才是语法。如果别人听不懂你在说什么，语法再好也没有用。

c. 我最需要感谢的是我的中国同屋。他教会了我很多在课本上学不到的东西。

d. 我跟我的同屋，在学习上 **hù** 相帮助，在生活上 **hù** 相照顾。

e. 虽然小叶每次考试都考得很好，但是她从来都不为她的好成 **jì** 而 **jiāo'ào**。

f. "New words" 的中文意思是 "生 **cí**"。"**Cí**" 就是 "**cíhuì**" 的意思。"生" 是 "**mò** 生"，你不认识，不知道的。"生 **cí**" 早就有了，不是新的，只是你不认识。

3.   Translate into Mandarin

Translate these sentences into Mandarin, using the structure or phrase in parentheses.

a. We're just about to graduate and leave China. The thing I am most nervous about is that I have too many things and I won't be able to carry them away. (NP 多)

b. I just arrived in Taipei a few days ago. I am a stranger to all the places and things. (对 NP 很 **mò** 生)

c. Nowadays everyone uses email. Who is going to spend a lot of money making a long-distance phone call? (打 … 电话)

d. When it comes to respecting one's teachers, American students and Chinese students are very different. This is a difference in culture. (在 … 上)

e. These last two years they have given a lot of help and guidance. (NP₁ 和 NP₂)

Focus on communication

1.   Dialogue comprehension

Study the Lesson 32 Narrative and Dialogue. Then, read the following statements and indicate whether they are true (T) or false (F).

a. (　) 大为被选为留学生的 **dài** 表在毕业 **diǎn** 礼上讲话，因为别人都不好意思去。

b. (　) 大为觉得两年的时间过得太快了。

c. (　) 大为和他的同学请老师们吃饭，表 **shì** 他们 **zhōng** 心的感谢。

d. (　) 大为的中文老师们不但教中文，而且还照顾学生的生活。

e. (　) 大为会用中文讨价还价，都是老师教他的。

f. (　) 大为的中国朋友和同屋带他们去 **guàng** 北京的地铁和酒吧。

g. (　) 这几天很多毕业留学生的父母都到中国来了。

h. (　) 大为认为，通过他们这些在中国学习的留学生，他们的家人也更了解中国。

i. (　) 大为认为，毕业以后，他们就跟中国没有关系了。

2. What do you say?

What do you say in each of the following situations? Type your answers, using characters where we have learned them, and email them to your Chinese teacher.

a. You are writing to your Chinese teacher. Tell her time flies and you didn't realize it's been five years since you graduated.

b. You are an elementary-school principal. On behalf of the teachers and students (师生), thank a company that donated (送) computers to your school.

c. Tell your mom not to worry. You won't go alone to an unfamiliar place at night.

d. You introduce your roommate to your parents. Tell them how your roommate takes care of you in your daily life and teaches you how to bargain in Chinese.

e. You are the valedictorian at your graduation. Finish your speech by telling everyone that graduation is a beginning as well as an ending. Wish everyone good luck and don't forget your dearest school and respected teachers.

f. Tell your parents to relax. Your new boss (老 **bǎn**) has high demands on you all but has taught you a lot. You think working with him *opens a lot of doors for you* (gives you a lot of good opportunities).

g. You are at a farewell party for your favorite and most respected supervisor at work. Thank him for teaching you so much and for taking care of you when you first started at the company. Tell him that you will never forget him (for your whole life).

h. You are at your little sister's school play. After the show, tell her you are proud of her.

3. Proverbs, fixed expressions, and literary expressions

Match each expression with the appropriate context.

A. **bìng** 从口 **rù**	B. 四 **jì** 如春	C. 生 **mìng** 在于 运动	D. 行行出 **zhuàng** 元
E. 愿者上 **gōu**	F. 严师出高 **tú**	G. 一言为定	H. 学会 **Pǔ** 通话, 走 **biàn** 天下都不怕
I. 远道而来	J. 年年有 **yú**	K. **gōng** 喜发 **cái**	L. **guāngyin sìjiàn**

a. 毕业以后你想做什么就做什么，我觉得，_____，大家不一定都要当 **yī** 生。最重要的是你对自己的工作有兴趣，能做好。

b. 年夜饭里头一定会有一 **pán** 鱼，表 **shì** _____。

c. 这个地方 _____，难怪什么时候都有很多人来这儿旅游。

d. 常听别人说，_____，所以你会说中文，去中国一定没有问题。

e. A: 星期六比较好。我星期天有事，不方便。

   B: 那就 _____，我们下个星期六见吧。

f. 你就别生气了。是你自己决定要买那件衣服的，_____，买回来以后发现衣服不 **héshì**，这不是服务员的错。

g. 我早就告诉过你，吃饭以前一定要先洗手，你没有听过 _____ 吗？

h. 我知道这个老师要 **qiú** 严、功课多、考试又特别难，但是 _____，你上他的课，一定能学到很多。

i. 过新年的时候大家看到朋友的时候，都会 **hù** 相说：_____。

j. _____，没想到才几年不见，同学们的 **biàn** 化都这么大，有的有孩子了，有的留学回来了，有的自己有一个大公 **sī** 了。

k. 你们 _____，我当然要请你们吃饭，再带你们到附近的名 **shèng gǔjì** 去走走。

l. _____，所以我从现在开始打算天天去健身房，好好 **duànliàn** 一下身体。

4.   Formal speeches on various occasions

Based on the scenarios, fill in the blanks to complete these formal speeches.

a. Scenario: A brand new bookstore, 三文书店, is opening today. The owner welcomes all the customers to their new store.

   Qīn 爱的 _____，大家好。_____ 大家来三文书店 …

b. Scenario: At a speech contest, a student, 方以家, begins his speech by greeting the teachers and students off stage.

   各位 _____，各位 _____，大家好。我 _____。今天我所要讲的是：中国现 **dài** 经济的 **biàn** 化。

c. Scenario: At a Chinese karaoke contest, the MC first welcomes all teachers, parents, and students on behalf of all of the students. Then he introduces the ten participants (people who participate in the contest) today.

   Qīn 爱的 _____、_____ 和 _____，你们好。_____，我 _____ 全体同学 _____ 你们来。现在让我 _____

   _____。

d. Scenario: At the same Chinese karaoke contest, one participant, 叶友文, introduces herself and says that she is going to sing 月 **liàng** (moon) **dài** 表我的心. It is her favorite song. She sincerely hopes everyone will like it.

   _____

   _____

   _____

Culture note: "月 **liàng dài** 表我的心"可能是中国流行音乐里最有名的歌。如果你有兴趣，可以去 YouTube 找一找。很多离开家 **xiāng** 的中国人特别喜欢这首歌。

e. Scenario: At a high-school graduation, the class valedictorian opens his speech by saying how time flies and their school life is coming to an end. He thanks the teachers on behalf of all of the graduates and begins his speech. Lastly, he wishes everyone a new start (no matter) whether they are going to attend college or begin work.

_____，没想到四年的学校生活 _____。在这里首先我

要 _____。…最后，我 **zhù** 各位

毕业生 _____，都有一个新的开始。

f. Scenario: At a high-school graduation, a teacher gives a farewell speech. She talks about how the first day of school seems like yesterday, and she can't believe they are leaving now. She wishes everyone good luck, hopes they stay interested in everything after they enter college, tells them to have confidence in themselves, and, most importantly, asks them not to forget their beloved school.

…_____ 好像是昨天的事，怎么这么快你们

_____？…最后，**zhù** 你们 _____。希望你们上大学以

后，_____，更重要的

是，千万 _____

_____。

g. Scenario: At an awards ceremony, the winner thanks his parents, saying "without them, I wouldn't be standing here today."

_____

_____

_____

5. Giving a speech

Read the speeches in Exercise 4 again. Pick two scenarios that you like the most, and write a speech of your own. Your speech should be at least 120 characters in length.

Scenario one: _____

Your speech: _____

_____

_____

_____

_____

_____

Scenario two: _____

Your speech: _____

_____

_____

_____

_____

6. Farewell letter

Using the speech in Lesson 32 as your model, write a letter to either all your classmates or to your teacher, thanking them and telling them how they have impacted your life in the past few years. Use the following procedure as you prepare your letter.

Part I. Brainstorming

a. Select the audience for your letter, either your classmates (   ) or your teacher (   ).

b. Make a list of ways that they have impacted your life and the things they have done for you.

c. Rewrite your list, organizing it so that it states each item in the order in which you want to present it in your speech.

d. Outline your letter so that it includes three parts. Use the following words to introduce each part: 首先, 其次, 最后.

e. Think about how to introduce and connect the information in each part of the letter. Use words such as 另外 and 还有 to do this.

Part II. Write your letter.   The opening and closing are provided for you. Your letter should be at least 150 characters in length.

Qīn 爱的＿＿＿＿＿＿＿＿：

我们马上就要毕业了。首先＿＿＿＿＿＿＿＿＿＿＿＿＿＿＿＿＿＿＿＿＿＿＿＿＿＿＿

＿＿＿＿＿＿＿＿＿＿＿＿＿＿＿＿＿＿＿＿＿＿＿＿＿＿＿＿＿＿＿＿＿＿＿＿＿＿＿

＿＿＿＿＿＿＿＿＿＿＿＿＿＿＿＿＿＿＿＿＿＿＿＿＿＿＿＿＿＿＿＿＿＿＿＿＿＿＿

＿＿＿＿＿＿＿＿＿＿＿＿＿＿＿＿＿＿＿＿＿＿＿＿＿＿＿＿＿＿＿＿＿＿＿＿＿＿＿

＿＿＿＿＿＿＿＿＿＿＿＿＿＿＿＿＿＿＿＿＿＿＿＿＿＿＿＿＿＿＿＿＿＿＿＿＿＿＿

＿＿＿＿＿＿＿＿＿＿＿＿＿＿＿＿＿＿＿＿＿＿＿＿＿＿＿＿＿＿＿＿＿＿＿＿＿＿＿

＿＿＿＿＿＿＿＿＿＿＿＿＿＿＿＿＿＿＿＿＿＿＿＿＿＿＿＿＿＿＿＿＿＿＿＿＿＿＿

＿＿＿＿＿＿＿＿＿＿＿＿＿＿＿＿＿＿＿＿＿＿＿＿＿＿＿＿＿＿＿＿＿＿＿＿＿＿＿

＿＿＿＿＿＿＿＿＿＿＿＿＿＿＿＿＿＿＿＿＿＿＿＿＿＿＿＿＿＿＿＿＿＿＿＿＿＿＿

＿＿＿＿＿＿＿＿＿＿＿＿＿＿＿＿＿＿＿＿＿＿＿＿＿＿＿＿＿＿＿＿＿＿＿＿＿＿＿

＿＿＿＿＿＿＿＿＿＿＿＿＿＿＿＿＿＿＿＿＿＿＿＿＿＿＿＿＿＿＿＿＿＿＿＿＿＿＿

＿＿＿＿＿＿＿＿＿＿＿＿＿＿＿＿＿＿＿＿＿＿＿＿＿＿＿＿＿＿＿＿＿＿＿＿＿＿＿

＿＿＿＿＿＿＿＿＿＿＿＿＿

Zhù ＿＿＿＿＿＿＿＿＿＿＿＿

你的 ＿＿＿＿＿＿＿＿ (friend, student)

＿＿＿＿＿＿＿＿＿＿＿＿ (your name)

Audio track listing

	Lesson 17	
Track 1	L 17 Narrative	0:56
Track 2	L 17 Dialogue parts A & B	0:53
Track 3	L 17 Listening for information 1	0:36
Track 4	L 17 Listening for information 2	0:17
Track 5	L 17 Listening for information 3	0:30
Track 6	L 17 Listening for information 4	0:31
Track 7	L 17 Listening for information 5	0:22
Track 8	L 17 Listening for information 6: Narrative & questions	1:22
Track 9	L 17 Listening for information 7	0:29
Track 10	L 17 Listening for information 8	0:21
	Lesson 18	
Track 11	L 18 Narrative	0:51
Track 12	L 18 Dialogue parts A & B	1:03
Track 13	L 18 Listening for information 1	0:33
Track 14	L 18 Listening for information 2	0:31
Track 15	L 18 Listening for information 3	0:46
Track 16	L 18 Listening for information 4	0:39
Track 17	L 18 Listening for information 5	0:26
Track 18	L 18 Listening for information 6	0:46
Track 19	L 18 Listening for information 7: Narrative & questions	1:24
Track 20	L 18 Listening for information 8	0:58
Track 21	L 18 Listening for information 9	1:06
	Lesson 19	
Track 22	L 19 Narrative & dialogue part A	0:48
Track 23	L 19 Dialogue parts B & C	0:47
Track 24	L 19 Listening for information 1	0:25
Track 25	L 19 Listening for information 2	0:34
Track 26	L 19 Listening for information 3	0:30

Track 27	L 19 Listening for information 4	0:26
Track 28	L 19 Listening for information 5	0:21
Track 29	L 19 Listening for information 6	0:29
Track 30	L 19 Listening for information 7: Narrative & questions	1:12
Track 31	L 19 Listening for information 8	0:47
Track 32	L 19 Listening for information 9	0:48
	Lesson 20	
Track 33	L 20 Narrative	0:38
Track 34	L 20 Dialogue part A	0:41
Track 35	L 20 Dialogue parts B & C	1:00
Track 36	L 20 Listening for information 1	0:26
Track 37	L 20 Listening for information 2	0:39
Track 38	L 20 Listening for information 3: Narrative & questions	1:15
Track 39	L 20 Listening for information 4	1:42
Track 40	L 20 Listening for information 5	0:34
Track 41	L 20 Listening for information 6: Narrative & questions	0:58
Track 42	L 20 Listening for information 7	0:42
Track 43	L 20 Listening for information 8	0:35
	Lesson 21	
Track 44	L 21 Narrative	0:37
Track 45	L 21 Dialogue part A	0:44
Track 46	L 21 Dialogue parts B & C	1:23
Track 47	L 21 Listening for information 1	0:42
Track 48	L 21 Listening for information 2	0:31
Track 49	L 21 Listening for information 3: Narrative & questions	1:01
Track 50	L 21 Listening for information 4	0:28
Track 51	L 21 Listening for information 5	0:46
Track 52	L 21 Listening for information 6	0:38
Track 53	L 21 Listening for information 7.1	0:38
Track 54	L 21 Listening for information 7.2	0:35
Track 55	L 21 Listening for information 8	1:39
	Lesson 22	
Track 56	L 22 Narrative	0:46
Track 57	L 22 Dialogue parts A & B	0:55
Track 58	L 22 Listening for information 1	0:44
Track 59	L 22 Listening for information 2	1:21
Track 60	L 22 Listening for information 3	0:25
Track 61	L 22 Listening for information 4	0:50
Track 62	L 22 Listening for information 5	0:21

Track 63	L 22 Listening for information 6	0:28
Track 64	L 22 Listening for information 7	0:39
Track 65	L 22 Listening for information 8	1:04
Track 66	L 22 Listening for information 9	1:35
	Lesson 23	
Track 67	L 23 Narrative	0:37
Track 68	L 23 Dialogue parts A & B	1:47
Track 69	L 23 Listening for information 1	0:28
Track 70	L 23 Listening for information 2	0:52
Track 71	L 23 Listening for information 3	0:22
Track 72	L 23 Listening for information 4	0:32
Track 73	L 23 Listening for information 5	0:25
Track 74	L 23 Listening for information 6	0:59
Track 75	L 23 Listening for information 7	0:36
Track 76	L 23 Listening for information 8	0:46
Track 77	L 23 Listening for information 9	1:03
	Lesson 24	
Track 78	L 24 Narrative	0:37
Track 79	L 24 Dialogue parts A & B	1:09
Track 80	L 24 Dialogue parts C & D	1:15
Track 81	L 24 Listening for information 1	0:33
Track 82	L 24 Listening for information 2	0:13
Track 83	L 24 Listening for information 3	0:35
Track 84	L 24 Listening for information 4	0:25
Track 85	L 24 Listening for information 5	0:44
Track 86	L 24 Listening for information 6	0:53
Track 87	L 24 Listening for information 7	0:29
Track 88	L 24 Listening for information 8	0:59
Track 89	L 24 Listening for information 9	1:03
	Lesson 25	
Track 90	L 25 Narrative	1:35
Track 91	L 25 Dialogue parts A & B	2:03
Track 92	L 25 Listening for information 1	0:34
Track 93	L 25 Listening for information 2	0:26
Track 94	L 25 Listening for information 3	0:12
Track 95	L 25 Listening for information 4	0:32
Track 96	L 25 Listening for information 5	0:29
Track 97	L 25 Listening for information 6	0:41
Track 98	L 25 Listening for information 7	0:57

CD 2: Lesson 25 (continued) – Lesson 32

	Lesson 25 (continued)	
Track 1	L 25 Listening for information 8	1:31
	Lesson 26	
Track 2	L 26 Narrative	1:35
Track 3	L 26 Dialogue part A	1:05
Track 4	L 26 Dialogue part B	0:34
Track 5	L 26 Listening for information 1	0:26
Track 6	L 26 Listening for information 2	0:26
Track 7	L 26 Listening for information 3	0:37
Track 8	L 26 Listening for information 4	0:28
Track 9	L 26 Listening for information 5	0:17
Track 10	L 26 Listening for information 6: Narrative	0:34
Track 11	L 26 Listening for information 6: Questions	0:18
Track 12	L 26 Listening for information 7	0:17
Track 13	L 26 Listening for information 8	0:43
Track 14	L 26 Listening for information 9	1:05
	Lesson 27	0:18
Track 15	L 27 Narrative	1:35
Track 16	L 27 Dialogue part A	0:37
Track 17	L 27 Dialogue part B	2:03
Track 18	L 27 Listening for information 1	0:26
Track 19	L 27 Listening for information 2	0:31
Track 20	L 27 Listening for information 3: Narrative	0:52
Track 21	L 27 Listening for information 3: Questions	0:12
Track 22	L 27 Listening for information 4: Recipe	0:35
Track 23	L 27 Listening for information 4: Questions	0:24
Track 24	L 27 Listening for information 5	0:44
Track 25	L 27 Listening for information 6	0:31
Track 26	L 27 Listening for information 7: Narrative	0:34
Track 27	L 27 Listening for information 7: Questions	0:22
Track 28	L 27 Listening for information 8	0:42
Track 29	L 27 Listening for information 9	0:50
Track 30	L 27 Listening for information 10	1:06
	Lesson 28	
Track 31	L 28 Narrative	0:50
Track 32	L 28 Dialogue parts A & B	1:23
Track 33	L 28 Dialogue part C	1:21